OUR LOT

How Real Estate Came to Own Us

ALYSSA KATZ

BLOOMSBURY

NEW YORK BERLIN LONDON

Published by Bloomsbury USA, New York

All papers used by Bloomsbury USA are natural, recyclable products made from wood grown in well-managed forests. The manufacturing processes conform to the environmental regulations of the country of origin.

Portions of chapter 4 appeared in *Mother Jones* magazine, September/October 2006.

LIBRARY OF CONGRESS CATALOGING-IN-PUBLICATION DATA

Katz, Alyssa.
    Our lot : how real estate came to own us / Alyssa Katz.—1st ed.
        p.   cm.
    ISBN-13: 978-1-59691-479-7 (hardcover)
    ISBN-10: 1-59691-479-3 (hardcover)
    1. Real estate business—United States—Marketing. 2. Real estate business—United States—Managing. I. Title.

    HD1375.K348 2009
    333.330973—dc22

                                                        2008054503

First U.S. Edition 2009

1 3 5 7 9 10 8 6 4 2

Typeset by Westchester Book Group
Printed in the United States of America by Quebecor World Fairfield

For my father

CONTENTS

1.   Almost like a Conspiracy   1

2.   The Rising Tide   27

3.   Subprime Time   54

4.   Into Oblivion   78

5.   Reaching the Limits   102

6.   Crime Spree   129

7.   Huffing the Fumes   156

8.   Tenants No More   185

Epilogue: Returning Home   213

Acknowledgments   229

Glossary   233

Notes   245

Index   267

One

ALMOST LIKE A CONSPIRACY

Chicago, 1972

SHE POURED ANOTHER GLASS from the vodka bottle. It was approaching three A.M., Indiana time, here on the campus of Notre Dame,
a couple of hours drive east from the city where Gale Cincotta had lived her
whole life. By day Cincotta was nominally a housewife, a mother of six boys
and young men living in Austin, a West Side Chicago neighborhood. But by
now she was working full-time and beyond, trying to rescue Austin and surrounding communities from a real estate plague that showed no signs of re-
ceding. It was, she would say, "almost like a conspiracy of people deciding
that this area was going to go."

Huddling in the dorm room with an ex-Methodist minister, who was
downing Jack Daniel's himself, Cincotta dragged on a series of Salems, the
smoke wafting over her platinum bouffant sprayed out into stiff cascades.

She always brought two bottles to organizing meetings, which often went
on long past midnight. One was for herself, and the other to help inspire the
other activists—student interns, career community organizers, and neighborhood residents like herself—to keep going. Cincotta used the vodka not to
dull the hurt, but to fuel her will to prevail over those responsible for the
destruction.

In West Side Chicago, it was hard to find a block that didn't have a vacant home, its furnace, copper piping, everything of value ripped out. Lots
of streets had four or five. Neighborhoods were turning ever more wretched,
saturated with empty houses and trashed lawns.

Investigators from the Chicago office of the U.S. Department of Housing
and Urban Development wrote up briefings for their division chief about
some of the five thousand foreclosed homes now abandoned in Chicago, as

he, unlike his superiors in Washington, vowed to crack down on the mortgage companies responsible for making the loans that led to their destruction.
Tens of thousands of dilapidated structures like them littered cities across the
country, their purchase made possible by a government program that was
supposed to make homeownership a possibility for anyone in America.

In Humboldt Park: "Very bad—should be demolished, a hazard to
neighbors. Water not shut off or drained—thruout building water damage. All radiators, bathroom and kitchen fixtures missing. Garage full of
debris. House boarded with cardboard-like material."

Near Lake Michigan: "Should be demolished right away. This house
could burn up at any time. House looks like it could fall in—it has been
completely stripped of everything. There is no plumbing, all gone. There
are no electric fixtures, all gone."

East Garfield Park, near the Kezdie El stop: "Structure in very bad
condition—plaster, glass and junk all over. Entrance unlocked. Chimney collapsing. Garage destroyed by fire. Interior littered with glass and plaster."

"House is littered with junk, furniture, cabinets, freezer, washing machine, mattress, dead cat, bugs."

"Dead cat in the middle of living room. House vandalized repeatedly,
furniture chopped up."

And on and on through the government's files, for block upon mile.

In 1972, in Chicago and in every other city in the nation, almost anyone
could get a home mortgage, including borrowers who didn't earn enough to
pay them off, on just about any house, for any reason. In many instances real
estate brokers simply fabricated information on the application to make it
look like a buyer who didn't qualify, did. ("Husband? I haven't seen my husband in six years!" one borrower told an auditor who asked whether she and
her spouse were both still working.) Real estate speculators descended to buy
flimsy houses cheaply and, with the consent of appraisers, resell them at absurdly high prices to first-time buyers. The money for the loans came from
a new and lucrative market in mortgage-backed securities—pools of thousands of mortgages packaged together by financial traders and sold as bond-
like investments. The more loans borrowers took out, the bigger that
bond-sales business would grow. And in the end all that was left were empty
and unwanted homes, whatever value they had now spent.

All those travesties seem utterly familiar today. These were, after all, hallmarks of the great real estate bubble and bust that has in the 2000s left homeowners choking on debt and the global financial system in shambles. Yet the feverish episode of frenzied real estate lending that ensnared the nation's cities almost four decades ago was remarkable, then as now, because it upended virtually everything that had until then been sacred about how Americans bought and financed their houses. And just like the recent adventure in lending beyond any rational limits, the mortgage disaster of the early 1970s was born from a lofty ideological conviction that enabled the basest of crimes and most foolish of gambles under its cover, insulated from almost any scrutiny until the damage was already done.

Owning homes would serve as a force to better the world—to build stronger families, more pleasant communities, financial security, a sharing of wealth through the generations. That idea has been embedded in the national psyche, not through any innate aspiration in the human spirit but by dint of methodical, deliberate salesmanship and an array of incentives seemingly too powerful to refuse. In the 1920s, an ambitious secretary of commerce named Herbert Hoover sponsored a national campaign for "Better Homes in America," introducing the effort by declaring, "It is mainly through the hope of enjoying the ownership of a home that the latent energy of any citizenry is called forth." Owning a home, Hoover insisted, "may change the very physical, mental and moral fibre of one's children." His agency sold hundreds of thousands of copies of a book called *How to Own Your Home.* It was distributed through furniture, lighting, and hardware stores, some of which folded their own advertising around the government tract. "Adults who have not already begun to save toward buying a home should start at once," the booklet advised readers. "Lack of experience should deter no one."

In the depths of the Great Depression, the administration of President Franklin Delano Roosevelt pressed for a vast new government home mortgage program not because they had any notions that homeownership would build better men or better places to live, but because they were desperate to jump-start a dead economy—and the construction and sale of housing would put people to work. A surge of housing development supported through the government's sponsorship "would affect everyone, from the manufacturer of lace curtains to the manufacturers of lumber, bricks, furniture, cement, and electrical appliances. The mere shipment of these supplies would affect the railroads, which in turn would need the produce of steel mills for rails,"

anticipated Marriner Eccles, an assistant treasury secretary whom FDR
would soon appoint as head of the Federal Reserve.

One third of the unemployed had worked in construction, during a
mad 1920s real estate boom fueled by—how did a nation forget this?—a
vast marketplace in mortgage-backed securities. In the early 1920s, real estate prices hurled upward by an astounding 50 to 75 percent a year. By
1933, a thousand homeowners were going into foreclosure every day.

By Eccles's account, FDR was distressed by how much his administration
was spending on the Works Progress Administration and other public jobs
projects. The trick was to find a way to juice up the production of housing,
putting those men to work, but without spending government money.

When Roosevelt gave his orders to create a self-perpetuating national
housing machine, no one had any idea what it would look like. Would it
make loans? Help homeowners pay for them? For answers his administration
turned to the auto industry, which had just done something miraculous:
during the 1920s, it had taken a nation that had abhorred debt and convinced consumers to borrow their way to a better life.

Until then, while many people held mortgages, most did so with the
taint of shame. Generations raised on Victorian values upheld "thrift" as the
greatest virtue second only to chastity, and the attitude extended to home
mortgages—they were a last resort, when all other options were gone. Most
homes didn't even have them, and a majority of Americans rented. Holding
a mortgage was considered more or less the same thing as being a tenant,
with little difference between owing rent to a landlord and a payment to a
bank.

All that changed when automobiles rolled into the world. Henry Ford was
famous for his policy of paying workers enough to buy one of his Model Ts.
General Motors had a different idea. In 1919, GM started its own loan company, the General Motors Acceptance Corporation, to fuel the sales of its
cars. Two years later, that financial arm saved GM—and installment loans
rescued the American economy from a depression before the Great Depression. When business ground to a halt in 1921, millions of workers found
themselves out of a job, and manufacturers ended up with piles of products
few customers could afford to buy. GM and other automobile companies began to aggressively market their installment plans, and crashed right through
the borrowing taboo. People wanted cars so badly they'd do almost anything
to get one.

By the end of that year, businesses and retailers found they could sell almost anything on installment plans, from sewing machines and pianos to newfangled radios and refrigerators. The 1920s were bought with a pyramid of debt. When the Great Depression finally hit, American consumers were $7 billion in the hole. That didn't count another $30 billion in mortgage debt.

Two of the men who turned thrifty Americans into a nation of debtors ended up in charge of the Federal Housing Administration, the New Deal agency that would build a way out of the Great Depression. This time, the hope was, they could use their genius in installment sales to get Americans spending again.

The FHA built on the success of the Home Owners' Loan Corporation, an emergency government agency that beginning in 1933 undertook an effort unprecedented in American history. It refinanced more than a million mortgages, and kept their holders in homes they would otherwise have lost to foreclosure.

To understand just how remarkable Roosevelt's project was, consider the prospects for someone who'd tried to buy a home in the 1920s. To assure lenders they weren't going to disappear without paying their bills, borrowers had to make a down payment of something close to half the entire cost of the house, and many who didn't have that much cash on hand instead took out a second mortgage to finance the down payment. The interest rate on that second mortgage could be 20 percent, or more. After all that, the mortgages usually lasted only three or five years; most borrowers expected not to pay them off in that time but simply to refinance—take out new mortgages—when the clock ran out, paying hefty fees for the privilege. In many cases the loans were for interest only, the principal sitting there month after month like a never-melting glacier.

Hence the need for the Home Owners' Loan Corporation. When the Great Depression hit, banks wouldn't or more often couldn't refinance the second mortgages, since borrowers had taken out far more money than the houses were now actually worth. The problem for unemployed borrowers wasn't just that some couldn't afford their monthly payments. It was that when the mortgage's term was up the remainder of the bill came due at once. Even though the house had fallen in value, the borrower would still have to pay the full amount owed. (In today's parlance, they were "upside down.") Most just refused.

The Home Owners' Loan Corporation refinanced more than a million home mortgages (average size: $3,028), and its success whetted enthusiasm for a continued government role in financing real estate. Once the new Federal Housing Administration was up and running, Roosevelt appointed as its head Stewart McDonald, formerly head of the Moon Motor Car Company of St. Louis. The executive who'd run GM's lending division, Albert L. Deane, helped the president's economic adviser devise the winning formula for the FHA: insure mortgages, to assure lenders they would be repaid in the event a homeowner defaulted on the loan, and make borrowers pay the premiums via a 1 percent fee on every mortgage.

These new government-backed loans were everything the 1920s mortgages weren't. They would run for thirty years, not three or five, and at the end of that period the borrower would owe nothing. Banks everywhere could make the loans, even if they didn't have a pile of cash to hand out, thanks to a new government fund, the Federal National Mortgage Association, which would soon come to be known as Fannie Mae. (At first the Roosevelt administration called for private financiers to create that funding pool, but none stepped up for the job.) Fannie Mae repurchased mortgages from banks, which gave the banks a reliable pipeline of funds to lend that they'd never had before. If anything happened to the borrower—if they missed payments, or up and disappeared—the government-managed FHA insurance fund would bail out the bank.

This new safety net literally built the American Dream. Over the next three decades, FHA and a no-money-down program for returning veterans insured loans for millions of new homeowners, about half of all the mortgages in the whole country. Most of these first-time buyers lived in single-family homes, in spanking new suburbs such as Levittown, New York, and Westchester, California—little houses, mass-produced and settled by the millions after the war and through the early 1960s. Thanks to the government support the homes were inexpensive, one to two years' salary (and this was back when most families had just one income).

But for all that time the FHA had refused to insure loans in older, poorer, and, most especially, blacker parts of cities. The agency's appraisers' manual, which determined who would and who wouldn't qualify for a government-insured loan, ruled out all kinds of homes as too risky—including those in neighborhoods that were "aging," "changing," or "racially inharmonious."

Row houses, places where lots of people lived in close quarters, and integrated areas were all verboten.

Whether or not they used the federal insurance, banks followed their own strict playbook, the American Institute of Real Estate Appraisers' manual, which advised lenders to seek eight signs of "neighborhood conformity": homes were safe bets for bankers if they were similar in style, configuration, age, size, quality, and price to the ones next door to them, and where residents shared similar ethnic backgrounds and household incomes.

These standards ruled out most loans in most American cities. For someone in Chicago or Baltimore or Toledo, 1966 might as well have been 1936. In large swaths of those and many other cities, a homebuyer just wasn't going to get a mortgage. "We are not social or welfare agencies," the Chicago-based lobbyist for the nation's savings and loans would explain. "We will not make loans at our own risk . . . in neighborhoods threatened with blight." The older and more industrial the neighborhood, the less of a chance there was of getting a home loan. In the mid-1960s, fewer than 3 percent of all the FHA-insured loans in the country were being made in central cities.

Like so much else in the late 1960s, all that had been sacred about home lending would quickly turn upside down. In June 1966, Chicago's West Side erupted into three days of window-smashing, rock-throwing, fire-bombing, and shooting after a police officer arrested a man who opened a fire hydrant on a broiling-hot day. One reason, the National Advisory Commission on Civil Disorders chaired by Illinois governor Otto Kerner would eventually conclude, was that homes in the neighborhoods where riots took place were already in dismal shape. Nearly a third of black Chicagoans lived in decrepit residences. Rents were too high, and people too poor. "The supply of housing suitable for low-income families should be expanded on a massive basis," the Kerner Commission continued. Government assistance in paying rent, the investigators concluded, would help more than anything. Martin Luther King Jr. had sounded the same note that summer, as his Chicago Freedom Movement staged demonstrations protesting the terrible conditions black Chicagoans were living in.

During that tumultuous summer, Charles Percy came to his own conclusions. The Bell & Howell executive had less than two months to go in his challenge against Paul Douglas for the U.S. Senate seat from Illinois and sought a knockout vision for how Chicago would avoid a future replay of the riots. Percy came to Sherman House, the grand old hotel on Randolph Street, to share his big solution with the Kiwanis Club of Chicago. For the forces he described assaulting American cities, Percy had a singular answer: "We must create and fortify a new spirit of independence, of self-reliance, of self-esteem, of human dignity, of creative initiative in the people who dwell there." Percy proposed that every American have an opportunity to own his own home.

"For a man who owns his own home acquires with it a new dignity," Percy orated. "He begins to take pride in what is his own, and pride in conserving it and improving it for his children. He becomes a more steadfast and concerned citizen of his community. He becomes more self-confident and self-reliant. The mere act of becoming a homeowner transforms him." Tenants were (yes, he said this) "slaves."

The speech was almost ridiculous in its optimism. Yet the notion Percy put out that evening conveyed a vast power. In the swirl of anxiety following the summer's riots, there was no shortage of prescriptions to cure whatever was poisoning cities, and virtually all of them had the government right in the middle of it, with grants for programs and slum repair and empowerment and every possible ailment. Here, out of nowhere, was a response that would not only leave the government almost entirely out, but also bring the formerly oppressed homebuyer into the light of economic success. He could then show his neighbors the way.

Amid a torrent of new Great Society programs that transferred cash to the poor and their neighborhoods, Percy's idea of spurring private investment in self-help and self-reliance got conservatives aroused. William F. Buckley Jr. raved about the Percy plan, calling it "the Conservative Answer to Public Housing." And others in Washington took notice. The brutal (and never-solved) slaying a week later of Percy's twenty-one-year-old daughter in their north suburban mansion only raised Percy's national profile, and probably won him the Senate seat. By the following spring he was running against Richard Nixon, George Romney, and Ronald Reagan for the Republican presidential nomination.

With support from some Democrats in Congress as well as a unanimous Republican front, Percy's program for universal homeownership—"the rebirth of the human spirit" in "the bountiful promise of land"—came to life as part of that year's massive housing act, the same bill that created the new

U.S. Department of Housing and Urban Development. The Johnson administration insisted on one fundamental change from Percy's vision. He had called for an independent nonprofit to run the homeownership project in partnership with bankers and community organizations. The White House simply modified its existing Federal Housing Administration loan insurance program and made it available, for the first time, in the areas that had previously been off-limits. The FHA was now, in effect, a front in the War on Poverty.

Via its insurance guarantee to lenders, which assured them of full repayment in case of foreclosure, the federal government made it possible for mortgage lenders to rain money—$100 billion of it, HUD secretary Romney would later account—onto parched land. Under the new regime, homebuyers living in Chicago and other inner cities weren't just eligible for loans. Lenders who signed up to sell FHA-insured mortgages were asked to do everything they could to make sure the buyers got them.

Normally government-insured loans could only be made in areas whose future property values were "reasonably viable." Under the overhauled rules, that restriction no longer applied in cities, or where homeowners of modest means were concerned. Now, the head of the Federal Housing Administration instructed home mortgage lenders, the only reason they *shouldn't* make a loan on an inner-city home was "if the health and safety of its occupants are seriously affected"—that is, if it was literally falling down.

Across the country, neighborhood destruction became a booming business, financed by the federal government. In Chicago they called it "panic peddling." In New York it was "blockbusting." Whatever the city and whatever the label, the scheme followed the same script everywhere, inflaming racial anxieties for profit. Real estate agents knocked on white homeowners' doors and announced, if they were polite about it, "You know, your neighborhood is changing."

White homeowners understood what that meant. The ghetto was coming. As new black residents arrived, they feared, crime would rise and home values would plummet. Blockbusting had already been entrenched for more than a decade, financed by small banks and petty entrepreneurs. Real estate agents made sure homeowners got the message by showing up at their doors—in the daytime, when housewives were home by themselves—with twenty thousand-dollar bills in their hand, an offer for their home. "If you don't sell to me today," they would inform the owner, "I'll be back tomorrow with nineteen." And sure enough, the agents did show up the next day with the nineteen bills. As they watched their white neighbors move out and new black ones move in, homeowners got daily phone calls reminding them that if they kept waiting to sell, they would barely make money at all.

The FHA-insured loans threw gasoline on that smoldering fire, so that instead of a few houses here or there, blockbusters could now crack open entire blocks and neighborhoods, confident that the government insurance fund would pay them back in the event borrowers went into foreclosure. Indeed, the insurance made it profitable to seek out the most impoverished and unreliable borrowers, since the sooner a borrower defaulted on a loan, the more quickly a lender would get paid back in full by FHA. Typically, a real estate agent would buy a house from a panicked white owner for a few thousand dollars and immediately resell it to a black buyer for two or three times as much. The FHA's staff of real estate appraisers certified that the homes were in fact worth the prices borrowers were paying—and some, with the enticement of kickbacks from mortgage lenders, approved prices far above the realm of reality, assuring the largest possible reimbursement to the lenders when the homes went into foreclosure.

The down payment was never more than five hundred dollars. If the buyer didn't have the money, the real estate agent would often provide it; if he or she didn't have a job, the agent might ask a friendly employer to invent proof of one.

Even as the number of FHA foreclosures began to mount into the tens of thousands nationally, another division of HUD kept loan funds flowing to the companies selling the mortgages. Through an entity called Ginnie Mae, the government agency was pooling FHA-insured mortgages together into securities, then selling them to private investors and using the proceeds to finance more loans to be sold under the FHA insurance program.

Gale Cincotta's neighborhood group tried everything they could to make the insane cycle of panic peddling and foreclosures stop. They hounded real estate agents to sign agreements that they wouldn't solicit panic sales, and picketed the front lawns of those who refused. They hooked up into a mega-group called the West Side Coalition. They held parties where they walked around the neighborhood ripping out hundreds of "For Sale" signs. They called back the real estate agents saying they were interested in selling, then invited ten or twenty friends to corner the agent in the basement, shouting, *"Out of our neighborhood!!"*

These skirmishes could be exhilarating, but it was like sending a posse out to hit termites with sharp knives. So the coalition started talking about where the money was flowing from—and where it wasn't. They started holding "bank-ins" at savings and loans on Chicago's West Side. Someone, probably Cincotta, took a look at the map of Chicago covering nearly the entire wall of one bank president's office, a bright border demarcating the boundary between the zones where the bank would make its own loans and those (black and Hispanic) territories ceded to FHA's insured-loan program and mortgage lenders determined to exploit it—and invented a new name for the great pestilence: redlining.

Who knows who came up that woozy night at Notre Dame with the idea of a national gathering of aggrieved neighborhood groups? It wasn't long before West Side Coalition interns headed out to O'Hare International Airport, the one place where they could find phone books for every big city in the country. They would look for listings that sounded like they could be for community organizations, and back at the office they called those groups, asking them to come to a big conference in Chicago that March. It wasn't a question of whether they would be interested, because the devastation unfolding in West Chicago was happening in their cities, too.

More than sixteen hundred people came to St. Sylvester's School on the West Side, from Baltimore, Denver, Newark, Detroit, St. Louis, Philadelphia, Cleveland, Pittsburgh, and beyond—all experiencing the same cancer Chicago had. They were black, Puerto Rican, white, and from racial and ethnic groups usually more often in conflict than in concert with one another. The walls of the auditorium were pasted with huge photo blowups of wrecked houses from all over the country.

Cincotta wore a button on her blouse that proclaimed "I'm Staying," and rallied the crowd with a coherent explanation for how they woke up at home like they always did, in the neighborhoods they'd always lived in, and found themselves in hell. "What for so long has been considered a natural phenomenon—change in neighborhoods, deteriorating cities—are not natural," Cincotta assured them. "It's a plan, and somebody's making a lot of money out of changing neighborhoods."

Cincotta had grown up Aglaia Angeles, an only child working in her family's Greek diner on Madison Street near Garfield Park. She married John Cincotta, a local gas station owner. John looked young for his age, and Gale matured quickly, but the difference between the two remained obvious—they had an almost thirty-two-year gap between them. She never finished high school, not with three kids by the time she was nineteen. Her wardrobe consisted of a series of floral and geometrically patterned house-coats draped over her immense frame, sometimes warmed up with a cro-cheted vest. Cincotta's pancake-flat midwestern voice was reinforced, when she was at the megaphone or podium, with a fist that in an earlier time might have rallied textile workers to the picket line.

Gale Cincotta and her fellow Chicago activists set out to replace the gov-ernment's scam-infested lending program with a healthy market in home mortgages—one that in many city neighborhoods simply didn't exist. Sav-ings and loan institutions, or S&Ls, made half of the home loans in the nation. These "thrifts" had originally emerged from a nineteenth-century movement to encourage workers to pool their savings together into coopera-tively run funds that they could turn to if they needed a loan to buy a home or start a business. With the great suburban boom of the 1950s, S&Ls thrived, and Americans could count on thrift institutions to meet their typi-cally modest banking needs.

Unless, that is, they lived in the heart of Chicago—or Brooklyn or Balti-more or just about any aging city or urban area in the nation. Plenty of sav-ings and loans, as well as commercial banks, still operated in these areas. But by all reports it was extremely difficult for even the most qualified borrowers in huge swaths of Chicago, especially on the South and West sides—and most of all if the neighborhoods were heavily black or Latino—to get mort-gages from those institutions by the early 1970s. Researchers from North-western University turned to the limited data available on the thrifts' lending habits and determined that while those institutions held billions in deposits from Chicago residents and businesses, they were indeed making pitifully few home mortgage loans to residents from many of the same neighborhoods.

On a May morning in 1975, Cincotta stood out among the suits in a sleeveless high-necked dress, her beefy arms folded across her chest and butterfly glasses perched on the ridge of her nose. She was a prime witness at a U.S. Senate hearing. "We are not asking for handouts," Cincotta stressed. "All we are asking for is a fair return on our savings into our communities."

She was making the case for a proposed new law that would force banks and S&Ls to reveal where they held their deposits and where they made their loans. When the Home Mortgage Disclosure Act became law, its sponsor, Senator William Proxmire, credited the research and community organizing of Cincotta's group for making it happen at all. Cincotta and her allies ultimately sought to obligate banks that had deposits from customers in a given neighborhood to also make loans there. The Community Reinvestment Act, hatched in 1977 by a number of different activists, including Cincotta, accomplished that. It required banks to demonstrate that they'd met the borrowing needs of their own communities. If they couldn't prove it, citizens' groups could petition to block banks' mergers and other major business moves.

CRA and HMDA together offered powerful ammunition for activist groups such as Cincotta's, which had been building their influence through public demonstrations designed to shame, goad, pressure, and ultimately encourage those responsible to help solve the problems they'd helped create. Cincotta and West Side Coalition members had started out with pickets on the suburban lawns of real estate agents who were using panic tactics and FHA-insured loans to buy and resell entire Chicago neighborhoods. Then the activists hounded HUD's regional administrator, massing in the lobby of his Lakeshore Drive high-rise and taking over a briefing he was giving to a packed ballroom of government officials.

By 1975 they were able to rally hundreds to take over the lobby of HUD's Chicago offices and compel President Ford's new HUD secretary, Carla Hills, to agree to stand before the group's members and answer questions about how her agency was going to solve the FHA crisis. Seven years later Cincotta's team coordinated groups around the country to besiege the Federal Reserve and get Chairman Paul Volcker to pledge to lower interest rates on loans for poor communities. That deal was sealed when a protester dressed as a shark—as in "loan shark"—scrambled atop the bronze doors of the Fed entrance, ready for the news cameras. Someone from a Bronx community organization had convinced a friend who wrote for *Saturday Night Live* to lend the land-shark costume that Chevy Chase used to wear.

Through these very public showdowns with the nation's top housing and banking officials, Cincotta had gone from fighting in and for her Chicago neighborhood to waging her war nationally as a ringleader of a group called National People's Action on Housing, banding together local organizations in other forsaken cities. She and her colleagues would figure out how the entire American mortgage system functioned, take it apart, and put it back together again as a machine for fixing broken neighborhoods. Bolstered by the Community Reinvestment Act, they would use community organizing to take on every force that stood between Chicago residents and access to home loans. It would be a kind of democratic coup, where the nation's financial powers would have to respond to the popular will.

Just one mighty institution remained to be brought on board with the project to finance mortgages in cities. For anyone looking to get a home loan, it was the most important by far—and it wasn't beholden to the Community Reinvestment Act. The Federal National Mortgage Association (FNMA), better known as Fannie Mae, was a New Deal creation intended to provide a pool of funds for mortgages so money would always be available to lenders, anywhere in the nation. Fannie Mae and its sibling agencies, Freddie Mac and Ginnie Mae, remained the only substantial sources of funds for a bank or other financial institution that made home mortgages.

In 1968, the Johnson administration had sold FNMA to shareholders for $216 million, to help pay for the Vietnam War. Ever since then Fannie Mae had been a "government-sponsored enterprise," receiving special privileges from the federal government that allowed it to borrow money cheaply from the Treasury. Every second Monday, Fannie Mae held an auction, at which it would buy the least expensive among the loans that mortgage bankers put up for sale—as long as those mortgages met Fannie Mae's stringent standards for prudent home lending. Thanks to the government sponsorship, the bankers could make more money by selling the loans to Fannie Mae than they could obtain elsewhere.

But Fannie Mae still wasn't, as far as anyone could tell, buying mortgages made to borrowers in neighborhoods such as Gale Cincotta's—decidedly urban, and now majority minority. Bankers earnestly trying to meet their new obligations under the Community Reinvestment Act reported that Fannie Mae still wasn't buying their loans from many urban areas, and that limited the banks' ability to lend in places such as Chicago's West Side. The government-supported company's refusal was all the more frustrating because its own charter required it to help finance housing "for low- and moderate-income families."

Fannie Mae's leadership, appointed by President Nixon, was keenly aware of the company's absence in inner cities. Indeed, they wanted to find a way back in—their way. Gas shortages and a gloomy outlook for Mideast oil signaled that the suburbs would stop growing and that the real estate industry's future therefore depended on turning blighted urban areas back into profitable territory. The company would soon inform shareholders that it was looking to increase its volume of business by 10 percent a year. Already, in its few years as a private company, Fannie Mae's earnings had been doubling and tripling annually. To keep expanding its business of financing the nation's mortgages, it would have to find unexploited terrain in which to flourish.

Gale Cincotta and members of her national network of activist groups weren't the only ones coming to understand that in the failings of the nation's housing finance system lay an opportunity to rewrite its rules, and in the process build a stronger, wealthier, and perhaps even happier nation. A former night mailroom clerk from Bensonhurst, Brooklyn, a redoubt of homeowners in the middle of New York City, had every bit as much determination to remake the business of real estate lending. He, too, was convinced that blunt and relentless efforts to get Washington to do things his way would bring the blessings of homeownership to Americans who never could have dreamed of it before.

But while Cincotta depended on an irregular army of thousands of working-class people and poor-by-choice community activists, Lewis Ranieri was a trader for Salomon Brothers, the most successful investment bank on Wall Street, and his partner in his project was the economic brain trust of the newly ensconced Reagan administration. Together they set out to create a system for financing home loans that would make far more money available, on far freer terms, than ever before.

Ranieri's vision for the new industry would be the antithesis of Cincotta's, even while it aimed for the same elusive goal of prosperity and security for all. Their two approaches came from extremes of the American political mind—one that believed that unfettered markets generate the greatest possibilities for broadly held wealth, and the other that believed in the necessity of ordering those markets to be socially helpful. For now, Ranieri and Cincotta's two utopias might as well have existed in parallel universes. But in just over a decade, the United States would have a president who embraced both at once, and pretended, like a child born of a doomed marriage, that the two weren't fatally incompatible.

Cincotta was building up regulations to obligate financial companies to do fair business with every American, regardless of where customers lived or the color of their skin or how much money they started out with. Ranieri believed that the best way to get to that ideal was to dismantle the regulations of a previous generation—cautious Depression-era strictures on securities trading that were preventing pension funds, insurance companies, and other institutions, collectively responsible for investing billions of dollars in other people's cash, from pouring their wealth into the places where we live. As more and more money flowed toward the nation's homeowners and the cost of borrowing went down, the market could at long last reach customers who had previously never had an opportunity to own a home.

"Lewie had this spiel about building homes for America," a Salomon colleague says of Ranieri in the book *Liar's Poker*, Michael Lewis's indelible portrait of Wall Street in the 1980s—and of Ranieri as its street-smart, loudmouthed, and hopelessly unfashionable embodiment. "When we'd come out of those meetings I'd say, 'C'mon, you don't think anyone believes in this crap, do you?' But that's what made Lewie so convincing. *He* believed that crap."

A team of traders at Salomon Brothers worked with Bank of America for three years, trying to create some kind of bond, made up of bunches of home mortgages, that they could convince large numbers of investors to buy. Ranieri joined the project in 1977, as it neared fruition. They didn't even have a name for what they were doing, until a *Wall Street Journal* columnist asked them and Ranieri came up with "securitizing." That is, they were taking all these mortgages and turning them into a security, like a bond, that could be bought and sold among investors.

The Bank of America bonds found few buyers. All but a handful of states had laws on the books forbidding pension funds and other investors entrusted with people's money from buying securities that weren't formally registered with state officials, measures designed to prevent the sale of bogus stocks. The Securities and Exchange Commission, too, required piles of documentation for each mortgage pool. The IRS was determined to tax the transactions. And even once Salomon figured out how to deal with the government's demands, few investors wanted to stick around for thirty years waiting to get paid as homeowners sedulously wrote their mortgage checks month after month. The hurdles to turning homes into readily tradable securities stretched out before Ranieri and his colleagues like a mountain chain.

Still, Wall Street "securitization" of mortgages had taken root, and the home business, under that gawky banner, would soon offer previously unimaginable opportunities for profit. It provided a swift solution to a mounting problem. In the late 1970s, the Federal Reserve's war on inflation catapulted interest rates to new heights; for homebuyers, mortgage interest zoomed past 15 percent. Savings and loans, the small local financial institutions that still made most of the home mortgages outside of redlined city neighborhoods, found themselves owing more money than they made, since they had to pay high interest rates to borrow funds but were collecting much smaller amounts of interest on loans they had made years earlier. The S&Ls' only hope was to sell those old mortgages to investors at a loss, and take a tax write-off. Meanwhile, no one was sure where affordable home mortgages were going to come from in the future.

The government-sponsored Fannie Mae, Freddie Mac, and Ginnie Mae could have supplied the solution. All three already did, or could, create mortgage-backed securities and thus generate from investors billions in new mortgage funds for the nation's homebuyers. Under their federal charters, they were exempt from the government restrictions on mortgage securities trading that so vexed Lewis Ranieri and his team; indeed, Ranieri's department had been created to sell Ginnie Mae's mortgage-backed securities to investors, and when Ranieri saw how much money there was to be made by buying up and reselling mortgages from flailing S&Ls, he persuaded Freddie Mac to create securities out of those home loans. Its sales of the Freddie Mac securities made Ranieri's division Salomon's biggest moneymaker by far.

But Ronald Reagan's election in 1980 opened up an even more attractive possibility for Salomon Brothers and other investment banks. They could now turn the creation of mortgage securities into a mass-scale, streamlined industry—and put themselves in charge. Like Salomon, the White House's economic policy office sought to unleash the power of private investors to pump vast sums of new money into the mortgage market. A President's Commission on Housing, consisting of bankers, real estate pros, and Washington political hands, helped shape and advance that agenda.

Under the Reagan plan, mortgage investment pools would succeed

S&Ls as the main source of funds for home loans. The administration and its housing commission were intent on putting Wall Street firms such as Salomon Brothers in command. In the process, they hoped to end the reign of Fannie Mae and the other government-sponsored enterprises that had been helping lenders finance home loans until now. "Eventually, the Commission believes, both FNMA [Fannie Mae] and FHLMC [Freddie Mac] should become entirely private corporations, without special access to the deep pockets of the Treasury," its members advised the president in 1982.

Working with Shannon Fairbanks, the deputy assistant for economic development in the White House Office of Policy Development, Ranieri became closely involved in shaping what the new, privately operated mortgage marketplace would look like. He met with the President's Commission, and together, almost by accident, they came up with the mortgage-backed security more or less as it's known today.

Their objective as they sat down in 1982 was no different from that of the toy company Coleco that year as it set out to sell millions of Cabbage Patch Kids. They were determined to mass-produce and market a product that, through simple variations on a formula, could lure their customers into a stampede to buy, whether they wanted a redhead, a preemie, or a bald one.

Investors in bonds, which mortgage-backed securities essentially are, seek predictable outcomes—and mortgages offer anything but. The biggest unknown on a thirty-year mortgage is the "prepayment risk": the possibility that a homeowner will either pay off the balance early or eventually opt to refinance with some other lender, and therefore not make all the interest payments that investors had been counting on. Statistically speaking, the longer an investor hangs on to the security, the greater the likelihood that he'll get stung by a borrower's prepayment and lose expected future proceeds.

To appeal to all kinds of investors—those who sought the safety that short-term commitments could provide, as well as those seeking high returns and therefore willing to take on the significantly greater risk of holding on to a mortgage security for a long time—Ranieri and the commission struck on the idea of carving up the pools into numerous slices, or "tranches," that let investors select the commitment that best met their needs. Investors who bought into the short-term, safest slices would get the bulk of the first payments to come in, until they were paid the full amount they'd been guaranteed. Then the next level of investors moved to the head of the line. Those who committed for the longest stretches of time generally were assured higher returns because they were taking on the greatest risks; payments from borrowers could run dry before those at the back of the line were fully paid. They were riding in the caboose on a train whose destination was clear but whose tail end might never arrive there.

To realize Ranieri's ambition for an unconstrained and fully private marketplace for mortgage finance, Congress would have to rewrite federal securities laws dating to the Great Depression, and meant to prevent re-currences of the abuses that had led to that cataclysm. With Fairbanks and a Washington attorney and Reagan housing commission member named Bernard Carl, Ranieri set about putting together a proposed bill.

The law Ranieri helped create, the Secondary Mortgage Market En-hancement Act, called on bond-rating agencies—at the time, Moody's and Standard & Poor's—to weigh in on each mortgage pool. As long as a bond got one of the top ratings from the agencies—meaning that in the agen-cies' opinions, investors ought to be confident of getting paid—it could be sold. While the Securities and Exchange Commission would oversee the trading of these securities just as it did all investments for sale, no longer would the U.S. government exclusively manage the market in mortgage-backed securities, as it had through Ginnie Mae. "We believe that the rat-ings services do offer substantial investor protection," Ranieri testified before Congress in early 1984.

The Colorado Democrat running the hearing, Representative Tim Wirth, voiced a lone and passionate cry of skepticism. Why set up private investment banks to do the same thing that the government-sponsored mortgage funds already could legally accomplish? And why trust the inscrutable, unaccount-able ratings agencies, which had already shown a tendency to give high scores to failing bonds?

Lewis Ranieri promised that putting private bankers and their sales forces in charge of mortgage securities would save borrowers half a percent on every loan, by allowing mortgage lenders to tap into a much bigger uni-verse of investors. The Democratic-run House joined the Republican-led Senate in handing Ranieri, and the rest of Wall Street, the keys to the na-tion's homes.

"We were now in a position to deploy all of the brilliant technology we had developed," hooted Ranieri, who spoke of his financial inventions

the way an engineer might refer to a supersonic jet engine. He had made
more money for the firm than anyone in its history—more, he claimed,
than the rest of Wall Street combined. Ranieri achieved what bankers and
real estate brokers had dreamed of forever: he turned homes into commodities as tradable, and impersonal, as stocks, bonds, and baseball cards.

A mortgage company with almost no money of its own, and unregulated
by any of the government banking agencies, could now go to Salomon
Brothers (or Goldman Sachs or Greenwich Capital) and get the funds it
needed to lend to customers, as long as its loans met the investment banks'
guidelines detailing the credit histories borrowers had to have and the maximum amount of debt a customer could take on compared with their income
and the value of their property. Computer tape reels made it possible to zip
all the related information over to the investment firm within minutes. The
fund manager would then take each pool and break it up into ranked
tranches, each with a different schedule for cash flow and corresponding level
of risk. The sales forces at the investment banks proceeded to market these
mortgage pool offerings to investors, especially pension and insurance funds.
In the coming few years, this new source of funds made it possible for
lenders that weren't banks—mortgage sales companies much like those that
had blitzed Chicago's West Side with FHA-insured loans—to go from making about one in five home loans to three in five. These lenders operated beyond the reach of the Community Reinvestment Act.

Lewis Ranieri left Salomon Brothers the following year, forced out in a
power struggle. It wasn't long before he began complaining that in a leadership vacuum, his industry was failing to deliver on the lowered interest
rates he had promised Congress. The financial gains from securitization
were substantial, all right, but Ranieri observed they were going overwhelmingly to a few savvy fund managers and investors, who quickly
found creative ways to capture the savings for themselves. In 1988, as
banking regulators warned of risky speculation among mortgage securities
brokers, Ranieri acknowledged that his invention could be a dangerous device if mishandled. "Just because a few people abuse the technology,
doesn't mean the technology is bad," he told the *Bond Buyer*. "I could use
the same argument about guns."

No matter. Ranieri, with the Reagan administration and Congress, had
rewritten history. Ranieri had spent three years pummeling and charming

every regulator whose favors Salomon Brothers needed to trade freely in mortgages. As Ranieri accurately assessed, looking back a decade later, "We won total flexibility."

The Reagan project to deregulate the mortgage securities market was supposed to eliminate Fannie Mae and Freddie Mac. Instead, the plot to kill the two agencies supercharged them into twin giants of home finance.

Fannie Mae and its sibling had many powerful allies in Washington, from homebuilders to mortgage bankers, who benefited from its government-discounted loan rates. With lobbying support from those partners, the agencies soon received permission from their regulators at HUD to take the loans they'd purchased from lenders and repackage them, as Ranieri's law now allowed them to do, into multilevel mortgage-backed securities engineered for maximum appeal to the widest possible range of investors. Salomon Brothers and other investment banks had advocated to exclude Fannie and Freddie from their new mortgage securities bazaar. Now the Wall Street firms had every reason to get along with them. The investment bankers would earn millions in fees by selling mortgage securities on behalf of Fannie Mae, Freddie Mac, and Ginnie Mae. The three government-sponsored enterprises together still supplied the funds for 95 percent of home loans, whether the mortgages were sold to consumers by banks, S&Ls, or, more and more now, minimally regulated mortgage companies.

When David O. Maxwell had arrived as Fannie Mae's CEO in 1981, the company was losing its shareholders a million dollars a day. Now, as President Reagan's second term came to an end, with the help of billions in new funds raised from investors through these mortgage-backed securities, it was again a profitable company. To make sure it stayed that way, Maxwell had begun toughening up lending standards, to reduce the chance that loans Fannie Mae bought would go into foreclosure. Those policies kept Fannie Mae's loans out of many city neighborhoods, even as the company's business was expanding.

Gale Cincotta was watching closely. Using data gleaned via the Home Mortgage Disclosure Act, her research staff drew up maps showing where Fannie Mae was financing loans and started calling what they saw "the doughnut effect": in virtually every city, they'd draw great rings radiating out from the center, with a big hole in the middle. Cincotta called Maxwell's office in the spring of 1988 to ask for a meeting with her members, at which they would propose how her group could help Fannie Mae fill the doughnut hole. She received the same response she'd been getting since 1975: none.

An unrequited call proved no deterrent. On an otherwise quiet Monday morning, the air buzzing only with the news that Nancy Reagan was consulting astrologers to determine her husband's public schedule, three yellow school buses pulled up in the circular driveway of Fannie Mae's brick headquarters, modeled on the mansion of an eighteenth-century Virginia governor. The buses disgorged demonstrators from Cleveland, Baltimore, St. Louis, Pittsburgh, Indianapolis. Still more yellow buses dropped off their passengers around the corner.

The organizers at the head of the group strutted in past the security guards, announcing they had a meeting with David Maxwell. The others massed in the lobby, their din amplified by plastic whistles, while the vanguard worked its way to Maxwell's office. "Come on out!" they shouted, and thumped with their fists on his door. "Come on out!"

The doughnut hole gaped because the Federal National Mortgage Association remained as picky as ever about which loans it would purchase. Homebuyers had to make a down payment of 10 percent of a home's price, at the very least; 20 percent was even better. Income had to come from a reliable and steady source, preferably a salary. Those cautious rules protected Fannie Mae's investors, but they also locked out a huge number of would-be homeowners.

Other urban activist groups had already succeeded in convincing some lenders to be more flexible, which they could be when they used funds from their own deposits to make the loans instead of selling the mortgages to Fannie Mae. The Community Reinvestment Act provided the means. Banks were now required to make loans or investments in their own backyards, no matter how desolate, and activist groups now had a way to block the expansion of any financial institution that didn't play along. Members of the Philadelphia chapter of Association of Communities for Reform Now, or ACORN, found a willing partner in First Fidelity Bank. Its members sat in conference rooms for hours and days, regaling First Fidelity executives with stories of ghetto economics, of household budgets concocted from odd jobs, tips, IOUs, food stamps, pillowcase bank accounts.

ACORN gave the bank a choice: it could count these sources of money as income for purposes of making home loans, or it could forget about its planned merger with Industrial Valley Bank. Miraculously, First Fidelity chose door number one. For the first time, a financial institution agreed to look at mortgage borrowers' income not as something to be documented assiduously with pay stubs and tax returns, but as an interpretive negotiation—a calculated risk.

The problem for First Fidelity and the other banks that soon followed was that unlike with their other mortgages, they couldn't make that risk go away by selling the loans off to Fannie Mae. These deals with banks such as First Fidelity remained quirky experiments in homeownership, and in the radical possibility that anyone, no matter how economically marginal, could achieve it. If Fannie Mae could get on board, that would change everything.

Maxwell, it turned out, wasn't in the besieged office the day Gale Cincotta and her hundreds of companions showed up. But his people who did ultimately greet them determined that here in their midst had fallen a golden opportunity. The reality was that to meet its growth objectives, Fannie Mae needed these poor people as much as the poor people needed them.

Julie Gould was there that day. As the head of the company's new Office of Low- and Moderate-Income Housing, she had been brought in to invest some of her company's billions into financing the construction of affordable apartments for rent. But here in this crowd of pushy capitalist radicals, another possibility presented itself.

Gould and her colleagues agreed to a meeting, and then more. "They had no idea who we were or where we came from," says Tom Schraw, who worked for Cincotta and organized the effort. The roster of activists looked nothing like the credentialed technocrats across the table from them. Schraw was a twenty-six-year-old self-taught data geek whose college mentor was Paul Wellstone. Next to him sat a nun from Cincinnati; a Cleveland mom who got involved because she was fed up with packs of stray dogs in her neighborhood; and, of course, Schraw's big, blond boss. They converged again and again in Washington over the months that followed, scraping together funds for plane tickets and armed with numbers proving that making home loans to low-income people in cities, even those who couldn't come up with down payments, would be a smart business proposition for Fannie Mae.

"We looked at: What was really driving your loan loss experience?" recalls Schraw. "We found that you're not really losing a lot of money on inner city neighborhoods." Using Fannie Mae's own spreadsheets, Schraw showed the executives where their big financial losses actually were: in places such as Texas, where plummeting oil prices had pushed a wave of layoffs and then home foreclosures.

Then Schraw and the other laypeople laid out a blueprint for how the biggest mortgage fund in the world could turn profit by selling homes to people who had never qualified for a mortgage loan before. "We're not trying to help you lose money," Schraw told the financiers in the conference room. "We're helping you make money."

To do that, the advocates advised the execs, Fannie Mae would have to do business very differently, and a little more recklessly. It would have to tolerate late mortgage payments, at least sometimes. It had to accept that old buildings in cities had some value, no matter what the appraisal manuals said. The company would have to lower its minimum required down payment, from 10 to 5 or even 3 percent. And it would have to allow borrowers to take on more debt, compared to their income, than anyone had previously considered reasonable.

As far as Fannie Mae was concerned, the proposal was a winner. "In order to grow our business after coming out of our financial issues, we needed to expand our market," Gould observes. "The first step was to create a lower down payment mortgage to allow more people to qualify." That proposition got further backup from economists from the University of Pennsylvania who had recently projected that lowering down payments and increasing borrowers' debt would raise the national homeownership rate by 3 percent.

After months of meetings, the organization that owned, in a sense, millions of homes had reached an understanding with a bunch of near-volunteers who possessed only smarts, persistence, gall, and a radar to find common ground. "The program is designed to demonstrate the soundness of mortgages to low- and moderate-income families and will ultimately lead to more flexible mortgage lending standards nationwide," Schraw informed readers of the National People's Action newsletter. In a test program in five midwestern cities, Fannie Mae would buy $50 million in home mortgages from lenders on terms it had never offered anyone else.

Borrowers could take out far more money compared with their income than other homeowners—up to 38 percent of their earnings—and wouldn't even have to have savings in the bank in case they needed extra cash to keep up with payments. Cincotta's group and the mortgage fund would watch carefully to see how well borrowers did at keeping up with their payments. Within two years, Fannie Mae had turned Community Home Buyers into a nationwide program backed by a billion of its dollars.

Fannie Mae's cooperation was welcome, but Community Home Buyers remained a limited experiment. Cincotta and other community investment group leaders resolved to keep looking for a way to flat-out require Fannie and its sibling Freddie Mac to do business in their neighborhoods on a massive scale. They finally found it in 1991, as Congress began to repair the disastrous legacy of its move almost a decade earlier to deregulate savings and loans. Hundreds of these once-modest local financial institutions had become insolvent, many after embarking on wild investment sprees on golf courses, casinos, shopping malls, and loans to girlfriends. A federal insurance fund was now on the hook for a projected $100 billion in losses. As House chair Henry Gonzalez turned his attention to ensuring that Fannie Mae and Freddie Mac would remain flush despite the S&Ls' stumbles, Cincotta, ACORN, Consumers Union, and other public interest groups decided that it was time to force the two institutions to purchase loans made to people with low incomes.

Their project got major backup from the *Atlanta Journal-Constitution*, which had just run a four-day, fifteen-part evisceration of the mortgage lending industry's systematic discrimination against black borrowers. "Whites receive five times as many home loans from Atlanta's banks and savings and loans as blacks of the same income—and that gap has been widening each year," began "The Color of Money." Or as the paper's editorial page put it, "Redlining: An Economic War Waged on Black Communities." The series would win a Pulitzer Prize.

Once again, Gale Cincotta waddled into the Capitol to make the people's case. "Secondary market purchases of low-down-payment loans to low- and moderate-income homebuyers is not yet standard procedure," she advised a Senate banking subcommittee in the winter of 1991. "It should be."

Indignantly, Cincotta reminded the Senate that only homebuyers with fantastic credit and extremely valuable houses could normally buy a home with just 5 percent down. Cincotta instructed, "The most important contribution the secondary market can make to increasing homeownership in this country is to change that outdated standard."

Congress agreed. It decreed that 40 percent of all the home loans Fannie Mae and Freddie Mac bought would have to be made to people who made less than the average income of their area. A share of those, in turn, would have to go to people poor enough to qualify for public housing. That was just for starters. In the future, the loans to lower-income families would have to become an even larger share, most likely the majority of the mortgage companies' business.

Though Fannie Mae's negotiators had objected to the requirements, the company's new CEO, James A. Johnson, had to make his peace with them. In fact, Johnson rewarded the activists generously, with sizable grants to help counsel homebuyers in the new programs. His company's future prospects now depended on the tens of millions of renters those grassroots groups spoke to and for.

Two

The Rising Tide

Holland, Michigan, 1996

H<small>E WORKED IN CONSTRUCTION</small> for a living, his specialty the muscular art of the tape knife and molding plaster into shapely interior walls. The cozy Victorian from the 1890s was a special test of Spencer Kasten's skill. Spencer and his wife, Lisa, had spent the past two and a half months gutting and rebuilding the place. The last inhabitant here, on this quiet street in the historic district of Holland, Michigan, was a cat lady with fifteen stinky life companions. The walls had crumbled behind fake wood paneling. Some previous renovator had the bright idea of spanning the ceiling with ersatz beams. Every window needed to be torn out and replaced.

"The foundation, roof, and plumbing—they had to be okay," says Spencer, listing the infrastructure he and Lisa made sure was solid. Everything else they could build themselves.

The Kastens were young, twenty-four and twenty-five, with the kind of energy you need to replaster every surface but the floor. There, they shredded room after room of carpet, exposing warm, wide oak. The laminate countertops—they had to go. Spencer and Lisa worked without pay or help, gladly, because this home was their own. They bought it with a government FHA loan. With the signature on the deed they were new people, homeowners.

Lisa wielded the toolbox and the checkbook. She also kept track of the family goals: "We knew the money we were spending on rent would not get us anywhere. We knew we wanted to have a family. We'd have a home where we could invest and start something." In 1996, homes in Holland's quaint historic district, a stroll from a walkable downtown, where independent businesses thrived and Lake Michigan was a quick drive away, were hot properties; few came on the market, and owners constantly found themselves fielding offers they had no intention of taking. The Kastens were lucky to find this fixer-upper, which had scared other buyers away.

As early June blossomed outside, Spencer brushed back his mop of blond curls and surveyed his handiwork—the concentric circular moldings around the hanging dining room lamp, the exposed wood grain (real) on the window seat near the front door, the delicately painted purple and green trim on the exterior. The house wasn't huge, and it had just one bathroom, on the stairway landing, for its three bedrooms. They couldn't even store stuff in the basement—too damp—and would have to rent a storage unit. But who could complain? They got the place for just $57,000, a typical price for the neighborhood, plus about $3,000 in closing costs.

Lisa didn't expect to hear from their Realtor again, so soon after they'd closed on their house. The agent called, with urgency in her voice. The people at HUD needed a couple, new homebuyers from somewhere out there, to come to Washington and talk about their experience. Could the Kastens do it? Like, in two days? Well, they reasoned, they would get a free trip.

Lisa is the writer in the family, and though she had never spoken publicly before, as instructed she located a notebook and pen amid the buckets of joint compound and piles of half-peeled linoleum, and put together some remarks. About how an owner takes pride in her home, and makes loving efforts to care for it. That it reflects on the owner as a person—someone who plans for the future. "Our home is no mansion," she wrote, "but to us it's the most beautiful house in the world." That would do. Lisa didn't want to screw up the speech.

Via the Grand Rapids airport—their trip was paid for by the National Association of Realtors—the Kastens got to Washington, where their escort took them to a cab with instructions to head for the White House. The White House? Neither of them had ever even registered to vote.

In the Oval Office, President Clinton was waiting for them. He asked them why they decided to buy a home. He asked them why they used a government FHA loan. Outside, on the White House lawn, aides propped up a photograph of the Kastens' half-finished home on an easel. With the president on their other flank, the couple stood on display alongside it, Lisa in a red polka-dotted dress and Spencer's slender frame almost drowning in a suit he rarely wore.

Plaster dust still in their skin, Lisa and Spencer Kasten found themselves actors in one of the showpieces of Bill Clinton's 1996 campaign for reelection. Standing next to the Kastens and the blown-up photo of their fragile new possession, the president nodded toward the nervous couple and called people like them the future of a prosperous nation. "Anything we can do to facilitate people buying their own homes and to speed the process along," promised the president, "will increase savings in America, increase security, and support families."

Clinton instructed the Secret Service to bring the Kastens in the limo with him to their next stop. In the backseat he had more questions: How had they found their home and their loan? How much had they paid? What were their closing costs? Then he pointed out the McDonald's where he bought his coffee after his run every morning. They were on their way to the Homeownership Summit, a grand event the Clinton administration pulled together at the Omni Shoreham to show off its efforts, over the previous year, to increase the number of homeowners in America to unprecedented heights.

The president's goals, which he first announced on June 2, 1995—proclaimed National Homeownership Day—were ambitious: 8 million new homeowning households over the next five years, and a record 67.5 percent homeownership rate. (That, compared with just 650,000 new homeowners a year in the previous decade.) One out of every eight renters, who couldn't or wouldn't have bought a home otherwise, would march into the ranks of the mortgage-holding mainstream.

President Clinton dive-bombed into office in 1993 with an immense economic agenda, geared toward pumping up the economy and lowering the ballooning federal deficit—which, if his advisers were right, would bring interest rates down. Selling people more homes was barely part of the plan. Lower interest rates were, rather, supposed to spur business investment; a lower debt, the Clintonians hoped, would free up money for job training and other efforts to put more money in Americans' bank accounts.

Clinton's National Homeownership Strategy, as it came to be called, began instead in a fit of campaign-trail rivalry, and with a scholarly expert on housing who decided he would rather make history than write about it.

Earlier in his career, Columbia University urban planning professor Marc

Weiss had documented the chaos of home mortgages before the New Deal and then the FHA's creation of suburbia. Through a serendipitous meeting with an old fellow traveler from the labor movement who happened to be running the presidential campaign of Arkansas' governor, Weiss forsook academia to work for the circus that was the Clinton campaign. He would be its liaison to urban development groups.

In the fall of 1992, as Clinton headed into a showdown with George H. W. Bush, Weiss called strategist George Stephanopoulos in a panic. The National Association of Home Builders was inviting the Clinton/Gore campaign to speak to its leadership—facing off with Vice President Dan Quayle. Unless the campaign could find another speaker, it would be Weiss up on the stage, not nearly as pretty as his adversary or his employers. Can we get Clinton? Weiss pleaded. Al Gore? Anyone?

In desperation, Weiss turned to an unfinished manuscript from his Columbia days, on the history of campaigns to promote homeownership. He proceeded to write its next chapter by making it happen. With a green light from Stephanopoulos, Weiss wrote a letter to the builders' industry group. Signed: Bill Clinton.

The letter told the homebuilders the bad news they already knew: home sales had dropped by nearly one quarter in the previous few years. Clinton called 1991 "the worst year for housing construction since 1945." And he told the homebuilders whom to blame. The rate at which Americans owned their own homes had declined for the past twelve years—starting with Ronald Reagan's first year in office.

With Weiss the dark-bearded professor as his medium, reading the letter to the homebuilders, Bill Clinton found himself promising that in his first year in the White House he would reverse the drop. "Homeownership, home building, home sales, home mortgages, and home values will once again be the rising tide that lifts all of America's boats," came the pledge.

The homebuilders, not suprisingly, loved the speech Bill Clinton never gave, enough to publish the candidate's message in its magazine. The Mortgage Bankers Association and the National Association of Realtors circulated versions for their members.

And so Weiss had to deliver what he—the now President Clinton—had promised. Once Clinton arrived in the White House, HUD secretary Henry Cisneros and his aides watched the numbers anxiously. Miraculously, they wriggled upward that first year, 0.1 percent, as four hundred thousand new homeowners bought in. Interest rates hadn't yet gone down, but Americans seemed to be acting on a newfound confidence in the future.

"Holy fuck," Cisneros exclaimed to Weiss. "We actually did this."

From there, the White House decided to go all out. In the summer of 1994, Cisneros sent a memo to Robert E. Rubin, then Clinton's chief adviser on the economy, outlining a plan to bring homeownership to an all-time high. Rubin was previously the cochair of the investment bank Goldman Sachs, and that gave him a special awareness of what a vastly bigger customer base would mean for the financial services business.

The reality was that the consumers the industry had depended on all this time were spoken for. More than nine of every ten suburban middle-class white households owned their homes. If the industry were going to grow, it would have to tap new borrowers, and HUD's research team concluded that those were going to be urban, black (only 43 percent were homeowners), Latino (41 percent), and people under age thirty-five (just 38 percent).

That last group was especially worrisome to the eminences of real estate and finance. In just a decade, homeownership among young people had fallen by nearly 5 points. The next generation of consumers were becoming renters instead of owners—Cisneros called them "lifers," as if they were in prison—a status that might well become permanent if their habits didn't change.

Invoking the twenty-fifth anniversary of the moon landing, the HUD secretary pitched the Clinton homeownership strategy as another Apollo Project. "MESSAGE: The Clinton Administration's Economic Plan has succeeded and is touching the lives of American families in a profoundly personal way: making it possible for families to become homeowners on a scale never before achieved," Cisneros bulleted out for Rubin. "The Clinton Administration is committed to extending the economic recovery by spurring housing production, which will translate into business and consumer confidence, increasing housing starts and home sales, and expanded economic growth and job creation." As someone at HUD calculated it, they would have to add one new homeowner every 24 seconds, 24 hours a day, 7 days a week, 365 days a year.

The White House couldn't do it alone. In August 1994, it brought representatives from the Mortgage Bankers Association, Fannie Mae, the

National Association of Realtors, the National Association of Home Builders, and other industry players, along with state and local government leaders and advocates such as ACORN and Habitat for Humanity, to Washington's National Building Museum to advance the cause. They were greeted by Rubin's deputy, Ellen Seidman, previously vice president for research and economics at Fannie Mae. That afternoon the White House would ask them all to pledge to do their part to propel the number of homeowners to new heights.

"The National Homeownership Strategy," announced the project's founding document, a compendium of a hundred steps to make buying a home cheaper, easier, and inevitable, "will attempt to help *all* American households become homeowners."

In classic Clinton style, the National Homeownership Strategy sought to sell Washington conservatives on the very thing they were trying to destroy: the sixty-year legacy of federal government involvement in housing. When Newt Gingrich and his Republican revolutionaries took over Congress that fall, one of the first things they did was cut HUD's budget by a quarter. Then they set out to eliminate the agency entirely.

But here, in the selling of homeownership, the Democrats had embraced a politically untouchable cause. No less a free market maven than Federal Reserve chair Alan Greenspan anointed the National Homeownership Strategy with a keynote speech at one of its early meetings, and even as they sought to take down HUD, Republicans never questioned the National Homeownership Strategy.

From its birth in the Great Society, HUD had focused on financing and managing inexpensive housing for those who couldn't otherwise pay for it. Now its staff experienced a culture shock. They were accustomed to talking about "affordable housing." Now the Secretary's policy aides instructed them to use the term "affordable homeownership" instead. "Housing," politically, signaled poverty, public housing projects, "Section 8" rent vouchers. Homeownership suggested the exact opposite: the great middle-class majority, responsible mortgageholders in stable communities.

Indeed, the Clinton administration expected its efforts to have a transformative effect. According to HUD's planners, homeownership would stabilize neighborhoods and build better communities because new prop-

erty owners would "exercise more responsibility over their living environ-
ment."

It was no accident that the R word—responsibility—was part of the vocabulary of the National Homeownership Strategy. This was a project of
mass behavior modification, in which millions of Americans would move
out from the liability side of the social ledger to bloom into assets to their
communities and the economy. The National Homeownership Strategy was
deeply connected to the Clinton administration's more infamous crusade
for personal responsibility: its overhaul of the welfare system, which for
the first time required almost everyone receiving public assistance to work
for their benefits.

Both welfare reform and the homeownership push were poised to herd
poor people from the raunchy outskirts of the economy into the eye of the
marketplace, as workers and then as consumers of financial services. Through
sheer numbers, this march of millions had the power to heave the American economy to new heights.

The Clinton homeownership crusade relied on two forces to get the nation there. One was a menu of deregulation, written with industry partners,
aimed at lowering the cost of building and financing a home. The other was
a campaign to transform public consciousness: "Instilling a can-do attitude
among those renters who have given up on the American Dream of homeownership will require a long-term approach, using both traditional and new
techniques of education, awareness, and encouragement," the homeownership strategy team predicted.

Introduced as social policy, welfare reform and homeownership evolved
into twin stars of Robert E. Rubin's plan to turn up the gas on the national
economy. Moving masses from welfare to work, generating budget savings
and tax revenues in the process, was an explicit part of the administration's
plan to eliminate the federal deficit. Clinton promised that deficit reduc-
tion would in turn bring interest rates down; the most important effect of
low interest rates would be to spur businesses to invest and expand, but
cheap money to borrow would also make homeownership attractive and
possible for those who didn't already live the dream. Around and around,
this virtuous cycle would keep gyrating, an economic machine that the
Clinton administration called the Community Empowerment Agenda. "An
expanding economic pie," as a leading theorist labeled it, would keep the
whole nation well fed.

In eight speeches leading up to Election Day 1996, President Clinton dug right into that pie, flavor: apple, with sweet words to tantalize future homeowners and their communities. Homeownership "encourages savings and investment, promotes economic and civic responsibility, and enhances the financial security of the American people," Clinton beamed as he announced his new project. "Perhaps most important, homeownership gives Americans pride in their neighborhoods and hope for a brighter tomorrow."

Clinton was drawing on a hot trend in policy wonk circles. His advisers, allies, and a growing array of philanthropists looked to homeownership as an anchor of a new prosperity for millions of Americans on the economic margins. Property ownership, as they saw it, would bring families out of tenuous economic situations—lives lived payday to payday, with little if any money in the bank—and mold them into people who saved for the future simply by dint of their mortgage payments, building home equity with every check.

"We really did believe that assets and wealth-building changed the way that people thought about the future, their planning horizons, their way of bulding wealth," says Michael Stegman, who headed policy development for Clinton's HUD and recommended the National Homeownership Strategy's goals (he's now domestic policy director for the MacArthur Foundation). Year by year, payment by payment, the new homeowners would move into what President Clinton liked to call the "economic mainstream." Rather than government spending its money on aid to families month after month, it would reward them for the desired behavior of saving for the future.

More profoundly, some especially ambitious thinkers postulated, getting poor people to acquire assets—wonk shorthand for homes and savings accounts—would actually change their consciousness, so that they would act in the world as someone with an investment to protect. "If a young mother owns her home, she begins to pay more attention to real estate values, property taxes, the cost of maintenance," social welfare expert Michael Sherraden postulated in a book that became required reading among reformers. The effects, he and others predicted, would carry on for generations.

Clinton saw few bounds to the power of homeownership: to set wayward young people on a course to success, to turn slums into orderly communities, to accomplish with a few pieces of paper what three decades of welfare had failed to do.

"We just had a report come out last week asserting that it may be that up to one third of our children are now born out of wedlock," Clinton said on the first National Homeownership Day, in 1995, in a speech viewed via satellite by housing and banking officials across the country. "You want to reinforce family values in America, encourage two-parent households, get people to stay home? Make it easy for people to own their own homes and enjoy the rewards of family life and see their work rewarded. This is a big deal. This is about more than money and sticks and boards and windows. This is about the way we live as a people and what kind of society we're going to have."

In practical terms, the Clinton administration's National Homeownership Strategy centered around a "partnership" with the real estate industry—homebuilders, bankers, Realtors—to do business with renters who had never owned a home before. Clinton's Department of Housing and Urban Development pushed lenders to sign agreements committing them to adopt more flexible loan policies and market their products to new groups of consumers.

Countrywide Home Loans, the biggest residential real estate lender in the nation, was the first to commit. Its CEO, Angelo Mozilo, was the president of the influential Mortgage Bankers Association, which also signed up to advance the National Homeownership Strategy. Countrywide was already in the process of launching a marketing campaign that reached where no mortgage lender had gone before: deep into formerly redlined city neighborhoods.

The home lender opened new offices in predominantly black areas of the District of Columbia, Los Angeles, Newark, Atlanta, Chicago, and other cities. It networked with local real estate agents and groups such as the Realtists, a national organization of black brokers. It made grants to trusted neighborhood nonprofit groups so they could counsel new homebuyers. It gave away a video, narrated by James Earl Jones, titled *A Feeling Called Home*, and unlike other lenders at the time, it made sure that all information was available in Spanish as well as English.

The pacts Countrywide and other Mortgage Bankers Association members signed signaled to their competitors and financial backers that expanding the market for home sales to formerly excluded groups would be a boon to their business.

The mortgage banks alone stood to make $500 billion in new loans. You'd think they'd be elated. Instead, they worried. "You'll be looking at people who are more likely to have employment histories that are a little speckled, or a credit history that has some nicks on it," the executive vice president of the Mortgage Bankers Association told the *American Banker*. "There is a prospect that those are going to be riskier loans." In that same article, American University finance professor Peter Chinloy predicted that lenders would look to lower the size of required down payments to bring in those new buyers. Borrowers who made low down payments, and therefore didn't have much of their own money at stake, were well known to be likelier to default on their payments than those who made high ones, and in the event they did go into foreclosure, a lender could end up saddled with a house worth less than the amount of the unpaid loan.

Clinton's man in charge of the homeownership project, FHA chief Nicolas Retsinas, shook off those concerns. "The perceived risk exceeds the real risk," he averred. The solution was to "price the risk"—charge a little more interest each month, perhaps, for those dicier borrowers—and make sure the new buyers got financial counseling.

Usually, corporations lobby politicians. But with his homeownership agenda, President Clinton chased the real estate industry like a horny prom-date suitor. In October 1994, Clinton came to the convention center across the street from Disneyland to tell the Realtors what he had in mind.

"I want to target new markets, underserved populations, tear down the barriers of discrimination wherever they are found," he proclaimed to cheers at the Realtors' annual convention. Pointing to sagging homeownership rates for young families with children, Clinton vowed to turn them around, and implored the real estate industry to do its part. "As they say back in Arkansas," he told the Realtors, "if you find a turtle on a fencepost, chances are it didn't get there by accident." The line got a big laugh from the Realtors, and no wonder: the president was committing to putting a turtle on every fencepost. By the time he came back to address the Realtors again, in the spring of 1996, they were on their way to selling a record four million homes that year.

Soon afterward, HUD secretary Cisneros applauded the news that homeownership was at a fifteen-year high. He was the official in charge of the nation's housing, but building better homes or better communities wasn't the focus of his remarks, made in a conference call with reporters and the president's chief economic adviser, Laura Tyson. He called the rise "a powerful engine of economic growth, creating jobs in the construction industry and in businesses that sell building supplies, appliances, and home furnishings." Then Tyson jumped in, to reassure reporters that an uptick in interest rates wouldn't break the upward momentum. "Housing affordability," she assessed, "will remain quite favorable."

Gale Cincotta happened to be in Washington that day, and she was irate. She was there to testify before Congress on how well Fannie Mae and Freddie Mac were measuring up to their new obligations to sponsor home loans for people of modest means. Cincotta looked around her and at the man next to her on the panel, formerly head of the National Association of Home Builders. "I am usually the only one talking about housing as shelter," she railed. "Everyone else is talking about how many refrigerators we can sell, how much carpeting, how many stoves, how many shingles, how much fencing, and it's how many jobs we can create."

Well, everybody but Bill Clinton. As the 1996 campaign plowed on, President Clinton began to weave his own personal tale into his rhapsody to the American homeowner. At the Homeownership Summit, with the Kastens onstage next to him, Clinton reminisced about the first house he bought, for $20,500, a thousand-square-foot hardwood-floored dollhouse of a home with a mortgage payment of $174 a month.

It was his way of proposing to Hillary, more valuable than any diamond. "Don't you think you'll have to marry me so I won't have to live there by myself?" he said he told his wife-to-be.

Lisa and Spencer Kasten still live in their cozy Victorian. Eleven years have given them a lot of time to fill the little house with artifacts they bought at antiques stores along the Red Arrow Highway, from other aging homes whose owners didn't value their parts—brass knobs, a folding screen, Dick and Jane–themed framed prints.

They can make their mortgage payments with no problem, on his income doing plasterwork and hers from her part-time job as a barista at JP's Coffee and Espresso down in the bustling Eighth Street shopping district. They did have to refinance, once, to pay for the adoption of their oldest child, Avery. Then they adopted two more, Elijah and Noah, filling the narrow bedrooms upstairs. All five of them share that bathroom on the landing, now painted a cheerful pink and green.

"I think we've outgrown the home we bought eleven years ago," Lisa muses. The gentle sun through the rippled glass of the living room window highlights her bleached hair and ruddy cheeks as she looks over at Elijah and Noah next to her on the couch. She wants to write the story of how she and Spencer came to adopt their children—black babies whose birth mothers agreed to give them away to be raised by blond strangers so their sons and daughter could grow up in a stable home.

Spencer doesn't see much of them these days. His current plastering job is in Ypsilanti, nearly four hours to the east, just shy of Detroit, so he stays there during the week and comes home to his family on weekends.

They'd like to relocate, somewhere where Spencer can work, but they can't. The housing boom and bust of the past few years had nothing to do with it; it bypassed Holland as surely as a hurricane would. They've tried to sell the house, asking $109,000, and have had no offers.

The theory was attractive. For a while, it even held true. During the late 1990s, economists, urban planners, geographers, and other academics produced a small forest of papers assessing the powers of homeownership—to make the poor wealthier, to turn disaffected individuals into citizens willing to spend long nights at town meetings, to keep a street clean. Until then, any case for the greater benefits of owning a home instead of renting had been a matter of anecdote and conjecture. "The validity of some of these assertions is so widely accepted," a HUD policy briefing acknowledged in 1995, "that economists and social scientists have seldom tested them."

With both the Clinton administration and Fannie Mae pushing the American Dream for people stuck in downwardly mobile American reality, homeownership, suddenly, was hot.

The research was paid for by HUD, Fannie Mae, the Federal Reserve, the Mortgage Bankers Association—institutions that stood to gain from increases in homeownership, lending, and property values. Another font of research on the social benefits of homeownership—and homeownership for poor people in particular—was Harvard's Joint Center for Housing Studies, funded by the real estate industry. The Joint Center's research, in the most literal sense, is market research, assessing opportunities for expansion and

profit; its more than sixty member-sponsors are building materials manufacturers (Sherwin-Williams, Andersen Windows, National Gypsum Company,
84 Lumber, Masco kitchen and bath cabinets), builders (Lennar, Beazer,
Pulte), Realtors, mortgage lenders, and investment banks. After he left HUD,
Nicolas Retsinas became the Joint Center's director.

The titles of the academics' papers track the hunt in progress:

- "Do Homeownership Programs Increase Property Values in Low-
  Income Neighborhoods?"
- "Simulating the Impact on Homeownership Rates of Strategies to
  Increase Ownership by Low-Income and Minority Households"
- "A Note on the Benefits of Homeownership"
- "Homeownership and Neighborhood Stability"
- "Incentives and Social Capital: Are Homeowners Better Citizens?"
- "The Decision to Own: The Impact of Race, Ethnicity, and Immi-
  grant Status"
- "The Social Benefits of Homeownership: Empirical Evidence from
  National Surveys"
- "The Economic Benefits and Costs of Homeownership: A Critical
  Assessment of the Research"

Yet for all the studies and the millions of taxpayer and private dollars ex-
pended to fund them, the research generated only glimmers of proof that
Clinton's project was actually going to work as intended—that as more and
more people became homeowners, at lower and lower levels of income, their
communities and their lives would improve as a result.

Some of the research unveiled towering barriers looming between the
Clinton administration and its homeownership goals. No matter how much
you lowered the down payment or increased how much debt a family could
carry, four out of five renters still couldn't afford to buy even the cheapest
homes on the block.

That last study on the list, funded by the Mortgage Bankers Association
and published in 2001, well after the first heady rush of these reports,
paused to consider how little anyone still knew about the consequences of
encouraging renters who weren't already wealthy to own their homes. "Raising national homeownership rates will require significant increases in homeownership among underserved populations," wrote the researchers from the

University of North Carolina. "We should have a more accurate assessment of the potential benefits and risks faced by these households before we persuade them to become homeowners."

Study after study grappled with a basic research dilemma: Does homeownership create better neighbors or neighborhoods? Or are neighborly and thrifty people more likely than others to become homeowners in the first place? The best the research could conclude is that homeowners stayed in one place longer, and that this tendency in turn led to greater community involvement.

Eventually, scholars found that once they set aside the various traits that tend to determine whether someone chooses to own or rent one's home, homeowners and tenants really aren't all that different. HUD housing policy architect Michael Stegman found that compared with low-income renters in similar neighborhoods, new low-income owners were actually less committed to "neighboring," whether that meant setting up a community play group or getting involved in a civic organization.

Some studies found that launching low-income people into homeownership wasn't always such a hot idea. While some moved up in the world, often the new homebuyers were purchasing the worst housing in the worst neighborhoods with the worst schools—hardly a solid investment. Two Yale School of Management professors compared the performance of real estate to other financial markets and concluded that during the 1980s and 1990s homes had performed worse than any other investment a household could have made. In forty states, there had been at least one five-year stretch of home price declines so great that someone who bought and then had to sell a house would end up owing more than the property was worth.

But those pessimistic voices were the exceptions, and mostly surfaced after President Clinton had left office. Industry didn't need to influence the outcomes of the research because it had already set the terms of debate. The Clinton strategy presumed that what was good for the real estate industry and economy was also good in the long term for consumers, and by extension the places where they live. The consumer found herself lashed to the prow of the ship. When the weather was favorable, everyone sailed far, and those farthest behind gained the most—within four years, the black homeownership rate had risen more than 7 percent, more than double the overall jump. But when the waters turned stormy, as they surely would, what would happen to the brave new homeowner?

As property values began to swell, that wasn't a question on many minds. What the studies couldn't prove, a few real-world experiments were tantalizingly showing off on potholed city streets: In some of the poorest and most blighted corners of the country, homeownership did seem to be working wonders. Formerly derelict city neighborhoods, places that had burned and buckled in the 1970s and into the 1980s, were importing new homeowners as anchors of stability.

There was the Nehemiah Program in the Bronx and Brooklyn, where local church activists and a civic-minded developer poured block-long foundations and then assembled modest brick homes on top of them. The nearly three thousand houses looked dinky, ugly, small. But they sold for less than $100,000 apiece, and clerks and teachers' aides and other working folks flocked to their low-slung promise. On those blocks, at least, fearsome neighborhoods were tamed with rose gardens and new residents with an investment to protect. They were in this for the long haul, since buyers signed agreements pledging that if they sold their homes in less than fifteen years, they could realize only a minimal profit.

Starting in Georgia and spreading across the country, Habitat for Humanity put hammers in the hands of the near-homeless to reclaim vacant houses. Usually, the new buyers received counseling on the responsibilities of homeownership, and stayed in the homes for a long time.

The Clinton administration started copying these shining examples, planting new homebuyers like seeds in rocky soil. HUD spent upward of $500 million a year to demolish deteriorating public housing and replace it with low-rise communities populated with owners, who it was hoped would be a good influence on the renters. The agency also quietly managed to sell public housing to nearly five thousand of its occupants.

HUD put another $50 million into "homeownership zones" that, like Nehemiah, laid down brand-new subdivisions in depopulated cities and imported buyers at low rates of interest. Those zones would have grown far more numerous if Congress had allowed it. Homeownership for Women (HOW) targeted single moms. Even poor tenants could get in on the action. Renters who received government Section 8 vouchers to pay for their rent were now able to take that money and put it toward a down payment on a new home as long as their income was at least $10,300 a year.

But ultimately the Clinton administration's homeownership dream depended on rewiring that battered division of HUD, the Federal Housing

Administration. With its public insurance fund providing a low-cost safety net that other loans didn't have, FHA could help lend more money—hundreds of billions more—to the new wave of homebuyers than anyone else.

There was just one problem. While Fannie Mae and the mortgage lenders it did business with were deploying new technology to get loans instantly approved, FHA lumbered like a mastodon. Under the first Bush administration, it nearly went bankrupt because its insurance fund had to pay back so many foreclosed loans. Government rules required every mortgage to be reviewed by a human being, who had to sift through mounds of paperwork. They processed those loans in eighty-one field offices. The agency had no flexibility to hire consultants to overhaul its technology, or even to write software to efficiently calculate prices. While other loans were getting cheaper and cheaper for consumers, FHA's layered on fees and delays. "We tried to do more," laments Nicolas Retsinas now, "but we didn't have the tools."

In 1995, the Clinton administration tried to turn FHA back into the fierce beast that led the nation out of the Great Depression by putting the seal of the U.S. government on home loans. Retsinas petitioned Congress to make FHA an independent authority, freed from stifling government procurement and management rules.

Newt Gingrich's Republican revolutionaries in Congress had no interest in helping Bill Clinton. They nixed the overhaul. FHA still insured one out of every eight new loans, but no longer could the Clinton administration hope to keep a leash on the vast new home lending market it was letting loose.

"That doesn't look like a plan to transform the American mortgage finance system!" Jim Johnson scoffed.

Well, Barry Zigas was trying, even if his needling boss didn't think so. When he had headed the National Low-Income Housing Coalition, Zigas sat alongside Gale Cincotta and other professional populists lobbying for those guarantees that Fannie Mae would fund loans for poor people. Then Johnson asked Zigas to work for Fannie Mae, to build that dream nation of homeowners.

At a meeting of the company's top execs, Zigas tossed out a number—some multiple of billions of dollars—for how much more of its own money Fannie Mae was going to pledge to make available for the nation's homebuyers to grab. Johnson threw it back at him.

Johnson was born into his suit and into power. His father had been the Speaker of the Minnesota House. Jim grew up to be a policy wonk and top aide to Walter Mondale. The Democrats' 1984 loss was Johnson's gain; he became a managing partner of Lehman Brothers, specializing in taking U.S. government programs and selling them to the private sector. One of his clients was Fannie Mae, and soon Johnson found himself on the mortgage giant's board, a master of both Washington and Wall Street.

When Johnson took over as CEO at Fannie Mae in 1991, staff found him tough to read—dry, conventional, pale, almost stiff. But Johnson spun a vision as florid as a Rousseau painting. He was looking for a figure, a concept, a mission that would literally change the American landscape.

A trillion dollars—that was more like it. Someone came up with the cheesy title "Showing America a New Way Home," under which Johnson resolved to lend $1 trillion by 2000 and make ten million new American homeowners in the process.

City dwellers, immigrants, black, brown and beyond, clock punchers and construction workers and anyone else who'd been locked out before: all of them would become part of the American Dream. Euphemistically, the company called its new target territories "communities in need."

Jim Johnson only needed to point to the *Atlanta Journal-Constitution*'s "The Color of Money" to show that he was embarking on nothing less than a civil rights crusade. A year after taking charge at Fannie Mae, he told the *American Banker*, "The evidence now is so overwhelming that there is discrimination in the housing finance system that I think it is really a social imperative that everyone who is involved in the system respond to the evidence."

Johnson was already working on test runs, and receiving guidance from Countrywide Home Loans, on how to make sure My Community Mortgage—the program born from the encounter between Gale Cincotta and Fannie Mae—would find its intended customers. By 1993, he'd made a deal with Countrywide to buy $2.5 billion in loans for lower-income and minority borrowers. Financially these homebuyers would be a motley lot, with no money in the bank, other debt to deal with, and less than stable employment histories. Every application that was rejected, Countrywide promised, would be reviewed again, to make sure that no one missed out on the chance to borrow to buy or refinance a home.

Then it was Fannie Mae's turn to sell homeownership to America's tenants. As a first step, Fannie Mae sweetened its product, irresistibly. Now that the activists' trial of 5 percent down payments for low-income buyers had proven successful, it was time to allow down payments of just 3 percent, as long as borrowers got a grant covering the other 2 percent and agreed to undergo homebuyer counseling.

In early 1994, Johnson was ready to unleash Fannie Mae's billions to the American public. He stood in Fannie Mae's lobby with Countrywide CEO Angelo Mozilo and other mortgage company executives at his side, promising, on their way to making that $1 trillion in loans, "a dialogue with every renter in America about their prospects for homeownership."

Fannie Mae's Washington pollsters had sized up the market for Fannie Mae—the country's roughly ninety-one million renters—and discovered what Zigas refers to as "a surprising amount of attitudinal resistance" toward homeownership.

"People like me don't get mortgages," they would say. Or, "I don't understand how to get a home loan." The polls found those views most pervasive among black and Hispanic people, those aged twenty-five to thirty-four, and people earning $20,000 to $35,000 a year.

To reach these reluctants, Fannie Mae went on an advertising blitz, spending some $50 million every year to spread the gospel of homeownership. "We have to offer them the necessary information to move through the home-buying process with a sense of confidence," Johnson wrote in *Showing America a New Way Home,* his 1996 paean to the blessings of homeownership. "We need a national consumer information crusade."

To advance the cause, Johnson teamed the former spokesperson for Ronald Reagan's 1984 campaign, John Buckley, with his old advertising director from the Mondale campaign, Roy Spence, who had since gone on to help make Wal-Mart the biggest retailer in America. Spence struck on a bold idea: The United Way was the NFL's charitable partner. So why couldn't Fannie Mae team up with a direct conduit to minority America— the NBA?

In 1994, Fannie Mae became a sponsor of a dozen NBA teams, including the Boston Celtics, Cleveland Cavaliers, Charlotte Hornets, Atlanta Hawks, and Milwaukee Bucks, airing commercials during games and sponsoring local homebuyers' fairs where visitors could meet the players ("the Home Team," as Fannie Mae liked to call them). Fannie proceeded to team up with the NBA itself as an official sponsor during its years of Michael Jordan glory. "It reached our target audiences: low- and moderate-income African Americans, and opinion leaders," says Buckley. Johnson told Buckley, as he gave him the assignment, "This will be the biggest political campaign you've ever run."

Fannie Mae targeted much of its advertising budget to Black Entertainment Television and made a sponsorship deal with Univision, the dominant Spanish-language TV network. In Fannie's ads viewers would see a family who looked like their own, sitting around a kitchen table and joking with one another, the merriment interrupted by a ringing phone. A rambunctious brother and sister grow quiet as their mother answers the call and her eyes tear up. The news is unexpected. "We got the home?!"

The advertising campaign explicitly targeted young families, new immigrants, and single parents. Fannie Mae's marketing department determined that 90 percent of all black Americans saw twenty or more Fannie Mae commercials in 1998.

"The public education campaign was supposed to get more people into the system," recalls Barry Zigas. "You look back at the TV ads and the message was: Owning a home is a fundamental aspiration; there are more opportunities than you think; and there are organizations and institutions that can help you." Like Countrywide, Fannie Mae opened satellite offices in cities across the country, to build personal relationships with local players in the real estate business and who, in turn, could help recruit elusive new homebuyers in their communities—places such as Miami's Little Haiti, Jingletown in Oakland, and the South Bronx. They could pick up a free guide on how to buy a home, in Vietnamese, Russian, Portuguese, Chinese, Creole, and any other language they were likely to speak.

That was just traditional advertising—TV, junk mail, and the like. The tax-exempt Fannie Mae Foundation would spend many times more on grants to organizations that counseled homebuyers and promoted the new opportunities for buying a home. Not incidentally, those grants bought Fannie Mae a national network of political allies who could be relied on to come to its defense as its growing earnings, made possible by Fannie and Freddie's unique government subsidy and their new power to sell mortgage-backed securities, began to generate increasing scrutiny on Capitol Hill.

The Ford Foundation became one of the many institutions seduced by the possibilities of what a $2 trillion company could do with all that money. In the 1960s, Ford had helped invent the community development corporation, organizations through which city residents across the country began to rebuild blighted neighborhoods. With nearly $100 million in Ford's funding, these organizations became lifelines for poor tenants, assuring them legal representation, organizers to help deal with landlords and get repairs on their housing, and opportunities to learn job skills.

In 1998, Ford shifted to a new agenda to fight poverty: It made one of its biggest grants ever to a program that would use homeownership as a path out of poverty. Ford spent its $51 million—nearly as much as the foundation devoted to all its antipoverty programs worldwide that year— to essentially create an insurance fund for Fannie Mae, to cushion the risk for the mortgage fund as it made more than $2 billion worth of new low-down-payment loans to people who had limited financial resources. "If we can demonstrate that low-income households previously thought to be un-creditworthy can manage monthly payments, the initiative could have the long-term effect of opening up lending practices across the nation," glowed Ford Foundation president Susan Berresford on the project's fifth anniversary in 2003. "And thousands of other low-income families considered high risk could own their own home."

Berresford pointed to the rising value of the homes—an average of 5.3 percent a year—as evidence that homeownership was pulling the borrowers out of poverty.

The rain of new wealth didn't fall consistently, Berresford acknowledged. Nearly one out of ten of the borrowers were falling behind on their loan bills, despite financial counseling. But look at the bright side, the Ford Foundation president suggested: four out of five of the borrowers had perfect payment records.

Faster and faster, the loans churned out. Fannie Mae's economists ran simulations of every possible factor that could increase the number of homeowners and determined that it was possible to lift the national homeownership rate far beyond where it had ever been—to three out of four American households. It would take a shift in the basic economics: Consumers would have to borrow more and pay less up front.

The memos to mortgage lenders kept coming, each heralding an innovation that would speed up and cut the expense of the formerly glacial process of approving a home loan.

- November 2, 1994   Income: On loans whose interest rates were set to rise later, it was all right to use the customer's early, lower payments when calculating the amount of debt they were going to carry each month compared with their monthly income.
- July 17, 1995   Credit: Buyers who lacked credit scores could get home loans based on evidence like canceled rent checks.
- September 26, 1996   Appraisals: From now on, lenders could have appraisers inspect just the outside of a house ("customers report significant reductions in the time and costs associated with performing an appraisal").

Fannie Mae's enormous investment in marketing was backed up with a second in technology, hundreds of millions of dollars' worth. Starting in 1990, years before most other big corporations dared, it had begun the switch from a clunky mainframe to a computer server network. When Johnson started, it took weeks for Fannie Mae to confirm with a bank that it would be able to buy its loans. The whole process happened on paper. By the time Johnson's people retooled the system, it took four minutes, boasted the company, to okay a mortgage.

A tech team labored to launch a groundbreaking system of automated underwriting, which allowed mortgage lenders to punch in vital stats about a borrower's financial profile and emerge with an instant yes or no. In close consultation with mortgage lenders, Fannie Mae designed the system to plug seamlessly into the lenders' own software for approving loans; the network tracked every step of the process, from the initial sales pitch to a customer all the way until a loan was sold to investors. Desktop Underwriter could even be used to approve loans that were destined not for Fannie Mae but for the Wall Street mortgage pools.

"Currently, it takes years to become an experienced underwriter"—to evaluate the viability of a home loan—Fannie Mae's chief information officer, Bill Kelvie, wrote in the trade publication *Mortgage Banking*, "but in a matter of months, we expect users of Desktop Underwriter to become thoroughly familiar with our automated underwriting system." In the

dorky Fannie Mae nomenclature, the workstations were "dream machines."

By 1998, a year that shattered all records for the American housing
market, Fannie Mae was financing or refinancing thirty thousand loans a
day. To keep up with all the borrowers clamoring for funds, it needed investors willing to risk hundreds of billions of dollars on the aspirations of
the American homeowner. The company created new programs to appeal
to foreign investors, especially in Asia, where collapsing currency markets
sparked a frantic search for safe havens for baht, yen, yuan, and ringgit.
When Fannie Mae offered up $3 billion in debt that year, Asian investors
scarfed up nearly half of it.

All this engineering had a groundbuckling impact. The national homeownership rate reversed its downward course and rose, first to 65, then 66,
then 67 percent, a record high. The number of homeowners grew by ten
million between 1988 and 1998, the year Johnson departed from Fannie
Mae, to sixty-nine million.

As Johnson had hoped, minority homebuyers accounted for much of that
growth; home sales to minorities rose by 30 percent in that period, while
those to whites actually fell slightly. Within Fannie Mae's own $2 trillion
business, close to half of loans were now being made to people who earned
less than most of their neighbors, and a growing share of those were going to
people in the bottom rungs of the economy. The business of selling home
loans to lower-income people was growing much faster than the rest of the
industry, doubling during Johnson's tenure.

"If you are not out there making sure that you are focused on cities and
low- and moderate-income families and minorities, your numbers will go
straight through the floor," Johnson told the African American MBA Association, the year (1998) that his company backed a record $1.5 trillion in
new mortgage loans.

More than anything, Fannie Mae made working people comfortable with
the idea of taking on vast debt as the price for participating in the American
Dream. From 1989 to 2004, mortgage debt for low-income people increased
by 46 percent, compared with just 15 percent for upper-middle-income and
5 percent for high-income. The total amount of home debt held by Americans more than tripled (by 2007 it would multiply sixfold).

Of course, other factors were at work, too—especially low and lower
interest rates, as Fed chairman Alan Greenspan cut them to keep the econ-

omy raging. During Johnson's tenure, the typical thirty-year mortgage rate dipped from about 10 percent to less than 7. But interest rates alone don't account for such a monumental shift in consumer behavior in such a short time.

Step by step, Fannie Mae built a home lending machine. And what that machine made, more than anything, was money. In 1999, Fannie Mae was doing better for its shareholders than almost any company in America. Fannie Mae stock outperformed the market—the crazy 1990s bubble market—seven times over, and then some. That was better than Coca-Cola, GE, Philip Morris, or Wells Fargo. A dollar invested in Fannie Mae in 1981 was worth $64.17 by 1999. In the eight years Johnson was with the company, its earnings per share tripled. The company grew in size ten times over.

Plummeting interest rates actually reduced Fannie Mae's ability to profit off of its holdings, but what it lost on interest earnings it more than made up for in sheer volume—the fruits of its great homeownership crusade. In 1988 the mortgage fund held $273 billion worth of loans. By 1999 it had more than $1.1 trillion.

The company's growth and profitability astonished even jaded Wall Street analysts. "Since 1990 there has been a belief that there is no way it could keep up its record earnings clip," Smith Barney analyst Tom O'Donnell told *National Mortgage News* in 1996. "The thinking was that profits had to level off."

Johnson's board rewarded him well for his feat. By his final year, in 1998, Johnson's annual compensation was $21 million. His dual-seated power— partly on Wall Street and partly in Washington—brought him still more. Johnson simultaneously chaired two of the most influential institutions in Washington: the Kennedy Center for the Arts and the Brookings Institution think tank.

Yet even in the giddiness of his company's breakneck growth—when he could go to the National Press Club and soberly tell reporters that "the drive to push the homeownership rate in the United States steadily closer to a point where every person who wants to own a home does own a home should define the housing finance industry in the next millennium"—part of Johnson's success was knowing where to set limits.

During David Maxwell's final days, Fannie Mae stopped buying loans where borrowers hadn't documented their income. Johnson also took pains to distinguish his company's 3 percent down payments from the no-money-down mortgages that were starting to pop up all over the place. Some investment bank might be funding zero-down financing, but not Fannie Mae. He conceded to the Council on Excellence in Government, "About 10 to 15 percent of American households are simply outside the reach of the economic proposition that makes a mortgage viable."

The timing, it turned out, was perfect. Just as President Clinton set out to mint millions of new homeowners, the mortgage industry was dying for new customers. In the early 1990s, descending mortgage rates prompted millions of owners to refinance their home loans. But by 1993, the sales forces found themselves propping feet on desks, waiting for phones to ring. They didn't. Interest rates were rising. Mass layoffs in the mortgage industry were beginning. Where could bankers turn for new customers?

At the convention of the Mortgage Bankers Association late that year, the hot topic, out of nowhere, was something called subprime loans. "This product is going to take off," predicted Paul Reid, who would soon become the president of the trade group.

Mortgage companies referred to them as B and C loans, for the grades their underwriters gave to borrowers with bashed-up credit. Each had its own definition of a "subprime" mortgage—many in the industry came to insist on tagging these loans "nonprime," as if to dismiss the suggestion that they are anything other than first-rate—but generally the loans went for 2 or 3 points above the usual interest rates, plus hefty up-front fees, to counter the risk of lending to people with less than ideal credit. These high-risk mortgages had another thing in common: As a matter of policy, Fannie Mae and Freddie Mac would not finance them.

That year, fewer than seventy thousand borrowers took out a mortgage from a subprime lender, out of more than eight and a half million new loans Americans took out to buy or refinance their homes. Wall Street investors had been wary of these freak mortgages, which, after all, were being sold to people who had already proven themselves unreliable at paying back what they owed. But as a trickle of subprime securities issues began to deliver sexy rates of return, bond buyers, such as pension funds, began clamoring to invest in subprime mortgages. Investment banks were eager to deliver.

In 1995, investors bought $10 billion in subprime securities; the year following, four times that. By the time Clinton left office, Wall Street investment banks would finance more than $316 billion in high-interest, high-fee mortgages. Subprimes accounted for one of every eight new loans, totaling $160 billion in new mortgages in 1999 alone.

Subprime consumer loans had in fact been around for a while—since the 1970s, when late-night TV shouted the opportunities from retailers such as Champion ("When banks say no, Champion says yessss") and the Money Store. In small doses, and at high rates of interest, you could use your home equity to borrow cash.

Then this sleepy and vaguely sleazy trade got a whole lot more interesting—and destructive. First, in an effort to help S&Ls weather the late 1970s, Congress lifted interest rate limits on home loans, and blocked states from imposing their own. Freed from three thousand years of laws banning usury, lenders could charge pretty much whatever they wanted. A $100-billion-a-year business was born.

In 1986, credit card debt stopped being tax-deductible. Mortgage interest, of course, still is. So a new business grew up overnight in swapping people's plastic debt for something a little more solid: their homes. Thanks to the lobbying of Lewis Ranieri of Salomon Brothers, the IRS overhaul that year also also made the trading of tranched mortgage-backed securities tax-exempt—opening the gate to their creation on a mass scale. Suddenly, companies purveying these new subprime home equity loans—which came with high interest, and a flurry of fees—had a place to sell them to. The interest, fees, and penalties on the loans more than paid for the risk the lenders and investors were taking—a risk of default and foreclosure up to five times greater than that for conventional loans.

There was little reason for lenders or investors to care about that risk. The borrowers may have been broke, but over time their homes had become worth quite a lot. That made them ripe for the taking. For lenders, the prospect of foreclosure was actually a chance to make money, by setting up borrowers to fail and reselling the house when they did. Loan companies didn't hesitate to exploit it.

Mortgage brokers and home improvement contractors began to cruise neighborhoods with low incomes and high property values, in places such as Boston and New York and Los Angeles, looking for homes that needed repairs and owners who needed cash. They sold prospects loans with interest rates upward of 20 percent—a rate so high that they'd never be able to repay.

One customer was James Hogan, an Atlanta janitor who'd never finished seventh grade. Hogan needed to make $6,200 in home repairs but ended up, after repeated refinancings, with a $32,400 mortgage he couldn't pay. By the time his home went into foreclosure, he owed almost $85,000.

It was no secret in Washington that these practices were savaging subprime borrowers. In the *Washington Monthly* magazine, journalist Mike Hudson wrote of annual interest rates as high as 41 percent, and loans that stole homes like they were nothing more complicated than a convenience-store cash register.

On February 17, 1993, just hours before President Clinton came to the Capitol to give his first address to Congress—it was all about his plans for the economy—the Senate Banking Committee held a hearing on what activists had started to call "reverse redlining": the practice of deliberately targeting desperate people with loans they'd never be able to pay back.

The Senate heard from witnesses such as Eva Davis, a widow living in San Francisco who needed to repair damage to her front steps from the 1989 earthquake. A yellow tag on her front door, placed there by the City of San Francisco, served as a beacon to a contractor and mortgage broker—the latter claimed he worked for FEMA—who told her the repairs would cost $6,000 and that they would help her get the money. By the end of the day, a loan officer had persuaded her to take out a much bigger loan, which would also include the money she owed on credit cards and other loans. (She didn't know how much, because her eyeglasses were broken.) Davis's income was not even $1,100 a month. Her new monthly payment would be $2,000, and that didn't count another $23,000 in up-front fees. Within five months, her home was in foreclosure. The sale was supposed to take place the morning of the Senate hearing.

Then a seventy-eight-year-old granddaughter of slaves who had lived in her house since 1936 testified about her ordeal borrowing money to fix a leaky roof. Annie Diggs of Georgia owed $343 on her old mortgage. She ended up borrowing $15,000, at 18.9 percent interest, from a company called Tower Financial, which then sold the loan to Fleet Financial. Five years later, the roof still leaking, her ceiling caved in, and though she'd paid $13,000 already, she still owed another $16,000. Diggs lived entirely on a Social Security check.

With some of the most egregious reports of abuses coming from his

Commonwealth of Massachusetts, at the hearing Senator John Kerry expressed dismay at the practices that led to such calamity—such as "no doc" loans, where borrowers didn't have to prove their earnings or assets.

"Incomes were inflated," Kerry went on. "Down payments were sometimes financed by the developers themselves as a second mortgage. Appraisals were falsely inflated." Worst of all, "negative amortization" loans made interest payments seem cheap, only to surprise borrowers with a massive bill down the road. "Suddenly it would balloon to such a degree that people simply never had a prayer of being able to pay this," Kerry marveled. "No one can accept that."

Three

SUBPRIME TIME

Orange County, California, 1996

H IS WIFE HAD BREAST CANCER. Between the Crohn's disease wrenching his stomach and the panic attacks that descended every time he got on the freeway, he could barely get to work sometimes. On top of all that, his Ford Contour was perpetually breaking down.

At forty-six, there was one thing Manny Palazzo could change, and that was his job. For the past year, since October 1995, Palazzo had worked at Long Beach Mortgage, where his title was senior vice president, credit and administration. For $83,000 a year, he controlled much more money than he'd ever earn, by deciding who qualified for the loans and how much they could borrow.

At a bank, that would have been easy. You'd write a manual describing how much income they have to have compared with debt, how much of a down payment they have to put down, and so on; instruct your loan officers to follow its guidelines; fire them if they don't. That was how it worked at Household Finance, where Palazzo had started his career in 1972 processing modest-size loans for people remodeling their homes or sending their kids to college. He worked his way up from there to become Household's head of underwriting—the guy who made sure the borrowers were reliable people taking reasonable risks.

But Long Beach was something quite new. It supplied mortgages, for close to the entire value of a home, to borrowers who had problematic credit histories—chronically late bill payments, even bankruptcies. In the banking industry, its mortgages were labeled "subprime" because the high likelihood borrowers would have difficulty making payments put the mortgages off-limits to the two major buyers of "prime" home loans, Fannie Mae and Freddie Mac. Subprime mortgage customers typically paid much more than prime borrowers for the privilege of borrowing. Not only did they carry interest rates of 9 or 10 percent while prime borrowers paid perhaps 7 percent, they also frequently laid out thousands of dollars up front, and if in the future they ever wanted to refinance into a less expensive mortgage, many borrowers had to pay thousands more. Quite a few subprime loans had "adjustable" interest rates—these rose and fell unpredictably over time, depending on conditions in the financial markets.

In addition to using its own sales force, Long Beach sold its loans through a nationwide network of mortgage brokers. Palazzo's unit was in command of the list—some nine thousand brokers all over the country, each charged with following Long Beach's loan rules to the letter.

It wasn't long before Palazzo realized that some of these brokers were getting extremely creative in finding ways to approve otherwise unqualified borrowers—in the process, netting themselves commissions. Worse, his own staff members were helping them get away with it, processing loans that misstated the financial details of applicants in order to get loans through the system. Even after Palazzo reported the breach to a supervisor, just as the Long Beach Mortgage Code of Ethics said he was supposed to do, no one took any action against the offenders.

Palazzo also was seeing what he considered to be an alarming number of exceptions to the guidelines that were supposed to limit how much customers could borrow based on their income, credit, and value of their home. The less attractive the loans and their borrowers looked, the harder it would be for Palazzo to do the most crucial part of his job. He sold Long Beach's mortgages—papers asserting claims on thousands of California bungalows, ranches, condos, and Colonials—to investment bankers, primarily at the Connecticut firm Greenwich Capital, whose stream of hundreds of millions of dollars the company depended on to stay in business.

Long Beach's agreements with investors allowed the lender to make exceptions, at its discretion, to its usual lending guidelines, but any broker or purchaser of mortgage-backed securities would have good reason to be alarmed if risky exceptions became the norm. Palazzo feared that the torrent of exceptions would put Long Beach mortgages in the hands of borrowers who didn't have the wherewithal to actually pay the loans back—and therefore put Long Beach Mortgage in danger of losing a lot of money for Greenwich's investors. That was already starting to happen.

Palazzo watched anxiously as the number of borrowers missing their bill payments began to climb sharply. If loans were failing, even a whiff of the stink would scare future investors away.

Long Beach was growing, quickly, from its base in Southern California, and it had just opened regional offices across the country. Already, the Northeast outpost was proving to be a problem. Its manager, Palazzo discovered as he prepared to sell the loans, was deliberately approving unqualified mortgages just to reach his sales quotas. One, Palazzo learned with alarm, was for a house with a tarp where a roof should have been. Since sales agents were paid commissions for every loan they could get a broker to close—and more, the larger the loans were or the higher the interest rate—they had a built-in incentive to tweak the applications.

It was no secret that Long Beach made numerous exceptions to its lending guidelines. That much the company disclosed to its investors, and indeed it was common in the mortgage business for a lender to ultimately reserve the right to make its own judgments about whether a given loan application was a safe prospect. But Palazzo was astonished at the mounting numbers of risky loans he saw come into his office. Sometimes he'd get paperwork on loans for more than the homes were appraised to be worth. By the time the mortgages came to him, there was nothing he could do but try to pass them off to the investors and hope they would agree to buy them.

The men who ran Long Beach were consumed with growth, and they pushed the sales force to churn out mortgages. "Countrywide is making $4 billion in loans a month," Palazzo's boss, Ed Resendez, informed him, "and here we are making $400 million. We need to get to where they are." In the brief time Palazzo had been at Long Beach, the company's loan business had already doubled. But he doubted more and more that he belonged there. He was a team player—"There are three things a man must do alone . . . testify, die, and putt," his memo pad paper read. Palazzo didn't think he could hold out on this one. "Won't it be nice when we can have our own company the way we want it?" he mused to a colleague.

Soon he'd get his wish. Lance Anderson had already tried to recruit Palazzo a couple of years earlier, for a young company called Saxon Mortgage that, like Long Beach, was taking subprime lending into the next dimension. Subprimes were still mostly the murky business of pricey home equity loans Congress had investigated two years earlier. Homeowners

might borrow $20,000 or $50,000 against the value of their house—
whatever the amount and however high the interest rate and fees, it totaled
just a small fraction of a house's worth, and for many homeowners this
was a "secondary" home equity loan, in addition to one's main mortgage.

But Saxon, like Long Beach, was working with a few ambitious investment firms to generate subprime mortgages that could be used to buy a
home or refinance a primary mortgage—a potentially more lucrative
proposition for the lender. Saxon, too, relied on freelance brokers, and it
allowed them to take extra fees when they got a customer to take a loan
with a higher interest rate than he or she qualified for. In the business, this
cash bonus is known as a "yield spread premium." In 1997 a federal judge
in Virginia would cite Saxon in declaring yield spread premiums illegal:
"The court is unable to see what service is provided to the consumer, as it
must under [federal law], unless it is the provision of a bad deal."

Long Beach and Saxon could make good money from those bad deals.
First they used custom software to qualify applicants who might not pass
muster through a traditional credit check but could be attractive risks if
they paid a little more or had to hand over penalties if they wanted to bail
out of the loan before thirty years. The interest and fees on Long Beach
loans were high enough to cover the losses even if a lot of borrowers
couldn't come up with the bills—the typical mortgage started at 11.3 percent and adjusted, usually upward, every six months. Borrowers who took
out these high-risk loans got no mercy: On day thirty-one of a late payment, a letter went out from Palazzo's unit announcing imminent foreclosure proceedings. If payment didn't arrive within a month, Long Beach
would file its case.

Palazzo knew how to make subprime loans look like winners to investment bankers. And so the ever-energetic Lance Anderson was calling again,
from Kansas City, asking Palazzo if the two of them could meet about Anderson's new venture. NovaStar Mortgage was about to go for an initial
public offering, joining a wave of fringe mortgage lenders generating cash
infusions from investors seeking high returns, which gave the lenders ample funds with which to make more mortgages.

In 1996, subprime loan companies were almost as hot as the Spice
Girls, and just as brazen. Even while the government wonks were looking
at the numbers and seeing that black and brown borrowers were the future

of homeownership, in the finance world it was increasingly clear that deadbeats would be their new profit center. Industry analysts saw opportunity in the mass downsizing of corporate employees across the country, who were turning to their home equity to help carry their household finances when income plummeted, and could only get a subprime loan because they had already missed mortgage or credit card payments.

Because Fannie Mae and Freddie Mac, with their advantages of government backing, so totally dominated the realm of safe, "vanilla," thirty-year picket fence mortgages, investment banks seeking juicy profits for their clients had to feed lower down on the credit food chain, making the kind of loans Fannie and Freddie weren't allowed to. And they needed hungry entrepreneurs willing to walk the high wire on investors' behalf—to promote and police the elusive space between intelligent risk and reckless idiocy in which it was possible to profit from lending money to unreliable borrowers.

Anderson would be the promoter; Palazzo, the policeman. At the Sandbar Lounge in the lush Hyatt on the bay in Newport Beach, they talked about having Palazzo run NovaStar's lending operation; how many loans they could push through on any given day; who else Palazzo could recruit from Long Beach. Plenty of people, it turned out: Everyone from Palazzo's old secretary from Household to Long Beach's head of risk management to the data entry clerk wanted to flee Long Beach Mortgage for the new opportunity. Pam Cirinelli, who was Long Beach's vice president of loan operations, was fed up with her inability to advance after a decade with the company. Her friend Leah Parra, who made $37,000 a year keeping the loan guidelines manual up to date, wanted to follow her out the door. Parra's cubicle was right outside Palazzo's office, and when she heard Cirinelli was going, she pleaded to come along. In the meantime, Palazzo gave Parra a homework assignment: Review NovaStar's draft loan guidelines.

In those sixty dense pages of mortgagese, Parra was inspecting the DNA of Saxon and Long Beach's spawn. Loan guidelines are to a subprime lender what the eleven-spices recipe is to KFC: It's the ticket to a vast universe of customers no rival's product can reach. When one company learned that a competitor was stretching its risks still further to make loans to a previously unqualified stratum of customers, lender number one would quickly revise its own guidelines downward to keep up, confident that their investment banker partners would approve.

With Palazzo as its traffic cop, Long Beach Mortgage was already pushing the limits of what anyone out there was willing to do. His company offered mortgages where customers didn't have to prove their income but could nonetheless borrow 75 percent of a home's appraised value, and it accepted customers who had recent judgments and bankruptcies on their records. Assuming they did document their salary, borrowers could take out loans amounting to more than half of what they earned—a huge amount of debt. One product, which it called QuickCredit, didn't even look at borrowers' credit card histories. This on-the-edge lending had been unheard of until now.

Palazzo had suggested to one Long Beach employee he tried to recruit that at NovaStar they would be building on Long Beach's aggressive lending strategies. Long Beach risk management head Ermete Vestri would later testify that Palazzo had mentioned, during a meeting in his office, "the possibility of copying policies and procedure manuals that Long Beach had established or created over the years, giving them a head start, a jump start." When Vestri decided he'd rather take a promotion from Long Beach than accept NovaStar's $100,000 salary offer, the founder of Long Beach retaliated immediately against Palazzo for trying to woo away his colleagues, and put his lawyers to work straight through Christmas week. When the courts reopened, Long Beach sued Palazzo and NovaStar for theft of trade secrets.

With the lawsuit, Long Beach CEO Roland Arnall was as much as warning his other employees what would happen if they jumped to Nova-Star or another new subprime lender. As Arnall prepared his company for its own IPO, he could ill afford to lose the very people who moved Long Beach's loans out the door. But his motivations ran deeper than immediate business concerns. Arnall intensely valued loyalty, and to his employees he appeared to feel personally betrayed by Palazzo's defection. Arnall was in the middle of a divorce. Long Beach Mortgage was the only thing he could count on.

Trust was a hard-won currency for Arnall, who was born into a family of Romanian Jewish refugees in 1939 Paris. The Arnall family survived World War II by living as Catholics until Roland was six. They eventually landed in Montreal, but Roland looked longingly across the border. He left college, moved to Los Angeles, and did whatever he could to make a living—selling eggs, then tomatoes, then flowers on street corners. When Roland Arnall saved up enough to buy a house, it was more than a place to live. With the proceeds from its sale he began to build a $3 billion fortune by financing real estate.

Arnall specialized in finding undervalued opportunities. If you've ever wondered who thought up the idea of putting fast food restaurants in the middle of shopping center parking lots—well, that was Arnall, who convinced property owners in L.A. and Orange counties that they could make extra money by developing acres of empty asphalt, and then lent them money on terms that eventually forced them to turn to him for more financing. He built office parks and thousands of modest apartments on cheap land in the formerly fashionable neighborhood of Wilshire Center, nestled among downtown L.A., Hollywood, and Beverly Hills.

In 1979 Arnall founded Long Beach Savings & Loan, two blocks away from the city's harbor. His timing would seem remarkably inauspicious. In California and across the country, savings and loan institutions were suffering mightily. Federal regulators had begun to grant other financial institutions new freedoms: Banks could for the first time pay interest on checking accounts, for example, and consumers now could put their cash into high-yielding money market funds and withdraw it at any time. But in the meantime, old regulations continued to limit the interest rate S&Ls, also known as "thrifts," could pay depositors, and restricted them to making home mortgages and small business loans.

As interest rates shot up into thin air, S&L passbook holders fled by the millions to money market funds and other accounts that paid far higher returns on deposits. When regulators finally did lift the interest restrictions on S&L deposits, that hardly helped the ailing thrifts because they couldn't afford to pay the higher rates: Their main source of income was interest from borrowers who had taken out thirty-year mortgages, most of whom were paying far lower rates than depositors were now demanding. Half of all S&Ls were now technically insolvent. By 1981, home mortgages were becoming hard for borrowers to come by.

Just as Lewis Ranieri and Salomon Brothers saw in this crisis an opportunity to convince federal regulators to create a new pipeline for home loan funds by setting up a loosely regulated market in mortgage-backed securities, Roland Arnall and other California real estate developers seized on S&Ls' misery to press state officials for a revolution in the lending business. In 1982, California decreed that S&Ls were no longer restricted to lending to consumers; they could now invest in just about any kind of venture. Following the recommendation of the Reagan administration, Congress took similar action.

Arnall proceeded to use Long Beach Savings to finance his own development projects. His thrift also became one of the nation's biggest players in a boom business of brokered deposits: taking funds from investors and putting them into accounts in other (formerly) humble savings and loans, where they would be protected by federal deposit insurance from any losses. Rogue S&Ls took those account funds and did, well, whatever their directors wanted to, since deposit insurance guaranteed that every penny would be paid back no matter how badly their ventures foundered. Some S&Ls used depositors' funds to build office complexes, casinos, and golf courses, whether or not there was a market for them. The most lawless just stole the money. By the time the savings and loan feeding frenzy had ended, some $160 billion had simply vanished. Cleaning up the S&L mess, and hundreds of failed institutions, cost Americans an estimated $125 billion.

When chastened regulators told California's wayward S&Ls that they would have to stick to their traditional business of merely lending money to consumers, Arnall resolved to push the enterprise of mortgage-making as profitably as it could go. He recognized that the unqualified mortgage customers Long Beach Savings had to turn away every day were actually a vast business prospect, worth a lot more than the safe 3 percent or so an S&L usually made on home mortgages. (Hence the banker's creed "3-6-3": Borrow at 3 percent, lend at 6 percent, and be on the golf course by 3.)

Arnall initially cultivated his own circle of investors willing to put up their money to finance risky home mortgages in exchange for relatively generous returns, but when he learned that on the East Coast, lenders such as the Money Store had teamed up with Greenwich Capital to transmogrify loans to unpredictable borrowers into profitable securities for demanding shareholders, Arnall was next in line to make a deal. In 1990, Greenwich Capital's investment bankers sold their first $70 million in Long Beach bonds, which essentially gave Arnall cash in exchange for a share of future payments on its mortgages. That cash, in turn, allowed Long Beach to make more loans.

Thanks to Long Beach and its maverick financial backers, in 1992 an unemployed widow in Pico Rivera named Stella Alviso—her husband had just been crushed to death by a gate in the Santa Clarita prison where he was serving for repeated DUIs—could buy a two-bedroom condo in

Whittier for $145,000. A friend who worked as a real estate agent set up everything, including the $96,000 mortgage, which started at 9.3 percent interest and was set to head up as high as 15.95. The interest rate would have been even higher had Alviso not paid more than $7,800 in fees. But what did she know?

"I always have other people handle my business, and I shouldn't have done that," says Alviso, who today lives in a studio apartment paid for by HUD and is compensated by L.A. County to take care of her four grand-children while her daughter finishes a welfare-to-work program. "That was so wrong." She thought the $250,000-plus from her husband's wrongful-death settlement would last forever and that her teenage daughter, already a mother herself, would grow up to live in the condo. But there was no way Alviso could keep up with mortgage bills of more than $800 a month, and in 1995 her loan went into foreclosure, with her owing tens of thousands more than she had borrowed in the first place, thanks to penalties and inter-est charges.

By then, the loan had been sold to investors, and those investors were get-ting paid. Willing to lend to quirky prospects like Alviso when other banks wouldn't dare, Arnall's subprime lending operation soon became so lucrative that in 1994 Long Beach closed down the "savings" part of its business and operated strictly as a billion-dollar-a-year fountain of home loans for people who couldn't otherwise get them. Most weren't buying new houses; instead they were borrowing against their current ones, and withdrawing cash or paying off other debts.

From early on, Arnall's aggressive business practices ran into trouble. Bank examiners noticed that black, Hispanic, and elderly borrowers, espe-cially women, were being charged much higher fees for the same loans than other equally qualified borrowers. In 1996, the Justice Department sued, and the company agreed to set up a $4 million fund to repay and educate cus-tomers. Yet Long Beach's system of compensating salespeople and brokers more for sticking borrowers with overpriced loans remained—indeed, this was a customary industry practice, one that higher courts would ultimately declare perfectly legal.

Palazzo was right to be worried about whether borrowers could repay his loans. Sort of. Over the next few years, one out of five of the loans in one group of mortgages his team sold to investors in 1995 wouldn't get paid back. Other runs of loans performed almost as badly. But through the alchemy of the credit markets, everyone involved in financing these mortgages still made their money—not only Long Beach, but also all the investors who had bought Long Beach bonds from Goldman Sachs, Prudential Securities, Salomon Brothers, and Credit Suisse First Boston.

In fact, even while Long Beach's borrowers were failing to make their mortgage payments, the ratings on the mortgage-backed securities that had bought their debts actually went *up*. First of all, Long Beach was making most of its money back by reselling the foreclosed homes. Meanwhile, the investment banks mixed the subprime loans into the pools with less risky mortgages, and took out insurance policies guaranteeing investors that they would be paid even if the mortgage pools failed to generate the promised returns. Ratings agencies Moody's and Standard & Poor's considered the resulting concoctions as safe as a pillow fight.

Long Beach wasn't only profiting off the interest payments. It also collected fees for creating the loans, more fees for billing customers, and still more fees as compensation for packaging its loans for investors. Those fees were the same whether they were lending to new customers or just selling to the same borrowers again and again, collecting more fees every time on bigger and bigger loans.

Losing his pioneering business to new competition was therefore a costly proposition for Arnall. In his lawsuit against Palazzo and NovaStar, Arnall demanded all of NovaStar's projected first-year profits, claiming that the upstart's business would have otherwise gone to Long Beach. The jury awarded him $21,498.30.

But really, Arnall's prospects didn't suffer. In its IPO, Long Beach Mortgage sold to shareholders in the spring of 1997 for $174 million. Arnall took 10 percent for himself. (His ex-wife was not pleased to later learn about this windfall, which Roland had failed to reveal in their divorce settlement.) Another $40 million went to set up Arnall's reincarnation of Long Beach. As if to describe his own infinite ambitions, he named it Ameriquest.

All that money was a poor measure of what Long Beach Mortgage had actually built in its few years of hustling on the Orange County end of the Garden Grove Freeway, the company name now a vestige of the deceased S&L's location miles away. Palazzo and Cirinelli were soon followed by other Long Beach alumni who spread, like milkweed, the secret of how to make a fortune from home loans to people who possessed nothing but the title to a house.

That same year, a Long Beach executive went to Countrywide Mortgage to start its new subprime division, called Full Spectrum. Another helped found New Century Mortgage, which Cirinelli later joined. Vestri later became president of Aegis Mortgage. Palazzo went on to run the lending operation for Option One, which was founded by Long Beach alumnus Bob Dubrish. And in 1999, Washington Mutual bought Long Beach when it sought a new subprime division of its own. At the real estate boom's peak in 2005, the Orange County companies spawned by Roland Arnall's operation at Long Beach Mortgage would come to make one out of every three subprime loans.

Subprime lending should have withered in the heat of Congress's scrutiny. Instead, it thrived beyond what its own inventors could have hoped. The 1993 congressional hearings did generate some regulations, but they proved hopelessly feeble, applying to just 1 percent of all high-interest loans out there.

In 1994, dozens of home lenders that had never been interested in subprime lending before, from Countrywide Home Loans to General Motors, decided to get in on its growth opportunities. Because their customers tended to be such high risks, at first most lenders wouldn't let them borrow anything close to the whole value of the home. But so many home lending and consumer finance companies were entering the subprime business and going after customers that by 1994, that rigid rule started slipping. Once IPOs and then investment bankers gave lenders massive infusions of capital, the lenders had to find homeowners who could spend it for them.

Hundreds of thousands of borrowers who already owned their homes refinanced their conventional loans with new subprime ones, stating that they would use the proceeds for home improvements or to consolidate other debts. By 1999, a million homeowners a year were discovering the miracle of subprime refinancing, which made money appear out of nowhere.

Year by year, increasingly sophisticated data analysis gave investors confidence to push the boundaries further—to allow companies like Long Beach to lend more, to people with worse credit, on onerous terms that made more money in the short term but that would, even the financiers acknowledged, have the unfortunate side effect of burying the borrowers deeper in debt some wouldn't be able to pay.

The very steps investment managers took to improve their own prospects—with devices such as prepayment penalties, which levied a hefty toll on borrowers who tried to refinance into a new loan or buy a new house—made it harder and harder for homeowners to keep up with the bills. The costs mounted faster than the property values or household paycheck ever would. The exec of one company that dove into the business in 1994 described his ideal customer as "someone who's a chronic delinquent, who is a self-employed professional, but doesn't know how to handle his money."

The business continued to cast itself as a resource for the poor and struggling. Soon after going public, Long Beach rolled out a loan specifically for people who had just gone through bankruptcy. "A car accident, a death in the family, downsizing—as long as we can determine it's been resolved," a Long Beach vice president promised, a borrower would get a loan.

Wasn't that what the community activists had been pleading for? "Lenders increasingly are providing loans to credit-impaired borrowers. As a result, they are providing credit to a previously underserved market and performing a valuable social function," explained a textbook for securities analysts.

To the public, news coverage promoted subprime mortgages as a godsend for homeowners in a financial crunch. "It lifted a whole weight off my shoulders," local homeowner Janice Demarchi told the *Cleveland Plain Dealer*. With a subprime loan of $56,000 from Third Federal Savings and Loan, she and her husband not only saved their home from foreclosure but also took cash out to pay the bills. "At least now I can hold my head above water a little bit."

The mortgage industry touted subprime lending as a foundation of the great homeownership crusade. "Our innovative industry has created a great way to expand homeownership by offering loans to those who can make payments, but who don't qualify for 'A' paper because of poor credit or bankruptcy," the former president of the Mortgage Bankers Association, Ron McCord, told his group's 1997 annual convention in New York.

Subprime mortgages did roll into the hands of seventy-five thousand or so new homebuyers that year, but these, it turned out, were rare exceptions. Most borrowers already owned their homes and turned to subprime mortgages to extract cash from home equity. Soon many also were learning what it meant to have bills bigger than what they could afford. McCord's own member loan companies reported that almost one out of eight of their subprime borrowers at any given time were seriously late on their loan payments. Subprime lending was in fact doing the opposite of what the mortgage bankers suggested: It was leaching the equity out of people's homes, and borrowers were ruining their credit in the process.

As early as 1995, analysts at ratings agencies such as Moody's reported a swelling number of subprime adjustable-rate mortgages going into default—that is, their payments just stopped. These subprimes were failing at triple the rate of similar fixed-rate loans. Moody's paused to note that this was only a problem for the borrower, not the securities investor, because the investment funds into which the mortgages were pooled carried insurance sufficient to cover any losses.

The notion that subprime lending was a way to help poor borrowers who otherwise could not buy a home live the American Dream was largely a fiction. It was a myth powerful enough to give subprime lending free reign for another ten years.

And so Margaret Newton of Philadelphia, who only wanted to redo the siding on her house—to cover up graffiti and keep the place warm, or so she hoped—instead ended up with a $15,500 loan she had no way of paying back.

Four strokes had left the seventy-six-year-old barely mobile and living on Social Security. This school custodian had bought her two-story Depression-era brick rowhouse for $7,000 back in 1968, the year FHA unleashed mortgages into the nation's formerly loan-starved cities. Twenty-eight years later, Newton owned her house free and clear, but it needed improvements she had no money to pay for. Newton was glad to hear from a vinyl siding salesman who said he could arrange financing to pay for his work. She did not read the loan documents, from United Companies Financial, and so didn't know that she was paying $3,000 up front for the privilege of borrowing $9,000, at a rate of 12.9 percent. Within a year, she had fallen behind on her payments. Along with other Philadelphia borrowers, Newton sued United Companies in a case that should have changed history.

By the time Bill Clinton was ending his second term, it was getting harder and harder for the mortgage industry to pretend that subprime lending was merely a force for empowerment of the poor. There were just too many stories of homeowners who had no idea what they were getting into taking out loans they didn't need, and if they weren't losing their homes, they were losing, through unnecessary fees that mounted each time they refinanced, tens of thousands of dollars that should rightfully have been theirs—those assets they had worked so hard to accumulate and that were going to turn them into more fully responsible Americans.

Instead, subprime lending joined malt liquor and the lottery as a corner industry that sold the promise of escape. As investment banks became looser in their lending rules, the more of a burden the loans became for many borrowers. Take United Companies, the Baton Rouge lender that had refinanced the loans for the plaintiffs in the Philadelphia lawsuit: Under its formula, borrowers needed just $400 a month left in their budgets for each household member, for all of their expenses beyond housing. United Companies would take the rest, thank you.

With a lawsuit filed by Newton and a few other borrowers, legal services lawyers tried to use that subprime law Congress had passed back in 1994 to do something that would seem very basic: hold lenders responsible for making sure that their borrowers could actually afford to pay back the loans they were taking out. The Home Owners Equity Protection Act bans "a pattern or practice of extending credit . . . based on the consumers' collateral"—that is, the value of their houses—"without regard to the consumers' repayment ability, including the consumers' current and expected income, current obligations and employment."

If this law had actually been enforced, it wouldn't just have prevented people such as Margaret Newton from losing what was in effect her life's savings. It also could have stopped the whole subprime nightmare in its tracks, years before anyone had conceived of a NINJA—no income, no job, (no) assets—loan or other absurd concoctions that set up customers with unpayable mortgages.

But in the Newton case, a federal judge refused to put the law to work. Congress had given the Federal Reserve a green light to decide exactly what was and was not too big a loan for a borrower to handle. And the Fed, under Alan Greenspan, had never weighed in, even as the subprime business continued to double its size every year.

That's not all the Fed didn't do as subprime lending settled in and took its seat on the couch, feet up. Federal Reserve Board governor Ned Gramlich would later reveal, from his deathbed, that he had urged Greenspan to have the Fed start overseeing subprime lenders, which the Fed could do when the lenders were owned by major financial companies such as Citigroup and HSBC. The General Accounting Office and a joint HUD-Treasury task force on predatory lending made the same recommendation.

Greenspan resolutely opposed any action. Even when subprime foreclosures snowballed into a global crisis seven years later, the Federal Reserve chair stood by his decision to allow loan companies' business to proceed without scrutiny: "For us to go in and audit how they act on their mortgage applications would have been a huge effort, and it's not clear to me we would have found anything that would have been worthwhile without undermining the desired availability of subprime credits."

Desired by whom? The notion of consumers clamoring for debt they otherwise couldn't get was largely manufactured by the lenders themselves. In 1998, Freddie Mac ran data on thousands of subprime loans through its own automated approval system and found that at least one out of every five of the borrowers shouldn't have gone subprime at all; they would have qualified for an ordinary loan, except a subprime broker got to them first with a sales pitch. Two years later, the new head of Fannie Mae, Franklin Raines, calculated that with a few minor adjustments to its policies, half of all subprime customers could qualify for a mortgage sponsored by his company.

As for the other half, the borrowers with truly lousy payment records, reformers faced a dilemma to which no solution was politically correct. They could try to crack down on all subprime lending, but that would mean confronting both the Wall Street firms that were financing the loans along with likely accusations that limits would deny opportunities to low-income black and Hispanic borrowers, roughly half of whom took out subprime loans.

Or they could continue to ferret out the worst abuses. That's what Clinton's Federal Trade Commission did, taking pains to distinguish between predatory lending, involving deceptive sales practices, from subprime lending as a whole. Associates First Capital, Delta Funding, First Alliance Mortgage: Each lender took its turn at the whipping post in what the FTC called "Operation Home Inequity," and gave back $300 million to consumers through settlements with the federal government. Among other transgressions, Delta got nailed for lending money without regard for borrowers' ability to pay.

But most of the subprime business carried on as usual. When Greenspan finally acknowledged subprime lending in 2000, he, too, characterized its mounting problems as the work of a few bad apples, engaged in what he called "aberrant behaviors." "Of concern are abusive lending practices that target specific neighborhoods or vulnerable segments of the population and can result in unaffordable payments, equity stripping, and foreclosure." He promised that the Fed was working to repair subprime lending.

Meanwhile, some 140,000 subprime borrowers were either in foreclosure or close to it by the end of 1999. Nine out of ten of them had refinanced an older loan. Entire communities of homeowners were in big trouble, the black and urban perhaps worst of all.

In Atlanta, even while foreclosures overall declined, the number resulting from subprime lenders more than doubled. In Chicago, foreclosures also doubled from 1993 to 1998, following a period in which subprime lending increased from three thousand to nearly fifty-one thousand loans each year. More than a third of the fourteen hundred Chicago foreclosures in 1998 could be traced to a subprime lender.

The experience in neighborhoods confirmed what Fannie Mae's market research also was discovering: Borrowers who were new to homebuying, especially if they were members of minority groups, tended to care more about how they were treated by the person selling them a loan than about the financial soundness of the loan itself. If it were a friend or a family member selling the mortgage or property, so much the better. Driving these decisions most of all was a desire to hear a bank say "yes."

As broke and bereft homeowners lined up in the waiting rooms of legal services agencies, CNN ran no special reports. Letterman never cracked jokes about being a subprime borrower. You didn't hear political candidates promise relief for homeowners who couldn't pay their loan bills. Not many people even knew what "subprime" meant. The catastrophe of unaccountable lending was entirely confined to downscale neighborhoods, far off the map of the America that mattered. Investors scarcely suffered. By 1998, many of them smelled the dangers and stopped investing in the riskiest parts of the pools. The resulting drought of funds put a brake tap on sub-prime lending's staggering growth and drove the most financially tenuous operations—including United Companies Financial—out of business.

By the time federal banking agencies got together and hammered out some rough ground rules for subprime lending, in 2001, it was already too late. First the Federal Reserve, then Congress, then President Clinton had already all done their part to make the subprime business massively more powerful. Together they dismantled the Glass-Steagall Act—a legal wall that, since the Great Depression, had kept the financial industry safely sep-arated into two parallel universes. In one, banks took deposits from cus-tomers and loaned out money. Basically, these were retailers. Those retail operations were forbidden from mingling with the other half of the bank-ing business, which bought and sold stocks and bonds. It's not hard to see why: The job of a bank is to protect depositors' money. The job of an in-vestment firm is to gamble with it.

But years of lobbying from banks and securities firms led the Federal Re-serve, under Greenspan, to make such huge exemptions that by the end of 1996 the law had become basically meaningless. In 1999, Clinton signed the Gramm-Leach-Billey Act, which eliminated its final vestiges. Under their new power to operate as holding companies with a multitude of subsidiaries, major financial institutions went right out and bought up subprime compa-nies. Citigroup acquired Associates First Capital in 1999, for $31 billion. HSBC took over Household Finance. Bank of America bought Equicredit, and later Countrywide. National City got First Franklin. And, of course, WaMu acquired Long Beach Mortgage. Subprime lending, which had until then been a marginal business, was now ensconced in the heart of the bank-ing industry—and at some of the very same banks that also were making piles of money by selling securities made up of those mortgages or could now begin to do so without restriction.

To stay in the subprime business, banks were going to have to conduct themselves more cautiously. Starting with North Carolina in 1999, states and cities began to pass their own subprime laws, attempting to stop in-creasingly flagrant exploitation of borrowers. The Mortgage Bankers Asso-ciation and its lobbyists went on the offensive, taking pains to distinguish harmful "predatory lending" from virtuous "nonprime" loans that ex-tended the gift of credit to the needy. "We must acknowledge that rogue originators have created a problem for legitimate originators," warned

Countrywide CEO Angelo Mozilo. "As an industry we must support the identification and swift punishment of unscrupulous players so they cannot further sully the mortgage lending profession."

More earnestly, the government-sponsored agency Freddie Mac started financing some subprime loans, with the idea that its involvement could help tame this beast and fulfill the elusive dream of affordable home loans for all. One of Freddie Mac's first subprime deals, in 1999, financed nearly $800 million in mortgages from Ameriquest, on its way to backing $5 billion in subprime loans. "Lenders who have been unable to originate loans in the subprime market will be able to do so, thanks to our tools," promised Faith Schwartz, who headed Freddie Mac's foray into what it called "alternative markets." Roland Arnall's nephew, Ameriquest's lead lawyer, publicly thanked Freddie for helping expand his company's reach.

That wasn't the only way Freddie Mac and its sibling Fannie Mae nurtured the newly supersized subprime industry. Since 1995, the two finance agencies had been investing in Wall Street–generated mortgage-backed securities. While some of their money went to buying shares of their own loan pools, more and more of it was going to purchase mortgage securities from the likes of Bear Stearns and Merrill Lynch. Unlike Fannie's own securities, these would come to be stuffed full of subprime loans.

How did Fannie Mae and Freddie Mac, those champions of stable homeownership, turn into the world's biggest funders of Wall Street–backed subprime mortgages? At gunpoint, basically.

It all started with the best of intentions, with Gale Cincotta and the activists who had demanded bank loans for the poor and urban. Remember what they won back in 1991: By now, nearly half of the loans financed by Fannie Mae and Freddie Mac had to go to low-income borrowers and urban communities. Well, those were the same people and places that were now turning to subprime loans in droves. Fannie Mae's lenders found that they just couldn't compete with the terms subprimes were offering customers— tiny down payments, low (seeming) interest rates, credit for the financially damaged, and instant approvals, without even a pause for the counseling that was obligatory for every Fannie and Freddie borrower.

Their solution? Fannie Mae and Freddie Mac began to purchase shares of Wall Street securities instead, from investment pools made up of a mix of prime and subprime loans. By buying prime-heavy portions of the securities as investments, Fannie and Freddie could meet Congress's quotas for the number of loans they had to finance for low-income borrowers. Their shares in the securities only included loans that could be purchased by the agencies under their strict guidelines. But because the riskier parts of the pools consisted almost exclusively of subprime loans, Fannie Mae and Freddie Mac were effectively putting their billions into financing subprime lending, with support from the federal government.

Under HUD secretary Andrew Cuomo, the Clinton administration gave a parting gift to the burgeoning subprime industry. Fannie and Freddie already had to make two out of every five of their loans to lower-income homebuyers. In October 2000, HUD raised that requirement to half of all the mortgages the two agencies financed. Out of those loans, more than a third had to go to people poor enough to qualify for a government-subsidized rental. To this brew George W. Bush added something quite peculiar for a conservative: a racial quota. Under pressure from the Bush administration, which had launched an investigation into their financing practices, in 2002 Fannie Mae and Freddie Mac together committed to finance $1.1 trillion in loans specifically for minority borrowers.

There was no way Fannie and Freddie could make those numbers, not with subprime lenders stealing their low-income and minority customers literally out of the parking lot, following mandatory counseling sessions. In line with their public-service missions and common sense, with few exceptions Fannie Mae and Freddie Mac still did not buy subprime loans. "These goals were very, very aggressive," says Barry Zigas, who was responsible for making sure Fannie Mae followed HUD's orders. "It was a struggle to meet them."

That struggle only deepened once the Securities and Exchange Commission opened an investigation into the agencies' accounting practices. A consortium of major banks, including Wells Fargo and Chase, was spending millions lobbying Congress to limit the power of Fannie Mae and Freddie Mac, which the banks viewed as unfair competition. The Republican majority proved receptive; the only question was going to be how tightly Congress would clamp shackles on the two government-sponsored companies. The White House also appeared to be targeting Fannie and Freddie for a takedown. The Bush administration's ideological fervor to obliterate government's role in business, and Fannie Mae's endurance, under CEO and former Clinton budget director Franklin Raines, as a stronghold of Democratic

Party power, rendered the agencies obvious threats. The White House launched a project—its operatives jokingly called it "Operation Noriega"—to seed doubts about Fannie Mae and Freddie Mac's financial viability, a strategy that apparently aimed at rendering those uncertainties into a self-fulfilling prophecy.

So while the low-income lending targets were absurdly high, Fannie and Freddie were in no position to shirk their obligation to meet them. In 2004 alone, Fannie Mae bought $90 billion in Wall Street–issued mortgage securities. Freddie Mac purchased $122 billion. By 2007, they held $257 billion. Together, Fannie Mae and Freddie Mac made up more than a fifth of the entire, increasingly vast global investment pool backing subprime and other oddball loans that hadn't been safe enough for Fannie Mae and Freddie Mac to buy in the first place.

By the time George W. Bush left office, HUD decreed, three out of every five mortgages financed by the government loan funds would have to go to the poorer half of America—to the very people who were now reveling in the seemingly boundless possibilities for borrowing one's way into prosperity.

September 11, 2001, didn't just usher in an age of fear and war. It also launched the greatest outpouring of debt the world has ever seen. Federal Reserve chair Alan Greenspan sharply cut interest rates to revive the nation's economy following the Al-Qaeda attacks and the collapse of the dot-com stock bubble. Those low interest rates rendered mortgage-backed securities a much more profitable purchase than Treasury bills or other popular bonds whose value tended to decline when rates went down. An enthusiastic array of investors from around the globe joined Fannie Mae and Freddie Mac in a clamor to buy mortgage-backed securities from Wall Street investment banks.

But the firms couldn't sell mortgage-backed securities if they didn't have mortgages. To drum up more business, they began to include in the securities loans that would have previously been considered too risky—loans that didn't just reflect damaged credit scores or a high amount of borrowing compared to a property's value or homeowner's income, but some combination of all of these.

As more and more new homebuyers came into the market, armed with cheaper and cheaper debt that allowed them to borrow more, home prices in parts of the country were beginning to climb sharply—places, from California, Arizona, and Nevada to Georgia and Florida, whose sun-powered population growth was luring homebuilders to carve out new subdivisions. With the help of developers and real estate agents, borrowers were now doing more than extracting cash via the loans. Those who already owned a home were discovering the power of leverage, using borrowing as a way to acquire property they could never before dream of purchasing.

One of them was Jorge L. Sotelo of Phoenix, Arizona. To understand how subprime lending captivated America, one only has to follow his borrowing career. Cheerful and polite, Sotelo, who'd immigrated from Chihuahua, Mexico, in the 1980s and worked as a carpenter, turned to FHA to buy his first home, in 1992. With his government-insured loan of just over $42,000, an interest rate of 8.5 percent wasn't especially onerous, since it amounted to just over $300 a month.

For the next eight years, Sotelo worked, thanks to a green card, and enjoyed his little two-bedroom wood house with the tile floors, though he would eventually want to move on to something a little more luxurious, in a safer neighborhood. In 2000, Sotelo refinanced with a loan from Ameriquest, a move that gave him more than $20,000, which he used to pay off other debts. The trade-off was a higher interest rate, at 10 percent, which would start adjusting in three years to as much as 16 percent. But for Jorge Sotelo, that day of reckoning never came. Two years in, Sotelo sold his piece of the dream for $102,000, more than double what he had paid for it.

With the proceeds he moved with his wife and two-year-old daughter to a brand-new neighborhood out in Avondale farmland built by Richmond American Homes, a builder active in a dozen states. Their new stucco spread measured an expansive twenty-one-hundred square feet. They lived there, and technically owned the house, but had to rely on someone else to finance the purchase. Thanks to too many missed bills, the Sotelos' credit was too crappy to qualify them for a mortgage, even one from a subprime company. So Jorge turned to his uncle José, who took out an FHA loan for $154,000, paying just 4 percent down. At the closing, immediately after Uncle José signed the mortgage, new co-owners Jorge and Claudia joined him on the deed, and the extended family settled in to live together.

Sotelo thought it was a joke when, in March 2004, his boss at a construction firm told him to prepare to meet the president, not of the company but of the United States. Jorge Sotelo would appear with George W. Bush as an exemplar of minority homeownership. The event was just two days away, and Sotelo was so nervous he barely slept until then.

"*No tienes que estar nervioso. Esto va a ser muy sencillo y muy divertido,*" President Bush reassured Sotelo backstage, just before hosting "A Conversation on Homeownership" at the Phoenix Carpenters Training Center, run by Sotelo's union. "This is going to be very simple and very fun."

Sotelo's fleshy face shone with sweat as he perched on a rough-hewn pine stool under the lights, a mic in his hand. Next to him sat a mother of three who had wandered with her schoolteacher husband into a homeownership fair and walked out with an appointment for a no-money-down first-time homebuyer program. On Bush's far side they were joined by a former resident of subsidized housing who had saved up her rent vouchers, under a new federal "self-sufficiency program," to buy a home in Mesa. Behind them loomed an enormous wood house frame, with the day's mantra stenciled below the eaves: A HOME OF YOUR OWN.

"There is a minority homeownership gap in America," Bush shared with the audience in the vast hangar. "Not enough minorities own their homes. It seems to me"—he paused to thump his palm on his chest, confessionally—"like it makes sense to help all people own their own homes." Bush peered down to a lectern to locate the number he was looking for. "Five point five new—million new minority homeowners into homes over the next five years." Whenever Bush spoke of the homeownership gap, he held his thumb and forefinger apart about three inches. Bush started giving these speeches on what he called "the Ownership Society" during his 2000 campaign, first airing that theme at a church in Cleveland.

In Phoenix, under the bright lights with the president, Jorge Sotelo said little about his new abode. "It's a better home now," he told Bush. "So you were upgraded?" asked the president. "Yes!" agreed Sotelo, smiling behind his mustache as the audience erupted into applause. "I've got a better life. Better wages. A better home," he said in his Chihuahuan cadence.

Sotelo and his wife also got an invitation that year to the White House Christmas party, though they had to pay their own airfare and hotel—no small sacrifice. Jorge had been promoted to foreman, but he and Claudia never had enough money, and both of them needed new cars. So they were grateful when they started getting offers for home mortgages that would let them get cash back in the transaction.

In the two years since Jorge Sotelo's convergence with George W. Bush, Jorge had turned from a pariah into a desirable customer. Stoked by a mortgage finance market that was now not only turning mortgages into securities, but also those securities into their own securities, called collateralized debt obligations, lenders and investors were on the hunt for new borrowers with bad credit, who as big risks commensurately brought the highest yields. Their enthusiasm was bolstered considerably by rapidly rising real estate prices in Phoenix, which were growing by about 16 percent every year, meaning that in an investment bank's calculus, even the worst-case scenario—foreclosure—would not result in much of a financial loss, if any. The values were rising because other homeowners and a swarm of speculators were making the same jeté the Sotelos already had: They were borrowing their way up into the biggest, nicest homes they could buy.

The subprime company Equifirst lent Jorge and Claudia Sotelo $246,000, at an interest rate of 6.9 percent. For now. Because this was an adjustable-rate loan, Sotelo's payments would vary depending on the rate banks charge to borrow from one another. In September 2007, the interest rate hiked up to 9.3 percent, meaning that their monthly payment jumped from about $1,600 to more than $2,000. And from there it could go up to nearly 13 percent. When the final bill comes due in 2036, they will still owe tens of thousands of dollars—a "balloon payment"—since monthly charges are budgeted as if the mortgage will run for forty years.

And that's all assuming they hold on to the house. Four years after his appearance with Bush, houses in the Sanctuary at Avondale are selling for nowhere near $246,000, so Sotelo owes more than his is actually worth. No bank will refinance the loan, no matter how good his credit gets. It also means he can't sell the house. Sotelo has paid his bills on time, but with his wife home now taking care of their fourteen-month-old son, he knows it's only a matter of time before they crash and lose their home, like so many of their neighbors. By the end of 2008, more than 8 percent of all homeowners in Avondale were in foreclosure.

Lately he's been talking to the loan servicing company about working out a deal to lower his interest rate. Sotelo's got it all figured out. With a low enough mortgage payment, they could cover the bills by renting the Avondale house to a tenant. He'd move his family out to a new place.

They'd be renting that home, right?

"Oh, no," says Sotelo, surprised at the question. "We'll own it."

Four

INTO OBLIVION

Cleveland, Ohio, 2006

A FEW TIMES EACH DAY and night, freight trains heave slowly over the rails at the dead end of East Seventy-sixth Street, their wheels politely screeching out rhythmic thumps. The steel for these tracks was once smelted here, by Polish and Czech laborers who could walk to Cleveland's factories from their front doors. Their wood-frame homes were modest. By today's sprawling standards, they resemble dollhouses.

Slavic Village's real estate strains to accommodate the twenty-first century. When Barbara and Robert Anderson's daughter gave them a sixty-inch TV after getting her first job out of college a few years ago, Barbara put it diagonally in the corner of their living room. Its main wall wasn't wide enough to fit the set.

But on the whole their house, five doors in from the dead end, has served the Andersons well in the nearly twenty-five years since they bought it, for less than $30,000. The intimate living room, festooned with pictures of grandchildren, gives way to a walk-through dining area, its long wooden table equipped with chairs for a dozen guests. The bright kitchen gives Robert enough room to marinate his grill specialties: shrimp, ribs, and the fish his grandchildren catch in Sandusky Bay. Up a steep and narrow flight of stairs the Andersons have created another living area, with deep maroon carpet and bedrooms on either side.

After Barbara's sister fell fatally ill with cancer in 1982, this was where the couple's five nieces and nephews came to live. Being homeowners, to Barbara, "meant a lot to us. We would be part of a neighborhood."

But what did "neighborhood" mean in Slavic Village now? By the close of 2005, another noise clanked louder than the freight trains: A scrap metal yard around the corner chewed aluminum and copper late into the evening. Raging development in China was driving up prices, and these commodities were plentiful in Slavic Village and all over Cleveland—in the siding of houses, and in eighty-year-old pipes.

The parts had been stripped from the homes of Slavic Village. That winter most of the houses on East Seventy-sixth Street looked like they were shivering in the January cold, naked. Scavengers had plundered the siding, the heating ducts, the wiring. From her weathered porch, Anderson watched them spirit away their haul in grocery carts.

The Andersons were the first black family in an all-white neighborhood that didn't want them. Slavic Village is the childhood home and present district of Representative Dennis Kucinich, a proud precinct of polka halls and kielbasa shops. The neighborhood never had money, and with integration came arson attacks against the Andersons and other black newcomers. Its East European population was dying out and the next generations moving on. The main allure of the neighborhood's cozy houses, their proximity to factories making everything from household supplies to car parts, had vanished with those jobs and virtually all of Cleveland's manufacturing businesses, first to efficient single-story buildings in the suburbs and then out of the region and the country.

Yet while racial conflict, unemployment, and depopulation all plagued Slavic Village, none accounted for the blight on these blocks. This neighborhood looks like a hurricane hit it.

"Such a small little street, and we have everything going on here!" Barbara Anderson says with a laugh, strutting through sidewalk slush in the wine-toned slacks and matching pumps she'll be wearing to church this evening.

Every night in January, her evangelical congregation holds a group prayer-and-project meeting, what they call "the Consecration" because the tradition started when Trinity Outreach Ministries celebrated its move to its home on Ashbury Avenue a decade ago. Tonight, Wednesday, the theme is civic affairs, Barbara Anderson's specialty. She's president of the Bring Back the 70s Street Club, a group that held its first meeting in her living room. In the year and a half since then, the club organized residents to clean up the piles of tires that until recently lined the rail embankment, brought in police to train neighbors in anticrime vigilance, groomed a new community garden, and stenciled curbs with house numbers so emergency responders can find addresses.

But each month the neighborhood had fewer and fewer house numbers to mark. By the start of 2006, financial trusts had repossessed half a dozen homes out of the twenty on the Andersons' block, and all six were hideously vandalized. Three other stripped and vacant houses had owners in name only. These, like the others, were in line to be sold at the Cuyahoga County sheriff's foreclosure sales.

For a week, Barbara Anderson had looked out from her porch at the latest addition to the museum of abandonment. Across the street from the Andersons, not long after New Year's, Wendy Wright asked her neighbor Will Lofton to hold her mail until the next time she came by.

Lofton wasn't going anywhere; he rented his house but was on his way to owning it, through a Bush administration program that let poor people who receive Section 8 rent vouchers use the aid toward a down payment. That following Wednesday, a moving company piled the Wright family's possessions in the street in a snow-flocked display of furniture, sheets, sweaters, and board games, punctuated with an orgy of nude Barbie dolls.

Household Finance hired the movers. It had bought back Wright's landlord's house at a sheriff's auction in December 2005. Household had already reclaimed the bungalow three doors down, at 3422 East Seventy-sixth, formerly home to a couple who had worked in the broom-and-mop factory down the street.

The Andersons' house only barely escaped the auction block itself. The $28,900 loan they took out when they bought it came with a 13.5 percent interest rate, not unusual in 1982. By the time they faced foreclosure in 1998—after Barbara left her job to care for Robert, who depends on a dialysis machine—they owed just $106 less than they had borrowed. The house was set for auction four times, most recently in the summer of 2003, and each time the Andersons managed to get the sale called off. In the final round, a group called the East Side Organizing Project helped the couple cancel the sheriff's sale and worked with a local bank to get them a lower-interest loan. And Barbara Anderson had found a new calling, as the organization's treasurer.

Part of Gale Cincotta's national confederation of activists, the East Side Organizing Project had been pushing for a dozen years to get home lending to inner cities, and especially to black buyers like the Andersons, whose likelihood of owning a home still lagged so woefully behind whites'. Now that they'd done it, those loans were metastasizing into a killer of neighborhoods.

Anderson knocked on doors all over Slavic Village, trying to help homeowners in trouble. All of her assets—her broad smile, her readiness to talk to anyone, whenever, that unyielding optimism that neighbors banding together can build a livable neighborhood—got her nowhere.

"You pass out literature and try to make people feel comfortable. A lot of people," remarks Anderson, surveying the empty husks of houses around her, "just give up." By now most of the owners, such as Wendy Wright's landlord, were investors who didn't live here, or even intend to own the properties for long. The houses here merely represented opportunities to borrow money from willing lenders, then cash in by selling to someone else doing the same thing. Whoever got stuck at the end of the line, unable to sell to the next flipper, would be the one to get the foreclosure notice.

"People come to strip the neighborhood," Anderson laments, as slush drips from her shoes in the afternoon sun, "to use it and abuse it and leave it." Though she works with one of the best advocacy groups of its kind in the country, and though she is an indefatigable community organizer herself, Barbara Anderson can do nothing about her own street, or to preserve her own life's investment in her home. Those homeowners who do hang on to their houses have little to show for their dedication. Researchers in Chicago concluded that for every foreclosure within the surrounding block or two, a home's value declines by nearly 1 percent. Violent crime increases at more than double that rate.

In 2007 and 2008, newspapers in places far from Cleveland—Tucson, Fresno, Atlanta, Palm Beach, Sarasota, Seattle—would duly report those findings as their cities and hundreds of others began to reckon with their own home loan hangovers. A parade of journalists from all over the world arrived on Slavic Village's waste-strewn streets to ask what had gone wrong, and how the entire global finance system was brought down by loans on houses that were barely standing.

But in 2005, East Seventy-sixth Street was already being sealed like a coffin, one nailed plywood window at a time. That year, 376 houses went into foreclosure in the neighborhood, joining hundreds of others that already stood abandoned. Three years earlier, this and other devastated nearby streets had been intact.

Slavic Village was already ill, part of a city and a region whose people and jobs had been leaching out for years. A Christmas card produced that year by the locally headquartered company American Greetings commemorated its greatest distinction: "Season's Greetings from Cleveland . . . America's Poorest City!" Yet the Midwest's dismal economy didn't entirely explain what had happened there. Northeast Ohio lost jobs and more jobs in the 2000s, yet the neighborhood had survived a time when unemployment was more than twice as high.

By 2005, Cuyahoga County's courts became so overwhelmed with foreclosure cases that the standard six-month procedure began to take a year and sometimes two. "Crushing is the word," Chief Magistrate Stephen Bucha says of the caseload he couldn't begin to tackle, during a pause between hearings in which few homeowners showed up to protest. Bucha was seeing plenty of laid-off steel- and autoworkers in his court, but he was certain that job losses alone didn't account for a crisis that he first saw brewing a decade earlier, before unemployment in Ohio began to rise. "It started because of changes in lending practices," Bucha concludes. "Banks were willing to make higher-risk loans at higher interest rates."

Actually Bucha got it wrong, on two counts. Lenders were not just willing, but also determined to make those high-risk loans. And these weren't banks at all, but unregulated mortgage companies that relied completely on Wall Street investment firms for their funds. The packaging of mortgages by the thousands into securities was on its surface the same business it had been back when Manny Palazzo had tried to stop Long Beach Mortgage from making absurd loans to unqualified borrowers. What had changed were the lengths the investment banks were willing to go to make more and more absurd loans to unqualified borrowers, and the amount of money they could make along the way by reconstituting those loans into securities—and those securities into still more securities—then selling them to investors.

Before, customers who didn't document their income could borrow up to 65 percent of the appraised value of a house. Now they could get 95 percent from one loan, and the other 5 percent from a second. Or buyers who might not otherwise qualify received a low introductory interest rate that would adjust upward, sharply, in two or three years. As long as real estate prices kept going up—as they did every single quarter, starting in 1994—lenders and investors would make money no matter what happened to the borrower. In fact, when borrowers had trouble paying, that was good for business. They could then be readily persuaded to refinance into a new loan, again with a low introductory rate, and lenders, securitizers, and a passel of helpers—insurers, lawyers, appraisers, title companies—got a fresh *ca-ching!* of fees.

The chain of transactions stretched farther and farther with each passing year, as investment banks built a massive and unregulated global business in "derivatives" of mortgage-backed securities—products that allowed them to repackage and pass along extremely-high-risk subprime loans to unsuspecting bondholders. But to understand what happened to Slavic Village, all you really need to remember is the lesson Chicago learned so painfully in the FHA debacle of the 1970s: Too much money is a far more destructive force than too little, when it's there to be made by plundering neighborhoods house by house and block by block.

In the year of Hurricane Katrina, a flood of money deluged Slavic Village and many other neighborhoods in Cleveland. This one didn't leave its victims stranded on rooftops or floating down muddy streets; it seeped in through transactions, tens of thousands of them, that looked beautiful on a spreadsheet. The tools that Wall Street uses to wring profits out of the places we live in were so powerful that they pushed Slavic Village, and almost every neighborhood in Cleveland, right over the edge. In just four years, starting in 2003, more than four out of every five home loans made in Cleveland and then securitized by Wall Street banks ultimately went into foreclosure.

If a securities analyst had only hopped on a one-hour flight from New York to Cleveland and taken a taxi to ZIP 44105, he could have seen what was in store for his portfolio. He could have talked to Nicole Farrow, who briefly owned the vacant house at the very end of Barbara Anderson's block, the one with empty bottles of Thunderbird on the porch and large holes carved in the drywall where fixtures used to be. The entire heating system was gone. The sink had been ripped out of the house's only bathroom, a fetid space in the basement. Just a few signs of life remained: "Destiny's Child" and "Aaliyah" scribbled on a bedroom wall upstairs; a baby bottle on the linoleum downstairs, near piles of broken glass.

In late 2004, Ameriquest Mortgage foreclosed on a speculator who lived in suburban Cleveland Heights. Ameriquest turned around and sold the house to an investor who buys up foreclosures, who resold it a couple of months later to Nicole Farrow.

Farrow made for an unlikely real estate investor: six months pregnant, racked with severe morning sickness that required repeated hospitalizations, and recently relocated from Las Vegas. "I didn't even have a job," she said, sitting in her mother's suburban dining room, its table covered with stacks of mortgage papers. What she did have was a boyfriend looking to close some real estate investment deals. " 'Cleveland is a hot market,' he told me. 'We can make good money.' "

The Seventy-sixth Street wreck wasn't the only Cleveland house Farrow purchased, with no money down. Starting in March 2004 and through that summer, Farrow bought six others in Cleveland and a condo in nearby Shaker Heights—all the houses ruins like this one, though she didn't know it at the time. Listed on the paperwork as the occupant of each of them, Farrow was able to become a multiple first-time property owner with nearly $500,000 in loans from a company called Argent Mortgage. Two years after Farrow bought the houses, all were in the process of foreclosure.

Cleveland's debacle was made of a few basic ingredients, the same ones stewing everywhere. Mortgage brokers fabricated information about borrowers (Farrow's listed her as a house painter). Appraisers conjured exaggerated estimates of property values. Attorneys and title agents who signed off on the papers pretended not to notice. And the money kept coming.

Ameriquest Funding, Bank One NA, Citifinancial, Argent Securities, Household Realty Corp., Countrywide Home Loans, Charter One Mortgage, ABN AMRO, HUD, the Federal National Mortgage Association— these were Barbara Anderson's new neighbors on East Seventy-sixth Street. In Slavic Village, subprime companies accounted for more than half of all mortgages in the mid-2000s.

As each house toppled into a Cuyahoga County sheriff's foreclosure auction in 2003 and 2004, an agent hired by the mortgage companies placed a bid—usually the only one—and the deed, literally, was done. Though not quite: The sheriff's staff was so backed up, processing 7,500, then 9,500, then 11,000 foreclosures each year, quadruple the number of a decade earlier, that it would take another five or six months before the bank had the ownership papers. The house was now "REO," real estate owned, while the bank looked for a new buyer.

Mark Wiseman sits in the back of a Cuyahoga sheriff's auction on a Monday morning, observing this utterly routine ritual of repossession, the first of 2006. "Ninety, ninety-five percent go to the bank," he whispers from his orange hard plastic seat in the back of the auditorium.

A few other bidders dare to make an offer. Todd and Yovette Gardner own their own house in South Euclid, but now they want to get into the real estate investment business. The Gardners plan to flip their new purchase.

"It's an investment, a way to make money," hopes Gardner, who kept his leather newsboy cap and jacket on in the auditorium. "I'm going to fix it up and sell it." The couple eyes a brick house near the Cleveland Clinic whose bidding started at just under $17,000. They'll end up buying it for $24,000 in cash, and borrowing another $19,000, at more than 8 percent interest, for improvements.

"Are there any other bids? Are there any other bids?" Over and over comes the question from the sheriff's stern auctioneer, almost a hundred times that morning. She spent the minutes leading up to the auction literally chatting about the weather (snowy) with the bank agents occupying the front row. After all, she sees them every week. One or two don suits for the event, but most carry themselves more like process servers or eBay entrepreneurs, jobs for which souvenir T-shirts and battered jeans do justice to the transaction.

"It's funny to see how the banks dispatch people to buy the houses, which then just sit there," Wiseman remarks behind a cupped hand, his wire-rimmed glasses trained on the front row as each agent strutted up to sign the papers. Funny, as in absurd, ridiculous, tragic. When he worked for a private law firm, Wiseman used to be the rare attorney whose job was to keep people, usually poor, from losing their homes to foreclosure. Then the Cuyahoga County Treasurer's Office hired him in 2005 to start a foreclosure prevention program, to stanch the huge losses to the county as property tax payments stopped coming.

First with his clients and then with the county, Wiseman watched in horror as a wave of home loans devoured his city, one neighborhood at a time. In his office across Ontario Street from the Cuyahoga Justice Center, winds from Lake Erie slashing through the gully between the buildings, Wiseman glanced toward the boxes of foreclosure records he had yet to unpack and review, to begin to figure out how to prevent the damage from getting worse.

His options are limited. The properties' owners of record are trusts—legal concoctions representing everyone in the world who possesses some piece, however small, of the securities that had swallowed the mortgage.

Nothing obligates the trusts' administrators to make amends. Just about everything the investment funds have done here is legal.

Determined to get justice, somehow, and more immediately the millions of dollars it would cost to start tearing down the blighted houses, Cleveland finally resorted in 2008 to filing a suit charging twenty-one investment banks, including Citigroup, Bear Stearns, Deutsche Bank, and Bank of America, with "creating a public nuisance." It went nowhere.

"Cleveland is the sacrificial lamb," Wiseman snaps, using a line he turns to often, "so the lenders can make more money everywhere else."

While Barbara Anderson watched her neighborhood get pulled apart, one slat of siding at a time, most of the nation was captivated by the spectacular view outside their windows. On the East and West coasts, the same flood of money that was deluging Cleveland formed a wave that any reasonably at-tuned surfer could jump on and ride. If you'd never owned a home, you likely bought one. (Homeownership reached its all-time peak at the end of 2004, at 69.2 percent of the nation's households.) If you already had a home, you probably bought a second, or took out a home equity loan, or sold what you had and moved up to someplace newer, bigger, better.

In a frenzy of demand, home prices were rising, by double digits every year, and that fact alone dictated a singular logic for the American home-buyer: The only sensible thing to do was to borrow as much money as possi-ble. The capitalist-minded borrowed to maximize leverage, and therefore gains; some thought nothing of moving their families two or three times to realize those gains. More and more had no choice but to go into massive debt. As a thousand mortgage products bloomed, allowing borrowers to take out more and more based on less and less, the price of real estate went up, too, putting places to live out of reach. Unregulated mortgage lending was making home mortgages more affordable, but at the price of making the homes themselves less so.

Back in the dark ages, when Lewis Ranieri sat down with Reagan's White House staff to create the private mortgage-backed securities busi-ness, we as a nation owed about $1.3 trillion on our homes. Now that his inventions had come of age, our home mortgage debt surpassed $11 tril-lion. Before, America's homeowners had a mountain of home equity as a reward for years of mortgage payments, at an average of 70 percent of a home's value. Leave out the twenty-three million households who've already paid off any mortgages they had, and today the typical borrower now owns just 20 percent of the place she calls her own. As the saying goes, they're renting from the bank.

Even as their debt piled on, until 2007 surprisingly few borrowers were losing their properties to foreclosure—perhaps 1 percent each year, far lower than any time in recent history. If they fell behind on their payments, after all, a property owner could always sell to someone else. Rapid price hikes guaranteed that no matter how much the seller had borrowed, the new buyer would pay more.

On the East Coast and West Coast, in the South—everywhere but in a few hundred miles' radius of the Great Lakes more or less centered on Cleveland—plenty of buyers, borrowers, and speculators took out more money than they could reasonably pay back. By the close of 2005, there was just one thing protecting them from the fate of their peers in Cleveland. Most borrowers were able to sell the property they'd bought, and make money doing it. In Cleveland and other downwardly mobile cities, there was no one left for investors like the Gardners to sell to.

The fallout rippled through the region. In 2005, 5 percent of all the mortgages in Ohio were either in foreclosure or were about to be; more than seventy-eight thousand Ohio homeowners had fallen months behind on their mortgages. The foreclosure rate was triple the national average.

Disasters like Cleveland weren't unfortunate accidents. They had to happen. The home lending industry was by this point addicted to volume—to bringing in as many new customers as possible. In 2006, the private market in mortgage-backed securities, the pools of thousands of loans banks buy from mortgage companies and then resell to investment funds, neared $6 trillion, and $1 trillion of that unfathomably enormous pile of money was bought and sold in that year alone. Two firms, Lehman Brothers and Bear Stearns, generated more than $200 billion between them by packaging those loans. Their fees varied, but generally an investment bank could expect to net about one quarter to one half of a penny for every dollar they threw out there.

Now imagine a bunch of men in suits scooping up all those pennies, and—thanks to automated systems that instantly sized up the qualifications of the loans they were buying—without having to stoop on their hands and knees. The growth of Citigroup's mortgage securities operation illustrates investment banks' lunatic rush to reap the fees before someone else did. In 2004, investors held about $3 billion in home loans in pools that Citigroup Global Markets assembled and resold. A year later, the division had more than doubled that. And by the beginning of 2007, it put together $23 billion in mortgage-backed securities. Based on the volume of loans it packaged in 2006, that division of Citigroup raked in mortgage securities fees that likely approached $250 million.

Citigroup's mortgage department would never have had that kind of freakish growth if it weren't for the subprime loans that became the standard currency in neighborhoods such as Slavic Village. By 2007, nearly half of Citigroup's mortgage investments consisted of such loans. Citigroup's volume of subprime loan business had increased thirty-three times over these lush few years.

Because they supplied the money, the investment trusts ran the show. They specified the underwriting—the basic ground rules for who would and wouldn't qualify for a mortgage, and under what circumstances. Record low interest rates had already snared virtually every homeowner or homebuyer who qualified for a "conventional" loan—those who made down payments of at least 20 percent, had high credit scores, and earned enough to keep mortgage bills below about one third of their incomes. Where would they turn for more customers? By 2004 Citigroup and the other investment banks had begun to accept mortgages into their securities pools with low almost everything: low credit scores, low down payments, next to no documentation of how much money one earned or had in the bank. By the end of that year, more than half the loans they securitized required little to no documentation from borrowers.

Low teaser interest rates brought in new customers; in two or three years they would see their rates adjust sharply upward. Many borrowers who took out these loans knew they likely couldn't pay the higher rate but were convinced—often with the encouragement of their mortgage brokers—that they would be able sell the property at a profit or refinance into a lower interest rate before the increase hit.

But as flexible as the boundaries of mortgage lending had become, home lenders couldn't really get around one thing: As mortgage companies were letting people borrow more and more money, all that phantom cash was propelling real estate prices far beyond what people could actually pay. Most Americans' incomes were barely budging. While banks began to tolerate borrowers taking on higher and higher levels of debt compared with their incomes, after a while the only way for a lot of buyers to qualify to buy the homes they wanted was for mortgage brokers to doctor their financial profiles. And so they and their brokers did.

Buyers of these securities received detailed warnings about possible problems with the loan pools—including, quite explicitly, the prospect that the financial picture of borrowers, from their credit to their assets, was simply untrue. Such disclaimers did little to deter investors, who could earn 9 percent interest every month by buying the loans billed as the riskiest.

They should have looked at who was selling the loans, and how they made their money. The ranks of mortgage brokers grew spectacularly along with the Wall Street securities that financed the loans, from about 7,000 firms in 1987 to more than 44,000, employing more than 418,000 people, in 2004. Subprime and other high-risk loans accounted for 43 percent of their business. (At the boom's peak they sold two out of three mortgages in America.) All of them work on commission, and the higher the interest rate on the loan, the more they get paid. Mortgage brokers team up with appraisers to tell them how much a house is worth, and therefore how big the loan ought to (or ought not) be. Even if a broker wasn't inclined to invent fictional jobs for his customer, a generous appraisal could make a stupid loan look safe, and therefore close one more deal. Across the industry, the rate at which mortgage companies denied loan applications dropped by nearly half from 1997 to 2001.

Subprime loans always had their risks, with foreclosure rates typically close to 7 percent. But the people retailing these loans carried none of it. Neither did the investment banks. First of all, they carried insurance policies on the pools, which bought them top endorsements from bond ratings agencies. (If a pool were to fall short of the top AAA rating, agencies such as Moody's helpfully sat down with fund managers to advise them on a remedy.) Under federal law, as long as Bear Stearns or Citigroup could reasonably claim illegal acts weren't readily discernible in the mortgage paperwork they received from lenders, they could not be held legally responsible for any transgressions.

Wishful thinking and a geeked-out obsession with data weren't all that kept investment bankers blind to the catastrophe already unfolding. They had, like Oedipus, gouged their own eyes out rather than face the consequences of their acts. So for now, Ohio wasn't on Wall Street's radar. In the investment pools, loans from that state made up a tiny percentage of each package of thousands, and Cleveland's foreclosure calamity kicked a mere dent in a shiny moneymaking machine.

On maps, the spread of Cleveland's foreclosures looked like a port-wine stain had collided with a Rorschach test. From Slavic Village straight east toward the city's most exclusive suburbs, and bleeding to the older towns bordering south, Cleveland was rapidly cultivating the nation's largest collection of abandoned real estate.

From his cubicle downtown, across the hall from the clerk who takes tax payments, Mark Wiseman started tracking foreclosures out in parts of the county that never had them before on any large scale, at least not since the 1930s. In South Euclid, down the block from a wooded creek where herds of deer gallop freely, a modern ranch with an in-ground pool stood rotting, its foreclosure, on a subprime loan, tied up in the homeowners' bankruptcy. South Euclid had about 200 vacant houses, where just a few years earlier it had none. Nearby Cleveland Heights, a progressive enclave where locals head for a latte or yoga, had another 200 or so vacant homes; 133 went to a sheriff's sale in 2004 alone.

Home appraisals were the dry timber of the foreclosures blazing through Cuyahoga. Ohio did not license appraisers, and brokers could handpick appraisers who would confirm the house was worth as much as the seller claimed it was, often twice as much as its actual value. Whoever owned the house called the shots. If a speculator sought to resell for a certain price, or an owner wanted to get cash back by refinancing, the deal could be done as long as somewhere in the neighborhood, someone had already convinced a lender to accept the desired number. In a city full of brokers and appraisers all doing the same thing, home prices quickly whipped up into cotton candy—sweet and artificially colored.

In the wealthy heart of Shaker Heights, where sprawling homes built in the 1910s and 1920s scatter around shapely parks and lakes, an eighteen-room Tudor mansion loomed vacant, its ballroom with vaulted wraparound windows ruined a couple of winters earlier by burst pipes. A speculator had bought it for half a million dollars, figuring he'd flip it—resell it quickly— for much more. When that didn't work out, he sold it to a phantom buyer, a postal worker who borrowed $1.1 million on his behalf, based on an appraisal of $1.3 million. In August 2005, Credit Suisse First Boston repossessed the mansion for the minimum bid of $233,334. It was one of seventy-four foreclosures in Shaker Heights that year. The last time Shaker had seen anything like it was in 1935, its worst year for foreclosures during the Great Depression.

A few blocks away, retired steelworker Steve Zsigrai found himself living with vacant foreclosed houses on either side of him. His ex-wife insisted on moving to the upscale suburb almost forty years ago. Now, Zsigrai laments, "Shaker lives in la-la land."

A massage therapist and democracy activist named Adele Eisner used to own, and live in, the cute little brick house to his left, with now-bare oak floors, and cracked slate paving the porch. At a sheriff's auction in December, Deutsche Bank bought back the brick house from Eisner. On an income of just $26,000, she had borrowed $197,000 from Argent Mortgage to refinance a high-interest loan on her new home and pay off credit card bills. She went into foreclosure less than eight months later, owing Argent $233,000. Eisner had borrowed nearly triple the county's appraised value of her house.

In 2004, Argent Mortgage sold more home loans than any lender in Cleveland, and it achieved that distinction within months of beginning to do business there. Argent blitzed the county with more than 45,000 loans between 2002 and 2004—this in a place that has only 620,000 homes in all.

Argent's growth in the rest of the nation was just as propulsive. In 2003 it sold $21 billion in loans. In 2004 the company made more than double that, over a quarter of a million mortgages. The year following, Argent was on track to selling $61 billion in home loans. Combined with its sibling company Ameriquest—another $39 billion—Argent was now the largest subprime lender in America.

Argent Mortgage became a successful organization by not really being one. It operated as a wholesale mortgage lender, which sold its products exclusively through freelance brokers. Argent itself employed hundreds of sales reps who made sure brokers pushed Argent loans to borrowers. But that sales force barely had any more ties to the company than the retail brokers did; they worked on laptops from their homes, and most were in or just out of college.

With a staggering selection of products by then ubiquitous in the mortgage business, Argent's account executives helped brokers find a loan product for pretty much any customer: borrowers who couldn't prove their income, borrowers who had horrific credit scores, borrowers who wanted to buy a second home, who wanted to pay interest only for five years, who wanted a forty-year mortgage. These options and more were priced on an à la carte menu. Argent rejected just one in six applicants.

And no wonder. Those account executives working out of their bedrooms and dens were paid on commission, starting at a quarter of a penny for every dollar they approved. The more loans they sold and the more lucrative those loans were for Argent, the more money they made.

When mortgage brokers submitted applications for loans, these salesmen processed the paperwork by computer, and didn't as a rule check the documents that demonstrated a borrower's ability to pay the loan, or the appraisals they were based on. For that, they relied on the information from the brokers.

But those brokers had every reason to twist, pump, and fabricate that information. They were paid fees for each loan they made. The larger the loans, the higher the fees. And following the standard industry practice, the higher the interest rate, the higher the fee the broker collected. Argent didn't do much to screen the brokers who sold its loans to customers—just a Lexis/Nexis background and a check on their credit. The brokers were reviewed much more loosely than they were supposed to scrutinize someone borrowing $20,000 to fix a roof.

That's because Argent Mortgage needed those brokers. By the time Ameriquest begat Argent in 2000, Ameriquest was already a pincushion for lawsuits, consumer complaints, protests, and other assaults, all of which were possible because the company could be shown to be responsible for the sales tactics of its employees.

Like quoting interest at rates lower than what ended up on the official documents. Having customers sign blank loan documents, and filling in the details—little things, like interest rates—later. Failing to tell borrowers that mortgages had adjustable rates. Copying customer signatures by tracing them pressed against a lighted Coke machine. Instructing borrowers on the amount of income they should claim. ("This number would bear no relationship with what the borrower may actually have been making; rather, the borrower was told that they would need to state the income at the instructed level in order to get the loan," a manager for Ameriquest's Silicon Valley retail office said in a statement, in one of hundreds of lawsuits against the company.) Inflating the appraised value of the home, which made the loan look less risky to investors. Pressing borrowers to refinance their existing loans, on the (false) premise they'd save money—whatever it took to sell a mortgage, Ameriquest's salesmen did it.

They were under extreme pressure to produce. Sales managers used the movie *Boiler Room* as a training video, pushing agents on the front lines to make up to two hundred sales calls a day. Their income largely depended on meeting aggressive sales targets. Sales agents had to follow scripts that blatantly misled customers into believing that taking out an Ameriquest loan to pay off credit card debt would save them money. Another widespread practice was to delay sending paperwork to borrowers until it was too late for them to back out. The sales teams' supervisors also oversaw Ameriquest's staff of loan processors—the workers who were supposed to screen out any applications that weren't up to snuff. If the processors wanted to keep their jobs, they would have to doctor loan applications into passing shape.

Responding to mass complaints that Ameriquest reps aggressively pushed customers to refinance over and over again and misled them about the cost of their monthly payments, forty-eight states reached a $325 million settlement with Ameriquest at the beginning of 2006. The lender agreed to disclose interest rates and fees up front, use independent agents at closings, and refinance loans only if a transaction genuinely benefits a borrower.

But the man who presided over those practices was already gone from the company. That winter, the Senate Foreign Relations Committee unanimously confirmed Ameriquest's founder, Roland Arnall, as ambassador to the Netherlands. "When we found out they were let go, and action was taken so that it never happened again," Arnall told the Senate during his confirmation hearings, about the managers of his sales teams at Ameriquest.

Arnall bought his new job. Starting in 2002, Arnall and his wife, Dawn, gave more contributions to George W. Bush than anyone else in America, including more than $5.5 million for Bush's reelection. Senate Democrats delayed Arnall's nomination for months while the states concluded their negotiations with Ameriquest.

Argent had no obligation to comply with the Ameriquest settlement. Ameriquest spun off Argent in 2003, and they became separate entities of a shared parent company, ACC Capital Holdings. The state attorneys general had considered hitting Argent, too, but found themselves flummoxed. How do you go after the company when freelance agents are the ones lying, defrauding, cheating, and manipulating to sell all those loans?

But investment banks kept providing Arnall with money, because his companies were making them so much of it. Citigroup, Bear Stearns, Merrill Lynch, Washington Mutual, and Ameriquest itself assembled and sold securities built out of Argent and Ameriquest loans. In 2007, Citigroup alone bought and resold twenty-seven thousand of them, totaling $3.8 billion.

Adele Eisner's loan, for instance, was part of a pool of more than four thousand that Ameriquest sold to insurance and pension funds, including John Hancock, American Funds, Manulife Financial, Lincoln Financial Group, and Fidelity. More than half of those loans were refinances that put cash into the homeowners' hands. In return, investors made 2 to 6 percent in interest every month; other Ameriquest pools could net investors 9 percent interest or more. Compound, of course.

There were only two ways for this delicious business to keep growing. One was by opening up new groups of customers. Ameriquest also was notorious for "flipping" loans, pushing consumers to refinance their mortgages over and over again.

When borrowers didn't earn enough to qualify, sales reps submitted applications full of fiction. In Cleveland, Catherine Chaney was earning about $1,600 a month as a hospital aide when a broker helped her buy her first home—a yellow bungalow just south of Shaker Heights, with a yard for her son and niece to run around in. An investor had picked the house up at a foreclosure sale, then sold it to Chaney for twice the price.

Chaney's first loan, from Flagstar, was well beyond her means, at more than $1,100 a month. She took out another loan, from Argent, but found that her payments were still too high. The broker who sold her the first loan called again, to see how she was doing, and told her she could lower her mortgage payment and get some cash for repairs by refinancing with Ameriquest. But she needed to make more money, he explained, to qualify.

"He wanted me to send a letter saying my income was three thousand dollars a month," recalls Chaney. She reluctantly wrote it. "I was locked in—it was like, 'Take this or be homeless.'" But the new loan wasn't cheaper. Her interest went up from just over 6 percent to nearly 9. Her old loan included property tax payments; the new one did not. And because Ameriquest al lowed her to borrow far more than her home's actual value, she found she couldn't sell the house or refinance it. Months behind on her payments, Chaney worked overtime and endured stress-induced migraines while negotiating with Ameriquest to get back her old interest rate.

Argent brokers ran beyond anyone's control. A survey on Cleveland's West Side found that Argent consistently made mortgages for double what Third Federal lent on houses right next door. FBI agents investigated a single mother living in subsidized housing who bought five houses in a day, and a night-shift postal worker who bought four, all with Argent loans and all in foreclosure. By 2007, one in four of all Argent loans in Cleveland would be sold at a sheriff's foreclosure auction.

For every dollar of home loans that the federal government guaranteed through the Federal Housing Administration, another fifty were now flowing through the Wall Street, Fannie Mae, and Freddie Mac mortgage factories. This was everything Gale Cincotta had fought for—and a worse nightmare than she could have imagined. Cincotta died of gallbladder cancer in the summer of 2001, aware, already, that history was repeating itself. "It is almost like an insanity," she had remarked at a congressional hearing on predatory lending a year before her death, "working in these neighborhoods where we were hit with so many FHA foreclosures." Cincotta had no idea that the worst was yet to come.

On the opposite end of Slavic Village from East Seventy-sixth Street, long, one-story homes huddle together on Mead Avenue. A demolition contractor named Vince Collazo lives here, a sturdy figure surrounded by eroding structures. Collazo grew up in Slavic Village and has no intention of moving from the neighborhood or the home he has owned since 2001. "I love the area. It's near everything," he says, gesturing from a curb crusted with sooty snow. "I don't know what people think about me for living here. Everyone took off. They think it's ghetto. I see it every day—'Oh, you still live here?!' "

"Here" is a street of a dozen houses, four of them boarded up. The bright turquoise one to the right, its windows shuttered, has been in foreclosure four times since 1990. The sea-foam green structure to the left of Collazo's home sits empty. Collazo had offered to buy the house from the old man and daughter who now lived elsewhere but still owned it—to tear down the termite-infested place and send Mead Avenue on its way to a fresh start. But in the perverse universe of subprime lending, the uninhabitable home was worth more to its former residents as a façade. Based on an appraiser's assertion that the property was worth something, Argent Mortgage let them refinance the structure with a $60,000 loan. Why should the owners let a wrecking ball near an ATM that produced that kind of money?

East Seventy-sixth Street turned out to be fortunate among the ranks of forsaken Cleveland blocks. The mortgage security trusts were buying those houses back at the foreclosure auctions, with hope, however dim, that they could find new buyers and recoup their losses. Mead Avenue was more like an orphanage without a caretaker. When houses went to auction around here—and, Wiseman guessed, in about 10 or 15 percent of Cuyahoga County's foreclosure sales—bank lawyers filed a motion refusing their return, and the homes sat stranded, with no owner at all.

Collazo made similar offers all over the neighborhood, to tear down houses that sat abandoned, but neither the City of Cleveland nor the real estate investment trusts were willing to extricate the homes from their legal limbo.

A few business owners like Collazo have tried to hold Slavic Village together. Seven Roses, a tin-ceilinged restaurant that looks like it's been in the neighborhood forever but actually just opened a few years ago, serves up pierogis, paczkis, and borscht to visitors who come from downtown for a taste of heritage. Third Federal Savings and Loan kept its headquarters on Broadway, in the heart of the neighborhood, and recently expanded it. After an earlier dalliance it stayed away from subprime lending, and thrived.

But local entrepreneurs were no match for the real money that was doing everything but bulldozing the neighborhood. Using funds freely available from mortgage brokers, speculators were descending on entire blocks.

Kevin Jackson remembered when East Fifty-third Street didn't have knots of young strangers hanging around in cars and empty lots. That wasn't so long ago, either. Jackson, a Cleveland police officer, and his wife, Andrea, had planned to sink deep roots into Slavic Village. In 1998, they moved into their handsome white-sided, black-trimmed frame home in the middle of the block. A nonprofit organization called Cleveland Housing Network, which restores abandoned homes and builds new ones, then sells them to first-time buyers, brought the Jacksons in as tenants, and allowed them to apply their rent toward a down payment. Kevin and Andrea were eager to stake their claim in Cleveland and become homeowners in the process.

After they moved in, the Jacksons watched as real estate flippers bought most of the occupied houses on East Fifty-third, seven of them with loans from Argent Mortgage. In November 2005, a federal judge sentenced the ringleaders of an operation that bought dozens of houses in and near Slavic Village from 1999 to 2002, reselling them to investors at wildly overappraised prices. Christopher Siedlecki, who has since pleaded guilty to fourteen counts of fraud, bought a house on East Fifty-third Street for $34,000. He then sold it to Lawrence Reasor for $61,500, in a transaction financed by a small mortgage company called Entrust. In 2003, Reasor refinanced with a $68,000 Argent loan; it went into foreclosure at the end of 2005.

Argent ultimately financed six other homes on the same block of East Fifty-third Street, all of them registered as "owner-occupied" and appraised at double and triple the value of their neighbors. Four are already abandoned. Because of cuts in federal block grants, the city had to suspend a program to demolish vacant buildings; now the houses just stand boarded up and decaying. Reasor's robin's-egg-blue rooming house is one of them. "I couldn't rent it out," Reasor says, sitting in his South Euclid living room. "It's a high-drug area."

A fatal problem for investors like Reasor was that money for rentals suddenly dried up when HUD cut funding for low-income tenants' housing vouchers. As rents across the country rose, HUD gave cities a choice: Local administrators could either cut the number of tenants who received the vouchers, or give each tenant less money. Cleveland did both.

The drought of voucher money contributed to the blight on streets such as East Fifty-third, as owners who bought at high prices expecting a steady stream of rental income found those payments dwindling. Many Cleveland voucher tenants never paid their share of the rent in the first place.

Now "For Sale" signs hang in front of owner-occupied homes up and down the adjoining street, Hamm Avenue. Everybody wants out. Hilda and Roberto Rodriguez, who've been here for more than thirty years, want to sell so they can move back to Puerto Rico. Across the street, Anika Pavlovic found her ninety-five-year-old father dead on the kitchen floor after a break-in. "Now is too much," she says, bundled in a parka on her slip of a front lawn. "Me go. Just house go. No more, me no."

Even when teenagers started using the windowpanes of abandoned houses for target practice, and parents on the block began to forbid their children to leave their homes, strangers and neighbors alike had left the

Jackson family alone, knowing that Kevin was a cop. Jackson used to patrol the street on his off-duty time, his Rottweiler at his side. Then one afternoon their sixteen-year-old son was beaten and robbed, on his way home, in front of an abandoned house on the block. The Jacksons packed up and got out of Cleveland. "That ultimately made us make the decision to move," says Andrea. "We were rent-to-own, but when we were ready to sell, who would we sell to?"

The newest Cleveland Housing Network project on the block gleams near the intersection of East Fifty-third and Hamm, its windows shielded with metal grates. The Jacksons watched workers spend six months building it. More than two years later, long after their family fled to suburban Garfield Heights, it still stands empty.

The auditorium of the Cuyahoga County Justice Center comes to order with the fatigued anticipation of a track before the first race. Men in work boots and quilted nylon jackets, who hope buying foreclosed real estate will bring financial rewards that previously eluded them, fill most of the chairs, though everyone understands that the mortgage trusts' agents own the front row. The trusts need the easy access to the auctioneer, since today they will be buying almost everything.

This morning's first auction is *Argent Mortgage v. Charity Stewart et al.,* starting bid $36,667. Argent had financed the home less than two years earlier, for a thirty-three-year-old grandmother who bought it because it was easier than renting.

Charity Stewart was already gone. The night before, Stewart took the garbage bags she had been piling at the front of her living room for a week, everything she could transport from her brief life as a homeowner, and brought them, and her seven-year-old daughter, Charday, to Charity's sister's apartment. Charity's seventeen-year-old son, Jamal, lives with Charity's mother on the other side of the neighborhood, so he can be near his high school football field and his new baby boy. Jamal's older child is in foster care, with a family preparing to adopt her.

Stewart had been the first person ever in her family to buy a home, and she was beyond ready to leave it. The heat never went on. The kitchen pipes froze. Electric bills were up to $400 a month in the winter, from the space heaters. And the dining room wall resembled a gallery installation, spattered dark brown and sculpted into stalactites of dripping plaster by a mold-infused leak oozing down from a busted pipe upstairs.

When the decay started, not long after they moved in, Stewart called Ameriquest, which sent her the bills. She expected the mortgage company to be responsible for the product she bought, just as her landlord once was. "They said it was on me to get it fixed!" she says incredulously. "I don't know what I'm paying the mortgage for." Hearing nothing back, she stopped paying. Argent went to Cuyahoga County Court that November and filed for foreclosure. Stewart had borrowed $85,000, and still owed $84,795.87, plus interest.

If getting out of homeownership didn't take much effort, neither did getting in. Stewart had to pay only $500 cash to purchase the four-bedroom beige frame, just outside Euclid. She would get a whole house, with her name on the title, for less than she was paying in rent each month.

Almost no one in Cleveland put their money down to buy a home anymore. Sellers nearly always provided the funds, and since they're forbidden to compensate a buyer directly—that would be illegal—they make a "contribution" to a nonprofit, which provides the funds as a "gift" to the buyer. With the mortgage boom rose a proliferating array of these charities, including Nehemiah, Ameridream, Liberty Gold, and local players, too, such as Buckeye and Ohio Mortgage.

Nonetheless, Stewart got a $10,000 loan directly from the seller of the house, a handyman-turned-real estate flipper named Steve Dragmen. (Dragmen says the loan was not for a down payment, but to qualify Stewart for the loan.) She certainly needed help. Stewart made about $30,000 a year as a machine operator at a bakery. The house cost $100,000, more than double what Dragmen had bought it for three months earlier. After Dragmen put $20,000 into overhauling the bathrooms, the kitchen, the carpeting, and the water heater, an appraisal company called American Dream green-lighted the selling price.

Dragmen sent Stewart to an Argent broker, who informed her she didn't earn enough to qualify for an $85,000 mortgage. Did she have any other income? How about anyone else in her family? Stewart's mother was on SSI disability, so the broker added "other income" of $693 a month to Stewart's mortgage application.

The application also notes that Stewart had $5,000 in her checking account. "Yeah, right," snorts Stewart. "I didn't even have a checking account at the time." What she did have, as noted on her application, was more than $26,000 in debt, including Charday's parochial school, medical bills, credit cards, and her own student loan. Plus she still owed Dominion East Ohio Gas more than $4,000. That would explain why she couldn't get the heat turned on.

Two days before the house is set for sale, Stewart lumbers around the house's cold and cluttered ground floor, her eyes red. She is six months pregnant, though she hasn't told anyone yet. "I wish I could just burn it down," she pronounces. The leak down the dining room wall has bloomed into a small waterfall. Stewart still has to pack the shower curtain and trash can and towels and toothbrush holder, all of them branded with Coca-Cola bottles. The glazed ceramic vegetables on the kitchen wall would have to come down. Charday keeps pulling her toys out of boxes. "Daughter, you unpacking stuff? We're packing stuff!" Charity instructs her.

Following sheriff's procedure, Argent will hire a moving company to photograph everything Stewart left behind and put the items in storage for thirty days. The movers will change the locks and pour antifreeze in the toilets. And they will put a notice on the door: THIS PROPERTY HAS BEEN SECURED AGAINST ENTRY BY UNAUTHORIZED PERSONS TO PREVENT POSSIBLE DAMAGE. This will be the third time in ten years the sheriff has auctioned 1430 Larchmont Avenue.

At Stewart's foreclosure sale, Argent is the only bidder. The auction ends in less than thirty seconds.

Three hours after Charity Stewart lost her house, her mother, Sandra, cooks lunch for herself and a friend at her place on Carl Avenue—panfried chicken, potatoes microwaved in a plastic grocery bag, rice.

Charity's dining room table, white and gleaming, sits in the next room, flanked by padded, high-backed chairs. Charity didn't have space for it at her sister's, and it isn't necessarily hers—she has a judgment against her for $850 she still owes Elgin Furniture, on Broadway. "I couldn't believe she would get rid of something she paid hard cash money for," Sandra says, glancing over at the table.

Sandra really likes living here, even though the location is too urban for her liking. "I want nice green grass down the street—not dirt grass!" she declares, voicing her opinion about the unmanicured chain-link-enclosed field that goes from her house all the way to the corner half a block away. The Cleveland Housing Network rehabilitated her house before she moved in, and over and over again, staff from the organization have offered Sandra the opportunity to buy, using her rent vouchers toward a down payment. She isn't interested. "You have to maintain it. It's a lot of responsibility. If the furnace goes out, you have to pay for it."

Such concerns didn't deter Charity. "She was always the one who wanted more than anyone else," observes Sandra judiciously. And for that accomplishment, Sandra is proud. For one year, ten months, and thirty days, her daughter was a homeowner. "She didn't tell us until she had the key," says Sandra. "It was beautiful. It was something no one ever did. It was a nice thing to do, like it was supposed to be."

Five

REACHING THE LIMITS

Sacramento, 2008

CLUSTERS OF COWS GRAZE a plain just past the ring of the California High School Rodeo. Off the roadside, swamp shimmers to the accompaniment of faint croaks. Red-winged blackbirds, Swainson's hawks, and blue herons flutter and swoop in long grass—pasture cleared from oak forests back when human settlers, predating the Gold Rush, discovered in the Sacramento Valley the most fertile farmland in America.

That agricultural land is disappearing fast—here in Placer County, at a rate of almost two thousand acres every year. For all the fruits ever squeezed from the earth in northern California, no venture ever yielded as much wealth as the one clanging behind a concrete wall a dung-pat's toss away from the cows' ranch. Willowy flags snap in a strong breeze. These medieval banners mark a subdivision of new homes—corporate America's most lucrative assembly line.

The high wall surrounding Lincoln Crossing, a new subdivision rising thirty miles north of Sacramento, encompasses sixteen minivillages under construction by seven different homebuilders. Each company marks its fiefdom with a flag. Off in the distance, Centex flies a blue-on-white standard. KB Home aspires upwardly with black and gold. Mighty DR Horton has claimed red, white, and blue. A teenager flails a cardboard arrow bigger than his body—it reads LENNAR—directing drivers to a row of red and black flags emblazoned with a mysterious "Z." On Kirkland Court, a cul-de-sac in a new "community" called Carriage Park being built by Lennar Corporation of Miami, Florida, they will find a mirage: houses under construction, while the rest of the real estate universe is collapsing around them.

Still little more than a slab of concrete abutting freshly paved asphalt,

55 Kirkland Court bears a stubble of protruding pipes and tubes. Next door, number 56 consists of an assemblage of wood two-by-fours, which carpenters are binding with metal hold-downs, anchors, trusses, and ties, then sheathing the exterior with plywood to help the frame withstand the Sacramento Valley's steady winds. All that pine brings a calming odor to an otherwise frenetic scene.

At 57 Kirkland Court, HVAC men dangle from rafters like bats, snaking heating and cooling ducts through the eaves. A plumber and his helpers carve out pathways for slender pipes. An electrician on a ladder tames braids of electric cords that will power number 59. Over at number 60, plasterers entomb them all in a sarcophagus of drywall. Not uncommonly, workers commemorate their presence with graffiti on the home's skeleton—a smiley face or, if they're angry at working conditions, obscene words for the subcontractor that employs them.

And so the houses evolve around the curve, acquiring windows, roof shingles, stucco, paint, cabinets, stain, grass, each in a prescribed sequence. On Kirkland Court, Lennar's production process offers a spectacle of efficiency wrung out of chaos. The tradesmen proceed in order from house to house, logging the necessary days or weeks at each stop, glancing when necessary at floor plans tacked to the wall—the Montreal (Plan 601), the Chateau (Plan 603), the Montecito (Plan 613), the Veranda (Plan 604).

As in the gestation of a baby, the most sensitive stage of homebuilding comes in its earliest weeks. Foundation and framing aren't just the most important parts of the process; they're also the most expensive. It used to be that builders of all but the cheapest houses would perch their structures atop beams braced against a concrete rim. This raised foundation kept a house away from its most pernicious enemy: water. Putting a nice home directly on naked concrete was unthinkable, since it would wick up water from the earth like a napkin. Then in 2000 Anderson Floors put a miracle sealant on the market, to be splashed by the bucket onto the cement. Now crews pour a foundation right on the ground—and cut $10,000 out of the budget. Usually, though not always, the sealant holds tight.

A builder can save tens of thousands more by building homes in the shape of simple boxes. The more twists the frame makes on its journey to enclose the structure, the more metal brackets and braces carpenters have to install, and all those parts and labor add up. Instead, most houses these days end up with architecture easily reproduced in LEGO.

Such are the measures necessary to preserve profit margins that during the boom hovered at upward of 20 percent. Like the builders of most new homes in Sacramento, Lennar is traded on the New York Stock Exchange. As with any manufacturing process, investors want to see fast turnover: land transformed into homes into sales. Once building inspectors are satisfied, the only details that count are the ones customers can see.

Around the corner, on Kinnerly Lane, models of the finished product are decorated to evoke stories of relatives never met and uplifting experiences yet to be lived. Home stagers call these emotionally stimulating props "memory points." The décor of the 3,179-square-foot Veranda imagines a wine lover whose daughter dreams of ballerinas and fairies upstairs. The Montecito II's five bedrooms suggest a *National Geographic* theme park, with kids' rooms dressed up as an explorer's tent, a jungle nursery, and an archaeological dig unearthing bones and pottery shards from the construction site here at Lincoln Crossing, a village born as a sales proposition. They offer a staged whiff of history for a place that has just literally appeared out of nowhere.

The true stories of some Lennar buyers in Lincoln Crossing are proving a lot less appealing. There's Darnisha Taylor, a gospel singer who relocated with her husband from Holland, Michigan, to join a congregation down in Elk Grove—they owe some $400,000 on their four-bedroom house but can find no buyers at $299,000. Or Ian Chi, a bottle-blond former Ameriquest salesman. He borrowed $510,000, the entire sales price, for his Veranda.

Like Taylor and about a dozen of his other neighbors, Chi recently received a foreclosure notice, and there's really not much he can do, since Lennar is now selling brand-new Verandas for $377,950. Taylor, Chi, and tens of thousands of Californians bought into the myth that home prices would keep going up, and proceeded to borrow excessive amounts of money. Now those buyers are expendable.

"The only real estate market I care about," New Home Consultant Joni Spitzer tells visitors who may wonder why Lennar is still building new houses in the spring of 2008, "is the one between me and the customer I'm talking to."

Rouged with an immense quantity of makeup, Spitzer is working from Lennar's sales script, repeating the same phrase one will hear from the company's New Home Consultants over at Sentiero at Westpark, or Terrasante in Natomas, or any of Lennar's fifteen developments still under construction at every compass point on Sacramento's periphery. Home sales around here are down to a bare fraction of what they were a couple of years ago, but Lennar's agents are still hustling to move product, at prices lower than anyone else's, including its own former customers. The company has to keep building to survive.

Like all Lennar sales agents and staff, and even company CEO Stuart Miller, Spitzer wears a plastic tag with her first name in capital letters, underneath the company's space-age logo. But she would be reprimanded if she were to call it anything but a "name badge." "Subdivision," "development," and "project" are also verboten—the new homes are rising in a *community*. A down payment, in Lennar-speak, is an "initial investment." Potential buyers are to be called "friends." And a house, of course, is a "home."

JONI is here because her brothers-in-law, Jeff and Guy Spitzer, used to run the Sacramento division of Lennar, the second-biggest homebuilder in the nation. The Spitzer brothers had come from Spokane, where their dad was a contractor who built public buildings such as schools and courthouses. In between working for their dad, Guy sold reference books door to door to get through college, and ladies' shoes during the school year.

Before Lennar came into their lives, Guy and Jeff used their know-how to start a little company called Renaissance Homes, opening their model houses the weekend President George H. W. Bush started the first bombing of Baghdad. Jeff's fluffy mustache and golden shock of hair had not yet turned white. He had learned the map of Sacramento like it was a game of Risk when he worked buying land for the homebuilder Richmond American. If Jeff looked like Einstein, his brother, Guy, looked more like Elvis. Guy did sales and marketing, and made time to play acoustic rock guitar on the side. According to Guy's credo, he didn't actually sell homes at all. "Somebody buys something. You don't sell it to them. They buy it because that's what they want." As their three work crews hammered out perhaps a hundred new houses a year, solid and spacious, the Spitzers became big players in a still small town, where it would be unthinkable to sell their product for more than $160,000.

Then Guy and Jeff found themselves on the front lines of a revolution. Filling a void left by collapsed savings and loans, the California state pension fund started investing state workers' retirement money into building new subdivisions, and for good measure bought millions of shares of homebuilders' stocks. Their billions helped usher in a new era in American real estate: the age of the publicly traded mega homebuilder.

The construction of houses was everything a stockholder's investment isn't supposed to be: erratic, slow, local. It takes years to get permits—especially in California, where environmentalists are rabid about protecting wildlife from the bulldozer. And every few years homebuilders had to endure slow "cycles" as predictable and unwelcome as menstruation. As a publicly traded company since 1971, Lennar remained a rarity, one of an odd dozen or so. As late as 1994, it was selling fewer than five thousand houses a year, at an average price of barely over $100,000.

But for homebuilders such as Lennar, the stars were growing brighter by the quarter. Plummeting interest rates, increasingly easy financing, the Clinton-era homeownership crusade: All of it was making their ungainly products both attractive and attainable. And everywhere they looked, stock analysts agreed that the homebuilders' untapped customers numbered in the tens of millions, from restless baby boomers with immense amounts of pent-up home equity to new immigrants seeking a fresh slice of the American Dream.

By the end of the 1990s, nearly sixty other pop-and-son homebuilders across the country, including Jeff and Guy Spitzer, had sold out to share-holders. Mutual funds, an emerging force on Wall Street through the swelling mass of 401(k) retirement accounts, owned much of their stock. To satisfy those investors, all of these homebuilders were now in a race to do the same thing: grow, massively. The race was on.

After passing on a torrent of offers, in 1996 the Spitzer brothers decided to accept the most impossibly compelling of them, from a young executive from Miami who had been sent on a mission to take over California. Lennar would buy their company outright, for $13 million. The Spitzers would run the corporation's northern California division, on their own terms. When Guy and Jeff went to meet their new boss for the first time, Stuart Miller asked and answered the only question that mattered: "What do you need? I'll give it to you."

Miller's emissary was making similar deals with half a dozen other California homebuilders. The company sought their local expertise, their relationships with subcontractors, and so on, but most of all it wanted one thing: their land. These little companies possessed thousands of acres of space that cost next to nothing, and Lennar bought it at sharp discounts. "We could use our strong financial position to strike hard," explained Miller to a home-builders' conference in 2000. For about $1 billion, Lennar had bought its way into forty-two thousand development sites in California alone. Half of the company's business would now come from that state.

With each acquisition, Lennar's stock price went higher and higher, to-ward a twentyfold increase. In just a decade, the company's annual rev-enues swelled from $650 million to more than $16 billion—growth that attracted still more investment and fueled more expansion. The company used its gains to buy another wave of local builders, expanding into nine-teen states in all. A company that had started out erecting FHA tract homes in Miami was now a teddy bear for Wall Street analysts who were desperate, as dot-coms deflated, for comforting news. "It remains ex-tremely undervalued," raved Citigroup as it predicted Lennar stock would hit $99 a share (when George W. Bush took office it had been worth less than $20). As the rest of the stock market went limp, homebuilders were suddenly sexy. Lennar was a must-buy stock of the moment—and with higher expectations it had to deliver, fast.

As Stuart Miller and his father, Leonard, acquired Renaissance and dozens of other local builders, they set out to unify Lennar's now far-flung operations under a single corporate Culture (the capital "C" is theirs), held to-gether with the sap of optimism. Lennar turned to two geniuses of behav-ioral science: Walt Disney and Dr. Seuss. After taking a course at the Disney School of Management, the junior Miller became convinced that Lennar needed a culture like Disney's, in which employees could be motivated to do anything to advance the corporation. The secret was to treat them, quite lit-erally, like children.

At regional executive meetings, the Spitzer brothers found themselves gathered cross-legged in a circle with colleagues for readings of *Oh, the Places You'll Go!*, while *Yertle the Turtle* served as a lesson in the perils of stepping on colleagues in the pursuit of personal gain. Stuart Miller was such a Seuss enthusiast that he took to writing his own adaptations under the authorship of "Dr. Steuss," until the Geisel estate put a stop to it.

Company meetings end with the Lennar Success University fight song. But by far the most distinctive Lennar ritual is "Scratchings from the Little Red Hen," or as it's known simply to the troops, "The Hen." Since 1994, Lennar employees have been required to memorize this reinterpretation of the classic children's poem and recite it on command at staff meetings and

Pizza Fridays. Stuart Miller himself has been known to deliver "The Hen"
for Wall Street analysts. Anyone who can recite the 350-word "Hen" in
less than one minute qualifies for membership in the Speed Hen Club and
wins a special pin.

Introduced during tough times for homebuilders, the verse prepares employees to press on with their cause no matter what the obstacles. "The Hen"
is Lennar property, but the story is simple enough to share. A hungry rooster
complains about a sudden shortage of worms, now that the wet earth has
dried after a rainstorm. But a determined hen won't tolerate his whining—
she starts digging in the hard earth, convinced that her meal lies just beneath. She spends a day excavating, while the indolent rooster mocks her as he
waits for the grub to return. He finds her in the evening, her eyes tired but her
belly full. All the effort was worth it, the hen declares victoriously—and it always is. *I've never seen a time there were no worms to get.*

Lennar was on its way to creating what the company calls its "homebuilding machine." With its fair weather allowing for year-round construction,
California, along with Arizona and Nevada, became the company's most
fertile ground: a place where houses could be coaxed into a predictable
process of mass production.

Now Lennar Renaissance was constructing more than a hundred homes
a *month* in Sacramento, and it was Guy's job, as vice president of sales and
marketing, to convince people to buy them. The secret, he was learning,
was to trigger buyers' emotions, specifically women's emotions. You can't sell
a new house without seducing women, who almost always are the ones who
decide which home is the place that feels like they do.

Emotion number one: *"O my God, I want it!"* Take a "friend" to the
kitchen and bathroom, make her see herself relaxing in the tub at the end of
the day, and you're well on your way to convincing her that the monthly
payment is worth it.

"It's a nicer home than I've got."

"I've worked hard all my life; look how much I sacrificed."

"I'll be the first person to sit on that toilet."

These are the rationalizations that Spitzer would hear uttered once the
buyer tried to make sense of her overwhelming emotions.

He also determined that buyers are motivated by fear. That one's family isn't safe. That the kids' schools aren't good enough. Located mostly in rural Placer County, which was quickly overtaking Orange as the whitest, most Republican part of all of California, the new Renaissance communities offered a blank slate with a tolerable commute, forty-five minutes if all went well, to Sacramento.

Then Guy Spitzer's sales force suddenly found buyers coming from much farther afield. Crazy property prices in the Bay Area, brought on by an influx of tech workers converging on the dot-com boom, were sending a flood of real estate refugees Sacramento's way—more than twenty-five thousand of them in the late '90s. Some were cashing in on their home equity and trading up. Others got on I-80 to check out what the newspaper ads promised; once they saw the model homes, they could never go back. By 1999, each new phase of ten or twelve Lennar products would sell out in a single morning.

Mark and Yolanda Adornetto were among the migrants, settling into a Lennar Renaissance development in Elk Grove, on the southern fringe of Sacramento, after renting for years south of San Francisco. Buying anywhere in the Bay Area was out of the question. Looking farther afield, they'd discussed purchasing an existing house, but Yolanda insisted on brand-new.

"We couldn't believe what we could get out here," says Mark, whose price to pay for a 3,278-square-foot, six-bedroom spread was an hour-and-a-half commute. Today Mark Adornetto has a fully online work life—writing résumés, teaching classes for the University of Phoenix, coaching the recently divorced. He does all of it from his home office.

And why? The model home, of course: "My wife in particular fell in love with it." In Lennar's taxonomy, the $345,000 model was a "Moveup II," designed for buyers who had already sold their first home, bought a second, and were ready for a more luxurious life. A previous personal bankruptcy proved no obstacle—with a $310,000 mortgage from subprime titan New Century, starting at 8.99 percent interest, the Adornettos had the keys.

In 2002, the year Mark and Yolanda bought their beige Spanish-style spread, Lennar built nearly two thousand other houses in Sacramento and its suburbs. By the time Lennar got to Lincoln Crossing and beyond, in 2005, it had built more than eighteen thousand. That's a kingdom bigger than legendary protosuburb Levittown, New York—in more ways than one.

Levittown's pioneering mass-produced homes measured 800 square feet. When Jeff and Guy started Renaissance, their homes were about 1,700 square feet. The new Lennar houses ranged from 2,200 to 3,800 square feet.

It doesn't cost much more to build a 3,000-square-foot house than a 2,500-square-foot one. Air is free, after all. But for a borrower seeking a mortgage, the jump in size could make all the difference. The bigger the house, the higher the dollar value it could be appraised for. The bigger the appraisal, the bigger the loan—and the more the homebuilders could charge for the house.

Low interest rates were like a gift from the Federal Reserve to the home-building industry. Every percentage point that interest rates dropped was equivalent to another $8,000 or so off the price of the house. The companies could have used that opportunity to sell cheaper homes. Instead, America's consumers craved bigger ones.

The typical homebuyer lives in a 1,800-square-foot home and wants one that's nearly one-third bigger. She would drive to the edges of an ever-spreading metropolis and borrow whatever it took to get it. When the home-builders' industry association, in 2007, surveyed people who had just bought or were thinking about buying a place to live, by far the biggest share of re-spondents, 35 percent, said they wanted a home in the "outlying suburbs." Just 7 percent of respondents said they wanted a "central city" life (sorry, Carrie Bradshaw).

And so at a time of spiking oil prices, global warming, infernal traffic, and ever-lengthening commute times, homebuyers voted with their wheels for more of the same—much more of it. In less than thirty years, as a nation we've more than doubled the amount of space we live in and therefore have to heat, cool, and power—space that accounts for as much green-house gas production as all the cars, trucks, and buses in America. In the process we also doubled the number of miles we collectively drive every year, to about three trillion. While the United States was heading into war for oil in Iraq, the nation's homebuilders were serving a feast of petroleum consumption and carbon gluttony.

The scene in Sacramento replicated itself on the fringes of Phoenix, Dallas, Las Vegas—anywhere with room to build, population growth, and min-imal risk of rainout days disrupting construction. Blanketing farms, desert, and any other flat land they could find within an hour's commute of a city center, a dozen-odd of the biggest companies came to build more than a quarter of all the new homes in the nation, pumping out some 400,000 new houses a year at the peak of the boom.

Lennar wasn't even the biggest player in Sacramento. That would be Centex, based in Dallas, which lives up to the Texas stereotype: Its homes' square footage is such a selling point that the company names its models based on their size—as in "the 4,731," also available at Lincoln Crossing. All told, homebuilders produced and sold more than 140,000 new houses in the Sacramento area between 1996 and 2006, typically larger than 2,500 square feet. At the peak of the boom, more than half of all the homes bought in Sacramento were brand-new—an extraordinary number, since in usual times, just one in eight or nine buyers purchases virgin property.

"I used to pity the poor guys who didn't increase their sales projection numbers by 10 percent a year, because they wouldn't be there in ninety days," remembers the Sacramento division president of another publicly traded builder. Lennar set its sights even higher. By 2002 it was reporting 20 percent growth every *quarter.*

All those hefty houses had to go somewhere. The race to produce set off a rush to seize the most important raw material—not wood, or Sheetrock, or aluminum, though all those mattered, too, but tens of thousands of acres of land.

Suddenly Jeff Spitzer's yearly bonus depended in large part on how much property the Sacramento division could buy access to. And, of course, his competitors were playing the same game, stocking up on tens of thousands of acres of farmland.

What Lennar typically bought was not the land itself but options to buy the property, once all the permits were in place some five to seven years down the road. In Sacramento, it teamed up with the area's most aggressive land investor, Angelo Tsakopoulos, to take care of the details of turning farms into subdivisions—and property worth a few thousand dollars an acre into a far more valuable asset.

This Brillo-browed entrepreneur, who had sailed from Greece to New York by himself at age fourteen, always seemed to get what he wanted. Sacramento County supervisors tried to halt sprawl in the early 1990s by banning development on the city's fringes. Tsakopoulos directed them to put miles of his holdings safely inside the area where building could continue. In a swath of rice fields north of the Sacramento River—another area beyond Sacramento's growth boundary—he managed to get approval for a massive development plan for an area so prone to flooding, and so ill protected against it, that the Army Corps of Engineers reported that only New Orleans was more at risk.

Fed by waters thundering down each spring from the Sierras, the Sacramento River regularly sees epic inundations. The levees holding the river back are made of porous earth and are more than a century old, which is why the houses on their banks sit on stilts. Floods are so serious a risk to Natomas basin homes and their occupants that in 2007 the federal government put a moratorium on building until many miles of levees can be raised some two stories higher, and Homeland Security secretary Michael Chertoff was moved to castigate the City of Sacramento for resisting. "We're still hearing, 'It's absolutely dumb because it's bad for development,' " Chertoff told an audience at Harvard. "Short-term economic impact trumps long-term—not only economic interests, but the long-term interests in life and health and property."

With the support of the City of Sacramento, which stood to reap millions in permit fees and sales taxes, Lennar teamed up with Tsakopoulos to blanket Natomas with nine thousand homes and ample shopping centers. When its construction crews started clearing the basin for development, they had to demolish condemned houses that had been abandoned after the most recent flood, in 1996.

Tsakopoulos's secret was to give local decisionmakers what they wanted—campaign donations, typically, but nothing was off-limits. He pledged up to $20 million to relocate the University of California Medical School to Sacramento and bring an outpost of Philadelphia's Drexel University to farmland in Placer County—and also made sure that county supervisors received his wife's baklava at Christmas.

When Tsakopoulous wanted to extend Placer County's zone of development west into wetlands that were home to endangered species, he made a proposition to Terry Davis, the head of conservation for the inland northern California Sierra Club: If Davis would help him get a key county supervisor on board with the proposal, Tsakopoulos would donate to the county another parcel of land he owned, with a guarantee it would never be developed. Tsakopoulos unfurled a map, and Davis immediately recognized the terrain. It was his own childhood stomping grounds in the hills. Somehow, the developer had learned this most intimate detail of his history. "I was kind of awestruck," recalls Davis. "He was offering me a bribe."

Even hardball tactics couldn't get acreage approved fast enough to satisfy builders' bottomless appetites for land. Property that had been going for $100,000 an acre came to cost $700,000 or more. By 2004, homebuilders were spending $70,000 to $175,000 just for a single lot to stick a house on. Land, in Sacramento and everywhere else, became so insanely valuable that Lennar made hundreds of millions of dollars every year just selling lots to competitors.

The local families who had built on Sacramento's formerly cheap space for generations had to look farther afield—a whole lot farther. John Reynen and Christo Bardis had been in the homebuilding business for four decades when they sold their company, Winncrest, to Lennar in 1998. (Bardis's nephew, Tom Winn, subsequently masterminded Lennar's Sacramento land deals.) As Reynen & Bardis, the two men decided to get back into the business on their own, and Bardis's twenty-nine-year-old daughter, Rachel, soon joined them with her own company, Corinthian.

Like any independent homebuilder, Reynen & Bardis had to front much of the cost of development themselves, putting their own homes and other personal assets on the line. Unlike a publicly traded company, theirs wouldn't be able to write off losses; they would be personally responsible for every penny.

To find land that could still yield a profit, Reynen & Bardis and Corinthian were buying it in absurdly far-flung places—such as rural Marysville, some fifty miles up the river, near Beale Air Force Base. The place had some issues. Once-a-decade floods that left fields littered with livestock carcasses were only the start of them. Registered sex offenders, meth fiends, you name it—Marysville's trailers and shanties were havens for California's unwanted. Some of the biggest beneficiaries of the construction boom to come were the prostitutes who hung out in the parking lot next to the local buildings department.

Reynen & Bardis tilled a thousand lots in the place it called Edgewater. Corinthian's work crews raced to get houses ready to sell, even when that meant setting up space heaters to blast plaster dry overnight or carving window openings into walls because there was no time to wait for the frames and panes to arrive. To offset the high cost of the land, Corinthian looked to cut corners in places building inspectors wouldn't care about, such as leaving out metal rebar from under the driveways—rendering the surface prone to crumble in just a few years—because it would save 45 cents a square foot. This is called "value engineering," and it's ubiquitous in the homebuilding business.

But even if buyers could notice, they wouldn't have cared. The average price of a new home in Sacramento was hitting $500,000. Out here on the final frontier of the Bay Area boom, for less than $300,000, Corinthian buyers could, as its ads promised, "Get the Home You Deserve."

"Nobody bought there because they wanted to live there," Kim Larios remembers. They bought there because they felt compelled to buy something, anything, at all. As Corinthian's community manager at Edgewater, in the summer of 2005 Larios was handing keys to buyers like a Carl Jr.'s shift manager making $1,300 a month and an enlisted man who figured he'd turn his house into a barracks-for-rent while he was off in Iraq.

Larios recalls when even those buyers stopped coming, and when those who had already committed did whatever they could to back out from their purchase contracts. It was October 2005. Twenty minutes closer to Sacramento, increasingly cheap mortgage financing put the products of Pulte, Beazer, Morrison, and other budget builders in Lincoln Crossing within reach—at least for anyone able to rationalize an interest rate that would adjust in two or three years. Edgewater had lost its reason for being, and Larios lost her job. Soon she would also lose her modest home in Carmichael, where Larios lived with her teenage son.

Rachel Bardis usually grinned with the force of two suns. On the afternoon she walked into the office crying, everyone knew it was all over. She'd tried to sell their remaining lots back to her dad, but he wouldn't take them. Christo Bardis had his own land to worry about. He and Reynen had borrowed close to $1 billion, personally, to buy it.

When John Reynen declared personal bankruptcy in 2008, he asserted that the land the partnership owned was worth just $637 million. At Edgewater, IndyMac Federal Bank filed for foreclosure on $15 million in loans to Reynen & Bardis. The land was now worth less than $7 million.

Two hours' drive to the northeast, Reno had briefly beckoned as the next frontier for Sacramento homebuilders, and Reynen & Bardis had jumped on board for ventures that included the planned transformation of Carson City's Champion Motor Speedway into a new home subdivision. Reynen still owed $47 million to a partner in its Nevada foray: Lennar

Renaissance. The only winners at the speedway now are bored teenagers, who find creative ways to decorate and dismantle its remains.

In his life after Lennar, Guy Spitzer works plotting acquisitions for a real estate brokerage that supplies land for malls, offices, and housing developments, awaiting the moment when it again makes sense to buy. The wall above Spitzer's office desk is draped in a map of the Sacramento area, on which vast areas of farmland are outlined in a bold border, indicating zones for new development. Humble Sacramento now covers a realm approaching the size of Los Angeles, stretching up fifty miles north to Yuba County and another thirty east to the El Dorado hills.

Some 180,000 home lots in the Sacramento region are still in the planning process. At the height of the boom, three out of every five new houses in Sacramento were being built by a shareholder-owned company. The bust that followed, not surprisingly, has taken an immense toll on the builders. Lennar's share price plummeted below $6 as unsold houses, massive price discounts, and stocks of land all became liabilities on the company's balance sheet. But even while some of the nation's biggest banks failed and Big Three automakers imploded, the big, Wall Street–traded national homebuilders remained afloat.

As its smaller rivals began to go bankrupt, the shareholder-owned companies took advantage of an IRS provision that let them charge losses against their earnings from the previous two years, generating tax refunds. In early 2008, Centex sold thousands of acres of land for less than a third of what it had claimed it was worth—and got $294 million back from the IRS. Lennar sold a stake in its land holdings to Morgan Stanley, and though it got just 40 percent of what the company had claimed the property was worth, thanks to the tax scheme Lennar anticipated reaping $800 million.

Republicans in Congress sought, unsuccessfully, to extend the IRS credit from two years to five, yielding even larger refunds to ailing homebuilders. For the publicly traded homebuilders that have remade the landscape, the current troubles are a mere setback in a long march across the nation. When demand for homes rises again, as it eventually must, those companies will probably dominate the industry.

"Homebuilding is just a way of moving land," says Spitzer. "It's like a lollipop. It's like a widget." Even when overwhelming demand swelled the costs of materials and labor at the height of the boom, a house itself only cost about $80 a square foot to build. So why were buyers paying $500,000 for a three-thousand-square-foot home? Five bucks per square foot went to Guy's marketing operation. All the rest was the cost of land, and profit.

Spitzer left Lennar in 2004, after he sized up his market and couldn't fathom who was left out there with the means and the desire to buy one of his products. Contrary to all economic logic, the more homes his company and his competitors built, the higher their prices grew. Each time Lennar released a batch of houses, it was standard practice to raise the asking price another $20,000 or so, to see if buyers would accept it. They always did. The asking price for the next round, after all, would be another $20,000 higher than that.

The Realtors' trade group carefully tracked how many families in each part of California could afford to buy a house, and as the prices for Lennar homes continued to elevate, Spitzer watched the number of possible buyers dwindle to a pitiful minority. Sacramento had become the sixth-least-affordable real estate market in the entire country, if you simply compared people's typical incomes to the average price of a house.

"I thought the party was over," Spitzer says with a shrug. "Everyone who could buy under any possible scenario had bought." One also detects a note of exhaustion, the product of years of missed dinners with his wife, who's a schoolteacher, and their three children. "No matter what you delivered to Wall Street, they would want more and more. This was a monster created by people trying to push the stock further and further."

He hadn't counted on the burst of insanity that was to come. Over the next couple of years, more than half the mortgages made by Lennar's lending division required only interest payments, and often less, which meant that the amount of principal borrowers owed actually grew every month. More than a quarter were subprime loans, for customers with bad credit. Few buyers put any money down.

These practices moved product, while setting up borrowers with mounting bills that would be difficult to pay off. Thanks to discounts it gave to buyers, Lennar convinced almost all of them to use the lending company it owns, Universal American Mortgage.

Who was purchasing all these houses? It wasn't just the *Real Simple* crowd. In Sacramento, one out of every six loan applicants in 2005 admitted that they did not intend to live in the house they were financing—

presumably, they were either intending to rent the property to tenants or to flip it quickly to a new owner. Many more didn't disclose that they were buying homes as investments, since mortgage rates are cheaper for buyers who promise to live in their properties. One local real estate geek analyzed the listings database and concluded that by the nadir of the insanity in 2006, two out of every five homes for sale in Sacramento and vicinity had been bought by someone seeking to resell within two years. Many were Bay Area homeowners who pulled cash out of their own homes and brought their Monopoly money to Sacramento.

Lennar didn't try to dissuade investors. "I've never felt comfortable discriminating against anybody," Guy Spitzer says glibly, "no matter what color their money is." Lennar also more than tolerated it when those investors, along with a few ordinary buyers, camped out at its development sites overnight—sometimes for more than a week—to secure one of a newly released batch of homes before they sold out. There was no question: The builders needed more land.

The City of Lincoln hardly lived up to the sobriquet. Its twenty-five hundred families were outnumbered by cattle and horses in the fields, and workers at the Gladding, McBean clay pipe factory at the terminus of G Street. Its downtown wore the charming shabbiness of what passed for old in California—shops and feed stores built a century ago. That was before Lincoln became the fastest-growing suburb in America.

Like many economically struggling rural towns, Lincoln seriously considered bringing in a prison. Instead, its board of supervisors decided it ought to grow—big. Starting in 1994, Lincoln bulked up to more than triple its former size by annexing land from the county—to the hills to the south, the fields to the west, wherever it could grow. The shape of the city's borders now resembles a lunging elephant, its trunk reaching for new territory to the northwest.

Lincoln's newest subdivisions are so fresh they show up on Google Maps' satellite views only as swirls in dirt, where they're not rendered as green fields. Homebuilders have erected more than fourteen thousand new houses within an archipelago of minicities blanketing the valley and hills. Looking across State Highway 65 south toward Roseville and Rocklin, one sees only roofs to the horizon.

This is nothing. Lincoln envisions growing to 120,000 people over the next two decades, which would make the Roseville-Rocklin-Lincoln agglomeration bigger than Sacramento itself. The farm town is following the playbook of its neighbors, which a little over a decade ago sprang out of wetlands and quarries, in the process doubling the area of Placer County that is covered in asphalt, steel, and wood.

When Rocklin's layer of lava proved impossible to dig through, the developer of 3,500 acres had Caterpillar invent a bulldozer with teeth eight feet long, and ran two machines almost continuously for a year. Roseville, the biggest of the three at population 106,000 and counting, annexed pistachio orchards and grazing fields from the county, and proceeded to borrow hundreds of millions of dollars on the municipal bond market to build roads, sewers, and other necessities. While developers contribute for some of it, most of that money will have to be paid back for years to come by the people who buy homes here. The bonds are like a mortgage, but for a city.

In hindsight, those debts may have been as reckless as a no-money-down loan on a house one can't quite afford. The cities' scheme, after all, works only if the homes have owners who are willing and able to pay the tax, and the homes are actually worth something in the first place. That's hardly a given in Lincoln, as a resident who goes by the nom de guerre of Paladin can attest.

When Paladin and his fiancée first came to visit Lincoln Crossing in April 2006, virtually every house had a "For Sale" sign, and they saw not a single other soul or even a parked car. On their first Halloween as residents, no trick-or-treaters came. When they did see cars in the driveway, they tended to be BMWs, Jaguars, and Lexuses. A builder called JTS Communities had sold every house in this corner of Lincoln Crossing to investors, most of whom secured outrageous and quite obviously fraudulent appraisals that allowed them to take out gargantuan loans far in excess of the properties' actual value. Paladin has been reporting these schemes to mortgage funds and the IRS, in hopes of punishing the lenders who profited from them.

Those owners who haven't gone into foreclosure yet are renting the houses out, which has led to an odd ritual on these serene streets. When a bank tacks a notice to someone's front door that the house is going to auction, the tenants start looking for a new place to live. There are so many other houses for rent in Lincoln Crossing that they don't have to go far. Like Alice at the tea party, they just switch houses when theirs is no longer in service.

The backyard at the corner of Heartland Court and Earlton Lane is tiny—a patio, really, covered in woodchips and slate—and so doesn't see much use. The four children living here play volleyball with a yellow balloon on the family room's spacious carpet, whose sullied condition alarms a pair of visitors, Scott and Cheryl, on this Saturday morning. Scott and Cheryl live around the corner with their own children, and considering that this house is less than two years old, they were hoping for something a little more pristine. But with their previous rental going into foreclosure, they don't get to be so choosy.

The mother of the kids looks only slightly less worn than the rug. She and her husband, whose left arm is sleeved in a tattooed Virgin Mary, will have to pack up the family in weeks, using the boxes they've already got piled in the corner of the dining room, and all they're fairly sure of is that they'll stay in the Lincoln school district. Even that is an uncertain proposition, since "future elementary school" is just a blotch on the Lincoln Crossing map. Lincoln's school district has borrowed $190 million to build new facilities, but it has already run out of money. The district has to worry about how to pay back all the debt now that its own homeowners aren't paying the bills.

This house was saved from foreclosure only because Paladin, who lives a few doors down from Scott and Cheryl on Hillwood Loop, bought the place from Bear Stearns in a preforeclosure "short sale" for $295,000. Now he wants to rent it to Scott and Cheryl, so they can stay in the neighborhood. Its former owner had borrowed $710,000 on two mortgages made directly by the investment bank's own lending unit. (By now the mortgage-backed securities business had become so profitable for investment banks that some, including Lehman Brothers and Bear Stearns, established or acquired their own mortgage lending divisions to help generate mortgages to securitize; these specialized in low-down-payment and low-documentation loans that real estate investors typically sought.)

Paladin bought his own generous house from Countrywide, for $389,000. Its original owner had paid a third more than that before going into foreclosure. JTS's corner of Lincoln Crossing is a monument to investment banks' losses, which, according to Paladin's carefully compiled spreadsheet, are heading toward some $40 million on these quiet blocks.

Every month another four hundred property owners in Placer County go into default on their mortgages, while other promised developments remain fields of dirt for the foreseeable future. But Lincoln will have to spend nearly $6 million a year just on bills for its own bonds on its biggest housing developments, while continuing to keep those new roads paved and the sewers flowing. If property owners don't pay, bond investors will be the ones to lose—just as they already have with failing mortgage-backed securities.

Flush with proceeds from the bonds, and on sales taxes from the shiny shopping centers in the middle of town, the formerly sleepy industrial town of Lincoln has been living large. The brand-new city hall is sided in marble, with a matching fountain in front. A fleet of gleaming white pickup trucks fills the parking lot across the street.

There's no way to blanket a rural valley with rooftops and $165 million in bonds to pay back and not expect it to become another place entirely. At City Council meetings, new residents share a litany of complaints on everything from convenience store lights (they blot out the stars) to the Union Pacific Railroad, which clangs through town day and night. Under orders from the city, Sierra Hay & Feed on H Street now must get its deliveries in the middle of the night, so it's been forced to cut back on its volume of sales. A new highway overpass scheduled to cut through the middle of Lincoln Crossing will relieve downtown's main drag from its traffic—and probably destroy it in the process.

"It's killing us," says Debbie Swindler of all the cars that now barrel down G Street without stopping. With her daughter, Swindler owns the Book Cellar, just across the train tracks from the feed store. Residents of the new subdivisions don't come to her side of the Auburn Ravine, the dividing line between new Lincoln and old—they stick with new shopping centers. Swindler grimaces as she concludes, "Lincoln stops at the Safeway."

The Mr. Pickle sandwich franchise on G Street is feeling the pressure, too. As the lunch rush dissipates on a Wednesday afternoon, a young city planner—ROBERT POETSCH, reads his City of Lincoln name badge—sits at a table across from proprietors Pam and Phil Lopez and informs them that they're welcome to paint the side of their shop's little wooden structure—once they pay the city a $1,000 "administrative design fee."

"We just lowered it from two thousand dollars," Poetsch assures the Lopezes. Then he adds, with the condescension of a parent looking to model a young child's behavior on an older sibling's, *"Roseville and Rocklin have the same design review standards."*

"I thought you wanted to bring people downtown?!" Pam protests, as she resolves to leave the weathered façade just the way it is.

"Can I add something?" A high voice chimes in from the table by the front window. Tisha Summers and her husband, Jason, have been listening in as they finish their sandwiches. "Everything has changed in Lincoln. Lincoln felt like a community. Now it feels like Rocklin and Roseville."

Summers moved to Lincoln when she was seventeen, to take refuge from teen troubles and live with an aunt who resided in the apartments on First Street. She remembers neighbors who were always around, and kept an eye on the many children who lived there. Now that she has her own son, who's eleven, Summers has resolved to be the same kind of supportive presence in his life, which means she doesn't work a job and devotes much time volunteering in his school.

"All those homes—it's not a community," Summers says as she gestures down the road toward Lincoln Crossing. She has watched the attendance at the Lincoln Fourth of July parade dwindle, and the Lincoln High football team descend from glory. Her commitment to her son means survival on one income, and that has excluded her family from buying a home here in Lincoln. They moved up Highway 65 to Marysville, to an older four-bedroom ranch house they could get for just $164,000—well in the flood zone, but also within their financial reach.

While longtime working-class residents move out, many Lincoln officials have moved up the hills, to the generous new homes they made possible. The city manager and his wife settled into a $761,000 Del Webb house at the top of the rise, with a view of the rooftops below. Lincoln's head of finance bought his home on a golf course, built by JTS Communities, for more than $1.2 million.

His subdivision achieved brief notoriety before it was even finished. On Christmas Eve 2004, two sisters from the nearby hill town of Newcastle helped friends break into several homes and set up kitchen timer devices atop buckets of fuel, spraying "ELF"—Earth Liberation Front—onto the cul-de-sac's asphalt. The bombs never went off, and the FBI promptly added the four to its list of successful terrorist apprehensions.

Standing on his tight front porch, Andrew Hennan keeps peering nervously at each car that passes into his street in Stonelake, an array of plump new residences just off the I-5 exit at Elk Grove Boulevard. The pear and apple trees, propped up with sticks, are still too spindly to either block the view or provide shade. Some sixty or seventy homes in Stonelake now sit empty, so every new arrival demands scrutiny. "I'm not confident in average people," Hennan confesses. He has watched them act utterly without judgment.

Sleeved in tattoos of a bull and Chinese characters, Hennan resembles a retired pro skateboarder (he actually works at a law firm that represents employers). From behind his front door, his three little Eskimo dogs sound like Cerberus at the gates of hell. Hennan doesn't know any of his neighbors. From what he can see, he doesn't want to, either. "These are asinine people making asinine decisions," he mutters, his blue eyes surveying the eerily still driveways up and down Waterfowl Drive.

The Mercedeses, the Land Rovers, the boats—as they started pulling out of their garages one final time, all Hennan could think about was the $250,000 he and his wife had invested into the house so far, only about half of which came from the sale of their previous place. As he saw it, his neighbors have as much as stolen that money from him. While other buyers here did make down payments, most proceeded to refinance their homes in exchange for cash. That included Yolanda and Mark Adornetto, around the corner on Harrier Way; their 10 percent down payment, and a couple of hundred thousand dollars more, came back into their bank account when they refinanced with Ameriquest for $464,000, after almost going into foreclosure a few months earlier. They refinanced again—Ameriquest's "account executives" always went back for more—for $550,000.

Hennan paid nearly that much for his place on Merlin Way. But now he's dealing with a more fundamental threat to his home's value, one that wasn't conjured through creative appraisals. His house, Hennan says, is sick. The trusses between the first and second floors appear to be separating. The exterior rear wall has a yawning crack across it, and he can find no Benjamin Moore color that disguises it. Windows leak.

Up and down these streets, other buyers complained of similar symptoms: drips, cracks, rot. To their list, the Adornettos added a bowed wall in the living room, and others that didn't line up; cracks in the foundation; a tub that shifted with the weight of a bather; a fireplace cover that didn't fit. "We started finding things right away—with the first rainstorm," Mark Adornetto recalls.

With the encouragement of a San Diego law firm, the Hennans, the Adornettos, and more than a dozen neighbors sued their homebuilder: Lennar. The company, they claimed, "engaged in a calculated course of conduct to reduce their costs of development by the use of substandard, deficient and inadequate design, construction materials and techniques." Repairs were superficial, the lawsuit alleged. The gloomy prognosis: "accelerated aging."

All over Elk Grove, homeowners received letters in their mailboxes asking about the health of their homes. Have you experienced leaks? Mold? Or anything else that would inspire you to join a lawsuit?

Hundreds of buyers of homes built by Lennar and its newly acquired local subsidiaries said yes. At Perry Ranch, on the far eastern edge of town, half the subdivision complained of troubles ranging from cracked stucco to jammed sliding doors. Across Elk Grove Boulevard, Lennar acquisition U.S. Home neglected to put building paper underneath stucco, which then leaked as surely as it rained. In another Lennar development, the lead plaintiff in a different lawsuit tried to light the fireplace on her first Christmas in her home, only to find smoke billowing into the family room because the chimney was too short.

Much of this doesn't surprise Mike Bocchicchio Jr., who supervised construction at Stonelake and for seven years ran Lennar work sites all over Sacramento. Elk Grove was the great test of the homebuilding machine. When Stonelake rose in 2002, he oversaw the building of 250 homes at a time, in two different subdivisions. Hundreds of men scrambled over rooftops in a race to meet deadlines.

"It was like Cecil B. DeMille," Bocchicchio laughs, as he often does, in describing the insanity of the moment. He has to have a sense of humor about those long, hot, frenzied days. Working as a superintendent for Lennar until 2004, he had to arrive at the work site at six every morning and stay until the sky was dark, and if he clocked out at less than twelve hours he'd be called in to HR. He never took lunch breaks.

Technically, Lennar doesn't build these homes at all; that work is left to local subcontractors. Circa 2004, crews worked on a couple of dozen homes at once, with no time to wait their turn: plumbers, electricians, HVAC technicians, and everyone else collided with one another in a race to meet deadlines. Speed was everything, even if that meant that a plastering job that ought to take two weeks had to be completed in one. Buyers were surprised to learn that their homes were finished months earlier than promised, and not sure whether to be appreciative or alarmed.

Not long after he first started working for Renaissance, in 1998, Bocchicchio and his wife bought one of the company's new homes, in Rocklin, enticed by the quality and value of the product: a frame "sheared" end to end with reinforcing plywood; lovely enhancements such as corbels on the outside and art niches within, cast in natural light from windows set near the ceiling.

Project by project, such flourishes started disappearing as construction schedules sped up and budgets tightened. Then the basics started to be compromised. When drywall deadlines shrank from fifteen days to ten, crews speaking only Russian were instructed through pantomime to plaster over tape while it was still damp, a sure way to produce cracks later. Stucco men's ladders and scaffolds were prone to punching through roofs because they'd had no time to properly pad them. Roofs were also vulnerable to plumbers trying to catch up on unfinished work without the supervisor noticing—they've been known to sneak in and drill a hole in the roof to access a vent. The tile layers had to get in and out within four days, down from the usual seven.

Skilled workers might have been able to handle such pressures. These weren't. A crew typically had two or three trained craftsmen working with seven or eight laborers who followed orders and winged it.

The materials began to falter, too. When a truck pulled up to deliver kitchen cabinets for Stonelake, Bocchicchio thought the supplier had sent the wrong order. What was particleboard doing here, in a Renaissance house? Then he looked at the order slip, signed by Lennar's head of Sacramento purchasing. Concrete counters, tile floors, and pressboard cabinets had become the new standard.

It all added up to a bizarre equation: The higher new home prices rose, the worse the product got. "If you bought a house at the peak of the boom, it's a crappier house," affirms Bocchicchio.

At Stonelake, the head of customer service was a former shoe salesman ill prepared to handle the wave of repair requests that began arriving as new owners moved in. "The poor guy was clearly overwhelmed," says Mark Adornetto, who'd call for help only to find that VINNY, the customer care rep, was simultaneously dealing with one neighbor whose bathroom was leaking into the kitchen and another with a mysterious stain on his carpet and yet another with a cracked foundation. Not all of the customers found themselves Tickled, Delighted, and Happy, per Lennar's customer service credo. "They just wanted us to sign and say, 'There's no problem,'" says Hennan.

Lennar and other major builders provide legal training for their staff, teaching proper responses to interrogations about construction quality. For example, if a supervisor were asked on the witness stand about whether they would say a procedure crews had followed was acceptable industry practice, the script would say, "I'm learning things all the time. I would be obliged to tell the story of what I learned from this experience."

But ultimately, homebuilders don't have much to fear from their customers. The structures are not only built by subcontractors; as a condition of getting the work, those firms are obligated to take the blame should any construction problems show up later. When Elk Grove's homebuyers sued Lennar, Lennar turned around and sued Deal Sheet Metal, Marticus Electric, Forsyth Marble, Blue Ribbon Stairs, and dozens more local companies.

Lennar wasn't the first homebuilder to force its local contractors to take the fall when problems cropped up. In California, KB Homes introduced the practice in the 1980s. Now it's the industry norm. The local businesses that do the construction work have to buy insurance, covering not only themselves but Lennar, too. And that was in the good old days. In the past few years, homebuyers have been filing so many lawsuits against homebuilders that no insurance company will sell the builders a policy. Instead, contractors have to wait until they're sued and have already laid out $100,000 in lawyers' fees; then an insurer might front them some funds, to be paid back when the case is settled.

"To be really frank, we're done," says a Sacramento contractor whose company works on Lennar jobs and who did not want to be identified for fear of being blacklisted. His family-owned company gets hit with lawsuits every week, and it's spending about $1 million annually on its defense, or roughly two thirds of what it now clears in a year. Process servers carrying flashlights wake him up in the middle of the night with summonses. "We're expendable—that's all there is to it," says the contractor, who still remembers when his business was done on a handshake, between families who knew one another. Lennar calls its contractors "partners." "I think of it as 'Partner, you're taking the liability and we're hitting the road.'"

The builders themselves "don't have much to risk," agrees Fred Adelman, a Santa Monica attorney in the business of suing homebuilders (including Lennar as a frequent target). "They can build an inferior product, because they have no exposure."

Such protection emboldens homebuilders to experiment with value engineering—finding savings by scrutinizing every nail, brace, and plank in an entire structure, then paring down as much as they can while still passing muster with inspectors. "Get me a letter" is a phrase managers use often—that is, a letter from a certified engineer attesting that a creative plan meets the building code. Lennar and its peers have in-house teams that scheme for savings. According to Bocchicchio, who formerly worked for Centex, during a value engineering push that company decided to put the wooden studs holding up walls two full feet apart, up from sixteen inches. At the same time it shrank the metal shields that seam roof lines together from eighteen inches to eight.

While saving money on the details buyers can't see, homebuilders find additional profit in selling them luxuries that are visible—granite counters, fine cabinetry, plush carpets, tile baths, and other model home highlights. Sales materials and agents constantly remind buyers of how little it will all cost on the monthly mortgage bill. For just $140 a month, signs in Centex model homes advise, they could buy $20,000 in options—to "take pleasure in the finer things in life as well as having your home feel custom and be a reflection of your success and good taste." Most buyers of new homes spend two to three times that on options.

"We used financing to sell houses, just like selling cars," explains the former head of the Sacramento mortgage division for one of the top national homebuilders. Upgrades, he notes, are an enormous profit center, just like cocktails and desserts in restaurants. Teaser interest rates and other gimmicks that made monthly bills look as low as possible helped consumers buy these things, but that alone didn't cover all of a buyer's costs. In California more than anywhere in the country, purchasers weren't just taking out one risky mortgage—it became de rigueur to have two. Often the first lender didn't even know about the second loan, which is why these mortgages are sometimes known as "silent seconds" (and other times as "piggybacks"). The goal, always, was to have the two loans cover most or all of the purchase price.

As the base of qualified customers dried up, the builders quickly dug deeper with second mortgages. In 2004, Lennar's in-house lender, Universal American Mortgage, made piggyback loans on about one in ten homes it sold in California, and nationally. By 2006 it was nearly one in three. Nearly a quarter of those loans were subprime, indicating that borrowers likely had lousy credit ratings.

By then more than half of its loans were exotic products that helped its buyers pick up homes beyond their means, especially interest-only and "negative amortization" loans, where monthly payments were low but the amount owed grew and grew—tolerable when home values are rising, deadly when they fall. At Centex, a third or more of the loans ended up being negative ams. Eventually the majority of all loans for new homes in the area were set up so that buyers paid interest only, or less.

These toxic trends were also promoted by the State of California. Governor Arnold Schwarzenegger appointed a mortgage company CEO as head of the state housing finance agency, charged with making homes more affordable for people with modest incomes in the most expensive real estate markets in the country. What the agency gave them was more of the same. Launched in 2005, the state's Interest Only PLUS program lets consumers with modest incomes borrow 100 percent of a home's value, yet not make any principal payments for five years. The state also began offering second mortgages, to eliminate down payments.

But even the most recklessly generous financing couldn't make it profitable for Lennar, or any homebuilder, to keep the formula for profit going. By 2004, construction supervisor Mike Bocchicchio, like Guy Spitzer, knew that he needed to move on. The breaking point was a strategy meeting run by Guy's brother, Jeff.

"Quality doesn't sell anymore," Bocchicchio was stunned to hear Lennar Sacramento division chief Jeff Spitzer announce as he outlined measures to cut construction costs. Spitzer's words came as a lament, from a homebuilder who had once taken pride in the quality of his work but now couldn't survive in a ferociously competitive business unless he slashed the expense of manufacturing his product. Renaissance used to construct homes for people to live in for a lifetime. Now his company was building them for buyers to resell.

Spitzer was effectively renouncing Lennar's prime directive—its "Z values." (Nobody is quite sure where the Z comes from, only that it shows up everywhere Lennar does.) Z value number one: Conduct our business with the highest degree of integrity, pride, passion, and professionalism.

Spitzer instead turned to Z value number five: Work efficiently to provide the greatest return to our shareholders. "People won't stay in their homes more than five years," he told his managers. "They don't care about the longevity of the components. It's a different market than it used to be."

Six

CRIME SPREE

Atlanta, 2007

THE PETITE CHÂTEAU LURKS just to the left behind the gatehouse, positioned, like a Vegas landmark, for maximum visibility. It greets residents of St. Ives as they enter the driveway every night, to remind them why they moved a good forty-five-minute drive (when there's no traffic, which is never) northeast of downtown Atlanta. Yearn for a villa? An English country estate, minus the estate? Perhaps a mash-up of Greek Revival and southern plantation, with a three-story glass arched entrance held up by eight Ionic columns and spanning fifty feet? Welcome home.

The grayish-white château at the corner of Wild Dunes Way, great iron lanterns pendulously flanking its doorway, weighs in at 3,184 square feet. For St. Ives, this is a modest place, clever at making its bold impression. In this two-decades-old subdivision, 736 little palaces of variously distended size roll on green drives adjoining a golf course, each marked with an identical mailbox bearing a fleur-de-lis. While the exteriors strive for wow, these homes are all about the insides, and only the landscapers spend time outdoors. St. Ives is a haven for retired Hawks and Falcons, evangelical entrepreneurs, and anyone else who can afford to lock the rest of Georgia out.

Like many other subdivisions in the Atlanta suburbs, St. Ives is also a magnet for mortgage fraud—for elaborate schemes that borrowed enormous amounts of money against impressive structures like the one at 1050 Wild Dunes Way. William McGill used to own this château behind the guard's gate, but he never had the pleasure of seeing it. He signed a contract to buy the house for $782,000 but never barbecued on the back deck or set a log afire in one of his two fireplaces, or even slept in one of its five bedrooms.

He probably would have felt out of place anyway, since he was a freelance graphic designer.

Down the road, another buyer picked up a modest (for here) redbrick place, one story with a shady wooden back deck and tiny hedges rimming the front. The little brick steps out front with simple iron railings evoke Queens. Twenty-five years ago, the buyer, Renee Donewar, was dance teacher to a two-year-old named Britney Spears. Now Donewar, too, was in the business of purchasing houses she never saw, and against which she signed her name to mortgages for hundreds of thousands of dollars, according to federal prosecutors. Like McGill's, Donewar's houses would soon go into foreclosure.

A secluded stone-faced haven, right across from the golf course. A vaguely hideous peach-cream stucco confection. A Greek-columned villa atop a grand flight of stone stairs. A modest, asymmetrical pile of stone, flanked by chimneys in the rustic English style. Eight homes in all, and on their façades they looked like all the others. But these were zombie houses.

Prostitutes came in and out of one of them, conducting their business in the aspirational surroundings. Another became a hideaway for an armed and dangerous drug-industry operative when law enforcement came after him on kidnapping, aggravated assault, armed robbery, and murder charges. Agents swooped past St. Ives's security gates in search of the suspect and his roommate, a bounty hunter. The agents retrieved the two men's weapons from the $798,000 house, an undistinguished stucco secluded behind trees; the fugitive himself was caught in L.A.

From her desk on the second story of the gatehouse, an embroidered white sweater buffering her shoulders against Atlanta's brutal summer air conditioning, St. Ives property manager Jan Pittman enforces the legally binding standards of this gated community. Colors must be friendly with white, beige, or brown. Builders choose from a short menu of brickface or stone, representing a brief spectrum of taste. Pittman, a zaftig blonde who hails from Yorkshire but has spent most of her life in the American South running communities of progressively higher status, tucks a thick book of architectural rules into a gift basket she gives to each new buyer, along with a gold St. Ives license plate.

Anything that grows—impatiens, rose bushes, bougainvillea, grass for the sloping lawns—has to come from a list of approved plants Pittman picks out personally. "The only thing they can do without permission," Pittman stresses, "is seasonal flowers." She levies a $250 fine every month for violations and unkempt lawns. It's been a nice injection of income for the St. Ives homeowners' association. The Bank of New York, Bear Stearns, Washington Mutual, and other financial institutions that now own the homes that McGill, Donewar, and their confederates had purchased as part of an organized mortgage fraud scheme here would rather pay her than do the yard work themselves.

Ever vigilant, Pittman did her best to ensure that none of the neighbors knew about the goings-on at the absentee owners' houses, but there was no retreating into denial: This fortress was now harboring a growing population of criminals, not counting those who signed phony paperwork for substantial mortgages. A tall white man with a knife grabbed a sixteen-year-old girl near the clubhouse, dragged her to the woods, and cut her shorts off. One of the homes had its entire kitchen ripped out by someone who'd been staying there. Most just stood empty, their homeowners' dues unpaid and lawns growing ragged. Giant rats ("the size of cats," Pittman says with a shudder) scuttled through their empty travertine halls.

The wildlife still asserts itself in this backwoods junction once called Shake Rag, whose red earth only recently spawned anything much more than kudzu and oaks. Today ZIP code 30097 is the wealthiest address in Greater Atlanta. And that made it a luscious target for those who would extract the ore of its real estate riches. Down the road just over the Forsyth County line, the same developer built St. Marlo, a golf course even more generously yielding of trophy homes, nine hundred and counting as woodchippers munch fallen trees on an ever-widening periphery. Here a miniature Moorish palace trimmed with medieval iron bolts and awnings cohabits with a White House homage on the grassy slopes surrounding a golf course. Each home makes its intentions known by the stone statues flanking its doors—greyhounds, lions, four-foot Romanesque urns.

But in St. Marlo, too, a few houses broke ranks, and more soon followed in the anarchy. A dented 1980s Toyota offended one driveway. Sheets and blankets hung in windows, instead of blinds. Grass and weeds grew with impunity. Fifteen people lived in one house, all claiming to be related. A dishwasher from an Alpharetta restaurant bought, and lived in, a $1 million home.

Behind St. Marlo's gates, a few cautious neighbors started taking notes. About the stone-fronted grand Colonial with two-story vaulted windows on the ground floor, down the road to the left from the gatehouse, where a

limo showed up, idled outside for a few hours, and departed, to be followed by two or three more during the night, and the master bedroom was
decorated with purple sequins, chiffon, a sea of candles, and lighting set to
bounce off the walls just so. And the one where once a week or so, an SUV
would pull into a cul-de-sac at the end of one street, rev its engine till the
wheels screeched, and shoot past a particular house. A package flung from
its passenger window was immediately retrieved by a man who darted out
from the house and back in.

The little neighborhood watch had a hard time recruiting eyes. The community was almost entirely white. Most of the newcomers were not. Vol-
unteers who tried to jot down license numbers, ask about who was related
to whom, and make other inquiries of their new neighbors could expect
accusations of racism in return, and not just from those being investigated. A small band of homeowners persisted, though they did buy guns
(and don't, even now, want to be identified publicly).

Their Excel spreadsheet was pretty basic. In one column they'd note
what a house last sold for. The next listed the most recent sale price, and
alongside that anything strange that might be going on. If the house sold
and then resold for much more money, trouble, inevitably, would follow.

As the list of suspicious houses grew, so did the St. Marlo police blotter.
One resident reported his Lexus was stolen by a former roommate on a cocaine binge. (The roommate thoughtfully left in its place a brand-new Ele-
ment he had stolen from the next county over.) Another got taken away by
the Secret Service, busted in a scheme in which he put fake bar codes on rugs
at Lowe's and Home Depot, returned them for credit, and sold the refund
cards on eBay. Someone else spotted the front half of a cat lying in a
driveway—it had been cut in two and its intestines removed, possibly by the
same culprit who had set another cat on fire. Sometimes bullets flew; one
pierced a rear window.

And yet the strange sales kept coming: $1.3 million, $1.4 million, on
houses that just weren't worth that much. Some of these homes were new.
Others had just been sold in foreclosure auctions. One of the foreclosed
houses went for $580,000 only to be refinanced three times in six weeks:
first for $780,000, then for $960,000, then for $1.2 million. The mayor
of Barnegat, New Jersey, and a retired schoolteacher were among those
who cooperated with a mortgage broker to buy homes for more than $1
million apiece, submitting paperwork to Long Beach Mortgage that lied

about almost everything—employment, bank account, down payment, whether they planned to live in the houses. (The mayor claimed she made $45,000 a month.) If anyone moved in, it was tenants, like the family with eight children the adults said were foster kids, which might have been credible had the supposed father not already been charged in New Jersey with making similar claims, falsely.

The homeowners tried to alert the county sheriff and the FBI, and got only baffled questions back. All other outlets exhausted, they finally turned the spreadsheet, forty addresses deep by the time it was finished, over to the IRS. Agents hunting down unreported income ended up investigating two dozen homes in St. Marlo, all of them sold for far more than they could ever be worth, to people who didn't come near to qualifying for the vast sums they borrowed.

All this could happen because these homes weren't homes. Like an inestimable number all over the country—most likely in the hundreds of thousands—the structures served as mere collateral for the extraction of mortgage funds, billions of dollars that were there for the taking for anyone who thought to ask. William McGill, Renee Donewar, and dozens of others who signed papers to purchase real estate in Atlanta and its suburbs were part of an organized scheme that gave them kickbacks in return for their signatures.

From there, at no point along the chain of those who participated in these mortgage transactions, trading in millions of dollars of debt at a time, did anyone think to stop them. Not the mortgage brokers who approved the deals. Not the lenders who marketed the loan products and provided the funds. Not the bankers who supplied the lenders with enormous lines of credit. Nor the securities firms that injected funds into this food chain by purchasing the morgtages from the lenders and packaging them into securities. For each of these players, every sale brought a shower of fees. Why would anyone object to a deal?

Where financial institutions saw a business opportunity, so did Phillip Hill, the man who lured McGill and Donewar with the promise of free money. At the 1996 Olympics, Hill had been hired to play a temple builder for the opening ceremony, wearing a collar and wrist cuffs that he clamped over his swelling muscles. He reused the props on the gay party circuit, where he showed up at parties in Miami Beach as studly Charlton Heston-esque décor, his neck almost as wide as his narrow head.

McGill's biceps are no match for Hill's, but even now in his midforties McGill keeps them firm with a steady training regimen. That's how he met Hill, he told people—at a Gold's Gym across the street from the DeKalb County airport. Hill's blue eyes looked into McGill's, and Hill told him about the prospect of making piles of money in real estate. And all he would have to do was sign some papers.

That sounded good to McGill. He and his boyfriend lived in a bunga-low in one of Atlanta's aging 1950s subdivisions, where they'd stayed for eleven years as renters and then owners but where more and more neigh-bors spoke languages they didn't. They looked forward to getting out, to what McGill described dreamily as "a better neighborhood." McGill and his boyfriend, Bryce Otte, had big debts, and not a whole lot of income. McGill had been working for a decade designing catalogs and earning about $35,000 a year, but making even that was getting harder and harder. Otte sold office furniture. They already had three mortgages on their home, totaling $249,000. And then there was the $36,000 McGill still owed on three credit cards, plus the payments for their Land Rover. They liked to live well, outfitting their little home with modern paintings and retro lamps. On their back deck, they enjoyed a hot tub.

McGill seemed to hear about the real estate opportunity everywhere he went. First people were talking about it at a friend's barbecue. Then McGill and Otte got invited to a Christmas party at Hill's sprawling white home, on an acre and a half around the corner from the governor's mansion. They peered around the grand circular driveway looking for Hill's Jaguar. Today, McGill smiles, his piercing eyes crinkling, and says he will only tell you all about his encounters with Phillip Hill if you pay him.

After all, that's how Hill operated. Between the two of them, in late 2000 and early 2001, McGill and Otte bought eleven condos and houses from Hill's companies, most of them less than a mile from where they lived. They never even visited the properties. But each time they signed for one, they'd get paid—$3,750 for some, $7,500 for others.

Hill himself had just bought the places. He picked them up in bulk from developers who were eager to get rid of them, seventy and fifty and forty at a time, and paid for them with cash borrowed from any investor he could charm. Meanwhile, friendly real estate agents hooked Hill up with luxury homes whose sellers were in a hurry to get out, including 1050 Wild Dunes

Way in St. Ives, the château just past the gate. That was the first of the residences McGill purchased.

In October 2000, Hill had picked up the minimansion from its owners of several years for $400,000. Then came the flip. Before it became an inescapable presence in TV listings, "flip," paired with "house," was a term used mainly by criminals and law enforcement. Titling a TV series *Flip This House* or *Flip That House* is like creating a show called *Theft Is Easy*. The programs feature sweaty and stressed-out investors bestowing their labors on homes that could use some help. On TV, their work is rendered as a public service, reviving old structures instead of going for a tear-down. But technically, flipping is and always has been the art of buying and reselling homes without doing anything other than signing a few papers, while pulling out as much cash as you can between the closings.

That was Phillip Hill's specialty. In three weeks, Hill took that $400,000 house and turned it into a $782,000 house. He bought the property using a cash loan from John Kruger, a former Apple Computer executive living in Atlanta. Hill had an appraiser value it—falsely—for sale at $790,000. Then two attorneys working for Hill drew up papers: McGill agreed to borrow $586,500 from New America Financial, a company that specialized in loans where borrowers didn't have to document their income. McGill listed the house as his "primary residence," and his bungalow as his former. And he declared that his income was $232,800 a year, with another $25,000 in the bank.

Then McGill borrowed another $213,831, also from New America. On top of that, he took out yet another mortgage, for $50,000, from Express Funding, at 12.3 percent interest. That brought the total amount of money McGill borrowed on the house to nearly $850,000.

One more thing: McGill agreed to transfer the property back to Hill immediately after the closing. McGill would still hold on to the mortgage, and Hill promised to make payments, on the mortgage, insurance, and taxes, and to the homeowners' association.

For putting his name and Social Security number on 1050 Wild Dunes Way and its associated loans, McGill received $20,000. Half of that he gave as a finder's fee to Christine Laudermill, a recruiter who found borrowers like McGill for Hill.

Laudermill worked as a mortgage broker. She also worked as a drug dealer. It was hard to say which was the sideline to which. On a tip from an informant, the Atlanta police would soon catch her selling cocaine. In her Peachtree Street apartment they also found crystal meth, hundreds of mushrooms, ketamine (liquid and powder), GBH, ecstasy, a bag of crushed Ritalin, and a 9mm pistol along with forty-three rounds. She had been arrested previously on a DUI, a meth pipe on the passenger seat of her black Porsche convertible. Laudermill pleaded guilty to cocaine trafficking, meth possession, and theft. When he sued Phillip Hill, Christine Laudermill, and other scheme participants a month after the second drug bust, asserting that Hill and company had violated the terms of their agreement with him, McGill would call Laudermill "a well-known social figure in and about certain segments of Atlanta's gay community."

Over the next few months, McGill and Otte got $3,750 each for buying the condos. They borrowed $1.8 million on Phillip Hill's behalf, on condos worth barely half that. Hill could take out these loans because he had a thirty-year-old mortgage company vice president—a Floridian who had formerly propagated Texas Roadhouse franchise restaurants—feeding him $8 million. It wasn't enough to buy every property Hill was looking to finance, but it sufficed to pick up twenty condos in one development near Buckhead and another twenty-six in a cluster of Spanish-style condos a short drive from there. Square-jawed, dark-haired, and ready to live well, Ted Tagalakis worked as an agent for a mortgage company called Ameristar. On each mortgage he brokered, Tagalakis would get to keep more than half the proceeds.

Hill wooed Tagalakis and Ameristar president Bill Hall at Bone's steakhouse on Piedmont. "It sounded like a home run," Tagalakis recalled later. Ameristar had a $10 million line of credit with National City Mortgage, part of a Cleveland bank that was aggressively expanding its home lending business. National City prearranged to buy a block of mortgages from Ameristar, which would then allow National City to collect fees for making the loans, more fees from customers for late payments and other transgressions, and still more fees for reselling the loans to investors. Ameristar got a special bonus for making high-interest loans, which all of these were, since Hill told Ameristar he didn't care how much interest his front men and women would commit to as long as they could take out the biggest loans possible. Tagalakis collected nearly $250,000 and spent it all, quickly, on food, wine, clothes, and trips.

The mortgage broker first met Hill by the badge-shaped pool at Carrington Park, a gated cluster of homey three-story pastel condos abutting the toll road in Buckhead. In the winter of 2001 Hill had set up his operation in the Carrington Park clubhouse. Buckhead was the perfect location, a designer-label neighborhood equally accessible to his sprawling holdings downtown and to the northern suburbs. Hill would soon relocate his home up the toll-way there, to a $5.1 million, fourteen-thousand-square-foot compound sitting on thirteen acres with a pool and a tennis court—purchased by a Florida nurse and then signed over to him, naturally.

Carrington Park was a whole lot more modest. Behind the gates with Hill and his entourage lived a little village of first-time homebuyers, divorcées, and transplants. A lot of buyers of these condos, newly on the market, were graduate students at Emory or Georgia Tech whose parents bought their places, hoping to make back some of the money they'd been spending on tuition. Hill borrowed $12.4 million from the project's developer to buy 76 apartments in bulk out of the 140 here, scattered along long open-air corridors where ceiling fans struggle to heave the still air. That averaged out roughly close to the prices real buyers were paying for apartments there at the time, perhaps $150,000. For the developer, making the loan to Hill was well worth it—he got to unload inventory and would get paid back quickly, since Hill planned to resell the apartments immediately.

Days later, Otte and McGill, along with twenty-five other buyers, paid ludicrously more for the places. One-bedroom condos facing the highway wall went for nearly $300,000; other apartments went for $385,700, $412,000, $344,100. Except, of course, these buyers didn't pay for them, didn't live in them, didn't even see them. In a kind of real estate Moonie wedding in which McGill, Otte, and dozens of others signed their papers, each of the buyers bought their properties and simultaneously transferred ownership back to Hill. With the deeds in hand Hill now had total control; in the future he could, if he wished, arrange for still more mortgage loans, sell the properties at a profit, or do whatever else he wanted with the real estate.

And so it went, all around condo developments across Atlanta: Deere Lofts, Peachtree Place, Concorde, Park Tower—all new or newly converted condos whose builders were hungry to move units. Hill's own son, Phillip Jr., bought twenty-two of them. In all, Hill's people, using more than a hundred front buyers and their phony paperwork, borrowed nearly $100 million on more than two hundred condos and fifty-plus sprawling homes in upscale country club subdivisions, including St. Ives and St. Marlo.

The other owners of Carrington Park didn't know what to make of the country-boy dude with the blond highlights who spent long days in the burgundy-walled offices, meeting with a stream of visitors amid paintings of the Tuscan countryside and maroon crushed velvet curtains. "He seems nice," they would say, especially the Emory kids, after meeting Phillip Hill. A nurse-administrator named Patty Conaway moved in here after a divorce, into a bright one-bedroom just the right size for herself and her miniature Doberman, and wasn't so sure. The condo owners were supposed to have a meeting the week Hill arrived to transfer the Carrington Park homeowners' association from the developer to themselves. Then they opened their mailboxes to find a notice announcing that the meeting was canceled.

Conaway rallied a bunch of her neighbors to meet with Hill in the clubhouse and ask what was going on. "There's no meeting, and there will be no turnover," Hill told them. And then he added, "*I* am Carrington Park." Hill and his companies now owned a majority of the units in the complex and therefore could legally control it.

The neighbors met again, about fifty of them this time, in the education room of the Home Depot around the corner on Piedmont. Hired security guards patrolled the door. The candidates for the board of directors, including Conaway, began to introduce themselves.

Hill had found out. He showed up with his son, daughter, and two business partners, all of whom now lived in apartments he'd bought at Carrington Park. He announced he was going to cast votes for his proxies—all the apartments he now owned. A representative from the management company spoke up: "You can't vote, because you haven't paid your dues." Hill promptly produced a check for $56,000. He had seventy votes versus everyone else's sixty. "You've made a mistake," he told the incredulous owners. "I'm going to do wonderful things for Carrington Park. I'm going to put in a heated pool. I'm going to make improvements. I'm going to get corporate leases. Why are you fighting it?"

The homeowners' attorney tried to answer. Hill fired him on the spot. Then Hill turned and fired the management company.

A few weeks later, Hill threw his fellow condo owners a poolside Italian feast. But the food and wine couldn't buy much. Following Phillip Hill's coup, the value of Carrington Park's condos rapidly collapsed, and it was obvious why. Hill had instructed his secretaries to hand keys over to visitors who brought money over in a bag. Every weekend one apartment turned into a party pad. The DEA, the FBI, and the ATF seized a town house and retrieved $4.5 million in cash. And then life at Carrington Park took a turn for the worse. Hill stopped paying electric bills, and one by one the public areas went dark. First the parking spots. Then the swimming pool, its pump immobilized. Hill's company collected the homeowners' dues and kept the money.

Next the mortgage investment trusts came. ABN/AMRO, Bankers Trust, Chase, Washington Mutual, Fannie Mae: over the next four years, half the condominium units in Carrington Park went into foreclosure. These were Phillip Hill's units, all bought with phony loans. The securities traders who bought the mortgages and packaged them for sale had elected to believe that the details on the borrowers and properties, as supplied by mortgage brokers and their affiliated lenders, were as true as a virgin bride.

New buyers found bargains galore, condos right down the road from Saks and Neiman Marcus, for $105,000 or so. Parents who'd hoped that selling the condos would help pay for college ended up stuck with apartments that some still haven't been able to sell. They can take some comfort knowing that Phillip Hill is now serving a twenty-eight-year sentence for fraud and money laundering. A close aide who lived down the hall from Conaway in Carrington Park is also in prison, as are the three appraisers who invented the home prices. For cooperating with prosecutors, mortgage company middleman Ted Tagalakis remains free. Bill McGill and the other straw buyers were never charged.

Conaway sits in her easy chair resting her swollen ankles after work, dog Brody scuttling on her lap. Reluctantly, she serves as treasurer for the homeowners' association, but she's glad not to be president anymore. Conaway waged a two-year court battle to kick Hill out of her clubhouse, turn over control to the residents, and get back tens of thousands in dues. She knocked on doors to collect a legal fund from her often recalcitrant neighbors. By the end, Conaway and the lawyer were the only plaintiffs' reps in the courtroom. She blinks slowly in the early evening light streaming in from her balcony and remarks, "It was infinitely more difficult than divorcing the man I was married to for twenty-nine years."

At fifty-six, she's much older than her neighbors, most of whom are living in the first home they have owned. She isn't going anywhere. Conaway is now stuck here, in the seven-hundred-square-foot condo with pale blue carpeting facing the Route 400 wall, with a glimpse of Atlanta's pointy skyline off to the left. She's carrying an 8.1 percent interest rate. She can't sell the apartment or refinance the mortgage.

Conaway and a friend next door both have their eyes on a two-bedroom at the end of the hall. It's still owned by Hill's right-hand man, Les Rector, and when Rector goes to prison, it'll be up for grabs. Conaway would like to move in there with her boyfriend, even though Brody growls at him. But the move remains a little game she plays in her head. She owes more than her own apartment is now worth.

Chicago had the Black Disciples and Insane Mafia Vice Lords, drug gangs that started dealing in real estate flipping schemes—and why not, since mortgage fraud in Illinois would get someone three years in prison, instead of twenty or more. Real estate deals proved a convenient way to launder money. Hundreds of people in a single Virginia town thought they were buying into an investment group, so they signed papers that got them houses in Indianapolis with mortgages far bigger than the properties were actually worth. In Dayton, Ohio, one guy took out twenty-three loans in the names of dead people.

It's hard to find a part of the country that hasn't been infested with mortgage fraud—a term that turns out to be quite difficult to define, but can be boiled down to any transaction where a buyer or seller lies to reap more money on a deal, or to qualify for a purchase they otherwise couldn't get.

That description, of course, would apply to much of the everyday business of the home trade in the mid-2000s. Realtors demanded that appraisers set their prices at a predetermined amount, or else the appraiser would lose their business. In 2006 alone, more than half a million borrowers took out stated-income loans. Lenders selling stated-income loans required only that borrowers write down their monthly earnings on the application form (declaring them over the phone was just fine, too); customers did not have to provide any paperwork to back up the claim. Many other loans were "low-doc," requiring minimal corroboration from sources such as tax returns and bank statements.

While many of these low-doc and no-doc borrowers were freelancers and others who can't readily provide a paper trail showing monthly income, untold numbers dressed up their applications. Among Fannie Mae's own pools of these kinds of loans, one out of every eight turned out to be premised on lies. A fraud-prevention firm that examined data on three million mortgages found that of those that went kablooey within a few months, somewhere between one third and two thirds were based on misrepresentations in the application process.

Mortgage fraud had little to do, for the most part, with hopeful homeowners fudging some numbers. This was organized crime. By the middle of 2008, the FBI was investigating nearly fourteen hundred rings of brokers, appraisers, and other real estate pros colluding to set prices and extrude as much money as they could. In the hardest-hit states—not incidentally, the same places where home prices were going through the roof—the FBI ordered its field offices to stop taking new cases on everything from environmental crimes to price fixing in order to track thieves stealing mortgage money. Wildlife and consumers, step aside—the feds were here to protect faith in the financial system.

Don't feel sorry for the victims. They supplied the weapons and the getaway car, on the assumption they would get a cut of the proceeds. Mortgage brokers looking for deals, prodded by lenders looking to meet their numbers, and whipped in turn by investment banks that demanded greater and greater volume, were begging for business, and more was never enough. As home values soared higher and higher, and the mortgage fees grew along with them, investment banks had no reason to look closely at all the thousands of loans that went into their mortgage-backed securities. With property prices increasing by 10 and 15 percent and more every year in Atlanta and many other parts of the country, few loans looked like losing propositions.

As the mortgage pools started losing money, pension funds stepped up to complain that they had been deceived into buying shares of these bogus loans. But the securities documents scream caveat emptor. The fine print indicated that if it turned out any of the claims about the underlying loans were untrue, investors could send them back to the mortgage lenders for a refund—and that if the lenders couldn't or wouldn't pay, the investment would lose value. Securities documents also quite clearly said that lenders could make exceptions to their usual loan guidelines if they felt like it. Mortgage fraud, perversely, was very good for business. Bigger loans! More closings! Refis (refinancings), too! Quite literally, everyone was in on the act.

No wonder, then, that real estate fraud is now the number one white-collar crime in the country. Reports to the FBI of mortgage fraud rose fourteenfold between 1997 and 2006, to almost forty-seven thousand a year. But while mortgage fraud has joined identity theft and e-mail viruses in the lineup of twenty-first-century plagues, booming, sprawling, blissfully optimistic Atlanta demonstrated a special flair for this kind of corruption, as if someone had plowed fertilizer into its rolling green hills. For four years straight, from 2001 to 2005, Georgia led the nation in reports of real estate fraud. At one point Georgia had seven times as many fraud reports for subprime loans than it should have based on the usual rates that banks factor into their projections, the way department stores budget for shoplifting losses.

From the moment it achieved statehood, Georgia earned a special place in the annals of land crimes. In the 1790s the U.S. government, the State of South Carolina, and Native Americans all had their own claims on the vast range of land to the west of the Georgia state line, all the way to the Mississippi River. But that didn't stop the Georgia legislature from selling the Yazoo Territory to speculators. Investors from all over the new nation, including senators, judges, and financiers, bought shares in the ventures. But once Georgians found out that their state government had sold off the valuable land for just $200,000, they turned their rage on their elected officials, burning one of their senators in effigy and threatening the lawmakers who'd agreed to the deal (and who were presumed to have received kickbacks in thanks). The legislature promptly repealed the sale of the Yazoo lands, leaving the property holders with worthless paper.

Two hundred years later, and Georgia still had the same problem: Speculators were selling real estate at lunatic markups. Property appraisers, who decided how much a house is worth and therefore how much could be borrowed, used to be like plumbers, tradesmen who learned the art at the hands of their fathers. But after appraisers got caught signing off on some of the savings and loan scandal's most preposterous adventures, reformers decided to open the business to new blood. In Georgia, anyone with a high school diploma could now take the test. Fifteen hundred did, and half of them got the job. These appraisers depended, totally, on lenders for their livelihood, and many proceeded to sign off on whatever prices they were told to fix.

Atlanta ended up with so many rigged home prices that the tax assessor for Fulton County has had to hire extra staff to walk the streets and figure out what homes are actually worth, since their sales prices are no longer reliable figures. In the worst-hit parts of the city, by 2007 just one in every eight homes that transferred from one owner to another were actually legitimate sales; everything else was a flip or a foreclosure auction. Homeowners were shaken into outrage over tax bills thousands of dollars higher than they should be, pushed upward by all the outrageously pumped-up prices on the houses next door.

The Phillip Hill scheme stands out only for its scale, and for the ease in which his decoys showed up behind the gates of some of Atlanta's proudest upscale retreats. And that he got caught. By the time Hill was indicted by a federal grand jury in early 2005, more than $80 million worth of his holdings around Atlanta had gone into foreclosure. But meanwhile, hundreds of millions more in ill-gotten real estate was also going back to the bank. At least fifteen subdivisions immediately surrounding St. Marlo and St. Ives also got hit. So did clusters to the east. Water's Edge, Country Club of the South (home to Whitney Houston and other luminaries), Sugarloaf, Smoke Rise, Laurel Springs, Moorings IV—in Atlanta, if it had a gate, a pool, and a name, it was infested with mortgage fraud.

All over Atlanta and its suburbs, people moved into homes for a week or a month, dragging in their possessions in garbage bags. Sometimes it was an adult, or several. Sometimes it was a large family, with many children. And most often, it was no one at all. Vegetation grows like crazy in Georgia's rich and warm soil, and soon enough it becomes easy to spot a stricken house: Weeds sprout so wild it becomes difficult to see the house behind them.

When a rogue Florida mortgage broker recruited a sidekick-girlfriend on Match.com and embarked on a fraud spree all over the Southeast, using the identities of dead and homeless people to pick up hundreds of loans, where did he end up? Atlanta.

What's striking, in hindsight, is how routinized the scheme quickly became, with a basic format and a few variations. If someone in charge— federal regulators, or investment fund managers—had really wanted to stop it, mortgage fraud could have been eradicated long before it roiled neighborhoods that thought they had done everything possible to flee crime.

Dennis Outlaw headed fraud investigations for Southstar Funding from the time it launched the unit in early 2004, when investment banks started sending back two or three fraudulent loans a month for refunds, until the

Atlanta-based subprime lender went under in mid-2007. By the end he was supervising a staff of eight and operating stings all over DeKalb, Cobb, and Gwinnett counties. Compact, slender, and intense, he's an Alabama native who moved to Atlanta for love and soon found himself stalking perps like a parole officer and a prison guard, both brought into a mortgage cash-extraction scheme by a former inmate's girlfriend, who happened to be a real estate broker.

Now working to help a security company devise fraud-thwarting tech-nologies, Outlaw has discovered that greater caution among lenders in the wake of the collapse of lenders such as Southstar hasn't really slowed down the fraud business, just slightly changed the script. Lending institutions lo-cated nowhere near the properties they're dealing with continue to rely on lightly regulated local appraisers to scout houses for them, and the meth-ods for calculating home values remain easily manipulable. All an ap-praiser has to do is point to a similar house down the street that recently sold for a similar price—which is usually easy because those nearby home prices are inflated, too. In the new fraud scenario, instead of flipping the house—buying, selling, and then reselling at a much higher price—perps build their entire haul into one transaction, whose details are buried in fi-nancial statements that don't become part of public records, if they're ac-curately documented at all.

Outlaw can explain the whole drama in less than a minute. "There are orchestrators, sitting in the background, who've identified: Here is a house on this street that's distressed"—it's got some sad story hanging from it, maybe a death or an overdue tax bill or a roof falling down. Or a looming job transfer might pressure a seller into taking less than his asking price, es-pecially if his employer will reimburse him for the difference. " 'I'm going to cut a deal with the owner to get the house at a very low price, but before I conclude that deal I'm going to find an investor, a young person I can convince that buying real estate is better than putting money in a 401(k).' You need a name, date of birth, and Social, concoct employment, go to an aggressive mortgage broker who doesn't do due diligence—he puts it up to four or five mortgage companies to see who's willing to bite."

The orchestrator arranges for a supersized loan in the name of the buyer, often for much more than the seller's asking price. Then two checks get cut at the closing. One goes to the seller at the asking price or thereabouts. Meanwhile, the orchestrator sends an invoice to the lawyer doing the closing, instructing that a second check be cut to a contracting company for repairs to the property. That company is owned by the orchestrator. And the repairs, needless to say, never get done. Many purchasers have no idea of what's going on behind the scenes, using their names and credit, or that they're getting set up to lose the home they're buying.

In 2005, the state passed the Georgia Residential Mortgage Fraud Act, which makes lying on mortgage paperwork a felony when it involves two or more homes, and makes anyone involved—brokers, appraisers, closing attorneys, and on and on—potentially liable for prosecution.

Georgia remains the only state with a law making mortgage fraud illegal, and for that, Georgians can thank the Georgia Real Estate Fraud Prevention and Awareness Coalition (GREFPAC) and its media-virtuoso cofounder, Ann Fulmer. A former radio reporter turned attorney turned stay-at-home turned real estate crime expert, Fulmer and other mad moms instigated the "All Broad Fraud Squad" after her golf course subdivision, east of Atlanta, got hit by multiple fraud rings. Since then Fulmer and the squad have appeared in *USA Today, Reader's Digest,* and *People.* Fulmer badgered bank lawyers, Georgia's attorney general, prosecutors, and anyone else who could help crack down on fraud until they relented and joined the cause.

The law is nice to have. But Georgia's subsequent drop in the FBI's rankings of worst mortgage fraud states has little to do with it; it's just that other states, above all Florida, Nevada, and California, have gotten much deeper into the muck. In Atlanta, authorities can't begin to prosecute all the cases they know about. The Fulton County district attorney, who covers most of the city, has just one attorney dealing with mortgage fraud. The Atlanta Police Department has one detective on the detail.

Meanwhile, the market pressures fueling fraud have only been gathering force. Atlanta's real estate market stagnated just as thousands of new homes and condos came up for sale. As their own construction loans come due, homebuilders are desperate to unload product. Cathy Makley lives on a cul-de-sac in an exurb called Dacula, fifteen miles beyond the twin water towers that boast GWINNETT IS GREAT/SUCCESS LIVES HERE. Wolf Creek broke ground in 2000, and even now the area is so undeveloped it just got its first Wal-Mart. The steep hills prompt striking vistas into valleys still half wooded, and buyers could acquire thirty-five hundred square feet of chunky space, with a charmingly gabled roofline, for roughly $250,000. A full-time mom to two sons, Makley fell in love with her house's wide-open kitchen, where she could prepare sandwiches, cookies, and sweet tea and call the boys over from their spot on the TV couch to come roam around the dining room table. And "If one more person tells me 'What a nice neighborhood you have,'" Makley says with offhanded cheer, "I'm going to shoot them."

A couple of years ago the syndrome started: the rangy lawns, the drug busts, the neighbors who didn't want to talk. New buyers introduced themselves to Makley and others with a warm "We're going to be your neighbors," but either no one moved in, or someone else did, like the family of nine from New Jersey whose children knocked on doors begging for food. Families with Section 8 government housing vouchers began renting homes that had sold for more than $300,000.

Mortgage fraud didn't find Wolf Creek; Wolf Creek's builder brought it there, along with the cement and timber. As the company struggled to sell houses—it had to move 220 in all—the builder's on-site broker began paying a resident of the subdivision a finder's fee for each buyer he brought in. He picked up six in one month. The recruiter also found people to lease the homes on the prospect of owning them, many of them single mothers who worshipped with him at New Mercies Christian Church in Lilburn, on the opposite end of Gwinnett County.

These were new homes, or just a year or two old. Yet all of the mortgage statements included vast sums for home improvement. The buyers, most of whom were from Nigeria, indicated that they planned to use the money to install home theater systems.

Eight homes on Makley's street alone, and more than forty in the subdivision, ended up selling for far more than their offering prices or the value of neighboring houses. Ambling up the steep hill from her small porch, she points to each in turn, remembering who lived there not long ago: five kids and two women who said their husbands were in Iraq; a tenant tied to one of the biggest drug gangs in Gwinnett; the lady who passed counterfeit checks at Publix supermarket.

Like homeowners in St. Marlo, Makley and her neighbors started a spreadsheet and passed it along to the authorities—who now knew, thanks to GREFPAC, that they ought to take mortgage fraud seriously. The state attorney general helped coordinate a massive raid in which a hundred cops busted down doors, forcing the residents to lie on the floor while they scoured the premises hunting for evidence that promised home improvements had been made. The recruiter was arrested and jailed on weapons charges. Inevitably, the homes began to go into foreclosure, and renters who thought they were finding a foothold on homeownership instead found themselves evicted.

Wolf Creek remains lined with "For Sale" signs, whose numbers have been multiplying. Like a great many homeowners in Atlanta and environs, the Makleys live at the mercy of corporate employers prone to transferring them from city to city. Transplants' haste in moving out makes their homes a favorite target for fraud.

For the past four years, Makley's husband, Morgan, has worked in the Atlanta office of Securitas, the security giant once known as Pinkerton. It's the longest they've ever lived anywhere in their eleven years together. Before moving into Wolf Creek, the Makleys lived in Charlotte, Macon (two months), Charleston, Charlotte again, and Jacksonville (three years). It's only a matter of time before they'll have to pick up and move again. Morgan just said something about Portland. Even more likely he'll get transferred to Kennesaw, fifty miles on the other side of Atlanta. "I'm starting to think: Does it make sense that we own a house?" wonders Makley. "Not really. The only reason we don't go broke is because the company pays moving costs." For now, she weighs every home improvement decision against its future returns. They won't finish the basement. She reluctantly put in a sprinkler system.

When they have to sell, they'll be competing against the foreclosures, the new homes just coming on the market, and a mass debut of new homes and condos much closer to the city. Greater Atlanta's five counties have issued more construction permits than any other metro area in the United States, producing seventy-three thousand in 2005 alone, and it has ranked number one since 1991. Local publications burst with ads for new developments: McIntosh Place, Dresden Heights, Dupont Commons, Copperleaf, Ivy Hall, Alderwood on Abernathy, Preston Park, the Gramercy, the Towns of Crescent Park—thousands of new units all chasing buyers.

Along I-85 heading downtown, drivers get daily updates from the billboard for Metro Brokers, one of the biggest real estate agencies in the area. Every driver in Atlanta knows its billboard, along I-85 heading downtown from Buckhead and the northern suburbs. Each morning, the billboard updates the city on the number of HOMES FOR SALE TODAY! It ticks up and up.

106,985
108,335
109,646

In Atlanta, foreclosure auctions take place on the gray stone steps of the Fulton County Courthouse on the first Tuesday of the month. The county is so crunched with foreclosed homes for sale that the sheriff runs multiple sales simultaneously, eight or ten of them hawking right next to one another. Almost always, it's the banks themselves that buy the properties back, since they have a vested interest in turning them around and converting a loss to a gain. Like any homeowner, they hire a Realtor and hope for the best.

For a while the banks found eager buyers. "I got a house for $150,000 that was worth $330,000. And I had a baby, so I was doing a lot of bragging. I remember taking a picture: The front porch was so big. I've got pillars. I'm king of the world!" Or so Brent Brewer thought. Brewer, an environmental engineer for the City of Atlanta, was convinced he and wife, Al-Yasha Williams, a philosophy professor, were getting a wild bargain when they bought their beige corner bungalow with the cute front and back porches in late 2003. They knew they wanted to live in the West End, right near Spelman College, so Al-Yasha could come back on breaks from work to feed their baby, and Brent could get to work downtown in five minutes. With elegant little historic houses on blissful tree-lined streets and thriving independent businesses on Ralph David Abernathy Boulevard—the Soul Vegetarian restaurant complex (braiding, massage, and colon cleansing available before or after dinner), Yasin's Homestyle Seafood, the Shrine of the Black Madonna—the neighborhood, clearly, was a find.

Their agent, who showed them more than fifty houses, told them the home was a foreclosure—and that it had previously sold, two years earlier, for $310,000. What they didn't know was that the buyer had also picked up another house nearby a month earlier for $300,000.

Indeed, Brewer's house on Oglethorpe Avenue had sold three times in total during the three years before he and Williams bought it. The first sale price, coming out of a foreclosure, had been just $23,900. In the West End and nearby neighborhoods southwest of downtown, real estate speculators could pretty much make up any price they wanted to. The streets of West End, Adair Park, Westview, Pittsburgh, and other neighborhoods began to fill with empty, boarded-up houses, all of them far too expensive for any real homeowner to buy. And all of a sudden, Atlantans had no idea what their own homes were really worth.

Brewer jolted out of his reverie with the arrival of the first tax bill. Their payment should have been about $1,300 all told. They were being asked to pay $1,700, because their tax assessment had gone up with their alleged property value. All over the area, homeowners were having the same experience, though most of them didn't have the two professional incomes Brewer and Williams did. So legitimate homeowners, too—even if they had possessed their homes for years, and had reasonably priced mortgages if they still had them at all—started going into foreclosure because they couldn't pay their tax bills. Brewer's neighborhood of 950 homes now has 300 boarded up. By the calculations of one local resident who has spent months in the Fulton County clerk's office reviewing property transactions, one out of five homes here has been sunk by mortgage fraud. In 2007, ZIP code 30310 had the second-highest number of foreclosures in the country, with 709 filings in just three months. Only Cleveland's Slavic Village, ZIP 44105, had more.

The houses will get pumped through the foreclosure mill five or six or eight times. Atlanta is planning to borrow billions to upscale a nearby area called the Beltline with condos, parks, shopping, transit, and all the other essentials of good urban living, but for now, the little homes aren't moving the way Lehman Brothers (now Barclays) and Bear Stearns (since acquired by J.P. Morgan) would like them to. The investment banks ended up with the properties after the firms sponsored mortgage-backed securities that included these homes' loans—and then those loans went unpaid.

Month after month, the giants of Wall Street hold on to these most unlikely of assets, paying for lawn care (if they're thoughtful) and taxes. They purchase the houses at foreclosure auctions when no other buyer will, grabbing this collateral at the lowest price possible in the expectation that they can resell the real estate and in the process recoup their losses from unpaid loans. They've come to possess vast portfolios of homes that barely remain standing, windows paneled with plywood and yards bordered with the final garbage load of their last tenants. Quite a few of the houses are humble shot-guns, so called because a bullet can fly without impediment from one room to the next, from the front of the house to the back.

Investment banks try to sell the abandoned properties the same way any owner would: through a Realtor. But foreclosed homes tend to cluster among their own, in areas where epidemics of falsely inflated real estate prices and correspondingly distended mortgage debts overtake entire neigh-borhoods, making it impossible to sell a foreclosed house at anything close to the amount of money borrowed. When all else fails, financial institutions turn to private auctioneers. In July 2007, the same month when two of its hedge funds imploded and woke a somnambulant Wall Street to just how toxic mortgage-backed securities and their derivatives actually were, Bear Stearns and its EMC Mortgage division put nearly three hundred near-hopeless Atlanta homes on the block. Bear hired the Real Estate Disposition Corporation of Irvine, California, to put a hard sell on its product. CNN's studios sit next door to the Georgia World Congress Center, where the auc-tion took place, but no one thought to send a camera crew.

In the standing-room-only ballroom, it was impossible to talk or to think. As the auctioneer and his tuxedoed helpers stretched in preparation to take the stage, loudspeakers blared Stevie Wonder and bidders sat, silently or shouting, clutching large green cards. Many spoke Chinese; others, Hindi. With a $5,000 cashier's check—the auctioneer's fee—they could get the keys to any of these homes. More likely they were looking for more than one.

The music quieted down, and cheers rose for Jeff Frieden, the auction company's spiky-haired CEO. After reviewing various technicalities—and making special note of the deposit-return guarantee if you used their part-ner mortgage company—he warmed the crowd with assurances: "The only bad real estate deals I did were the ones I didn't do. The market always cy-cles back every five to seven years. I think it's a great time and opportunity to buy real estate."

And with that, the auctioneer and his crew sprung into action. A real es-tate auctioneer can't work a floor of nearly a thousand people on his own; he needs a support team to help him zero in on bidders, and goad them into moving their prices upward. The assistants wore the adrenaline-weary glaze Wall Street traders get after a couple of years on the job, and once the auction began, it became clear how they got that way: their job requires them to emote, for hours on end, like they're courtside at the NCAA Final Four and put this month's salary in the betting pool. As spectators looked on somberly, the auctioneers galloped through the aisles and exploded in hysterical theatrics of cheers, fist pumps, and elaborate hand signals, all designed to generate a climate of urgency. Female assistants to the assistants passed out buckets of candy periodically to keep the energy high.

The auctioneer used another maneuver to pump up bids. "Who will give me $465,000 on a home previously valued to $860,000?" he implored. "Take a look at that value! Take a look at what this home was previously valued at!" What he doesn't say is that many of the houses on sale here today carry prices that were conjured in pursuit of mortgage fraud.

The bidding got competitive for 1108 Welch, "previously valued at $250,000. We're starting at—how about that?!—$29,000!" The auction came down to a war between Steve Patel, who had already purchased five other homes that morning, and a group of eight investors who bought even more, concentrating all of their purchases on ZIP 30310 and other fraud-pummeled areas nearby. They argued fiercely among themselves at the closing table, though about what no one could hear in the din.

Patel won 1108 Welch Street for $47,500 in cash. For reasons unclear, he didn't close the deal. A closer look at the flimsy, one-story ranch would give any buyer second thoughts. A yawning gap between the front door-jamb and porch overhang suggests a foundation far out of alignment. Rainwater floods the entryway. A month later, Bear Stearns sold the place to a company called Zion Investments, which bought three tiny, ramshackle homes in all from Bear Stearns and GMAC for less than $50,000 and moved to flip them. A month later, one sold for $64,000, to an investor who already has a trail of eleven Atlanta foreclosures in his name.

For Michelle and Joe Polite, the ultimate buyers of the house on Welch Street (they also own a nightclub downtown called Sugar), it will take a lot more than that to make their purchase habitable again, if that is indeed its destiny. This sad structure was bought and sold eighteen times in eight years, going into foreclosure four times along the way, in 1998, 2004, 2005, and 2006. In Georgia, foreclosure sales can happen in as few as two months after a mortgage goes into default, because the cases don't go before a judge. Instead, houses get spit right back into the market, where they're prone to getting mugged again for their mortgage money.

After each foreclosure, 1108 Welch Street crawled back onto the market for more abuse, gaining value, on paper, at every step of the way: $32,000, then $40,000, then $77,000, $118,000, and $132,000 until reaching its apogee of $250,000 in the summer of 2005.

The run-ups happened blindingly fast. Following the 2004 foreclosure, Fannie Mae literally handed over the ramshackle little house to a real estate investor named Eyal Livnat, along with the $93,000 in unpaid loan debts still weighing on it. At the end of August Livnat passed it on to a buyer, who took out a $132,000 loan from a company called Fast Funding. On March 1, 2005, Fast Funding bought it at a foreclosure sale for $115,000, and resold it to yet another buyer for $129,000 (by backdating documents by a year, Fast Funding was able to rely on older, higher appraisals to set the price). That buyer then flipped the house for $250,000.

Following its usual process when a property first goes into foreclosure, Bear Stearns paid $195,500 on the courthouse steps for 1108 Welch Street, which sits on a block where the earth embankments are quickly eroding and every other house is for sale or for rent. But while the investment bank got to write off its losses, its responsibility for fueling a cycle of neighborhood destruction ended there.

Investment banks that trade in mortgage securities armor themselves with legal language absolving them of blame. The mortgage companies that issued the loans simply asserted that the loans they make comply with consumer protection laws and that all the facts in the paperwork are accurate. The investment banks did little more than inquire about the mortgage lender's procedures; rarely did they actually inspect even a sample of the loans, never mind the properties themselves.

In Georgia, for a fleeting few months, it was actually possible to hold investment banks responsible for the origins of the loans they held. In 2002, consumer lawyers and AARP persuaded Georgia's then governor, Democrat Roy Barnes, to sponsor a law that would for the first time make the Wall Street securities pools liable when they sponsored fraudulent loans. That provision applied to only some mortgages—those with high interest rates and fees. But the law's sponsors would have included all loans if they could have. "It's a matter of compromise," says Barnes now, "getting through what you can get through."

Barnes comes from the financial business. Before his 1998 election as governor, he launched a couple of banks himself and sat on the boards of others. "I'm a capitalist through and through," Barnes avers. But he found himself outraged at the interest rates lenders were charging some borrowers, and the impunity with which they made loans they knew mortgageholders couldn't pay.

"You have to be responsible for this if you make these loans," the governor remembers telling lobbyists from the Mortgage Bankers Association of Georgia. "If it's on the face of the documents, you should have taken notice."

The lobbyists were undeterred. Banking industry contributions to state legislators poured in, with $160,000 from Ameriquest alone. The ferocity of the opposition stunned State Senator Vincent Fort, a history professor who helped sponsor the law. Ameriquest chief counsel Adam Bass, who is Roland Arnall's nephew, requested a meeting with Fort personally, only to have the senator assail Bass for his company's role in preying on minority communities.

Ultimately the bill's target was not the lenders but the security pools that bought the loans. "This scam, this business, this predatory lending could not exist at the level that it does without the collusion of Fannie and Freddie, the ratings agencies, the Wall Street investment firms, and the banks," Fort says, his words still true six years after the fact.

Fannie Mae became the lending bill's most visible opponent. Its CEO, Franklin Raines, wrote Governor Barnes, asking him to exempt Fannie Mae and Freddie Mac, and warning direly that the proposed predatory lending law "could unintentionally shrink the availability of responsible credit for the most vulnerable consumers."

As Fannie Mae and the mortgage investment banks asked the governor to back off, as Barnes recounts it, "I told them they were buying from a bunch of crooks." Just to make sure that the bankers got the message, he vowed to scour the country to fill the vacant job of state banking commissioner with the most radical consumer activist he could find.

But any hope of bringing the likes of Bear Stearns and Lehman Brothers to court for their role in mortgage fraud and predatory lending ran aground when Barnes lost reelection that November, a martyr for his efforts to remove the Confederate stars and bars from the Georgia state flag. Standard & Poor's, the ratings agency whose imprimatur assures investors in mortgage-backed securities that these loan pools have value, announced as the new Republican governor took office that it would no longer rate pools of mortgages that included loans from Georgia. Fitch Ratings concurred.

The campaign to unravel Georgia's groundbreaking lender-liability law wasn't only a backroom affair. Nationally syndicated conservative radio host Neal Boortz, whose show broadcasts from Atlanta, railed against the law repeatedly. His listeners probably didn't know that before he became a radio host, Boortz worked as a real estate attorney. Mortgage lenders became some of his show's regular sponsors.

The legislature and Governor Sonny Perdue promptly amended the law to remove all but the most exorbitantly expensive loans from its oversight and to limit how much a plaintiff could win by suing a financial institution.

None of it ended up mattering anyway. That summer, Bush administration banking regulators overrode Georgia's law, and by the following year they had effectively barred all states from creating their own regulations on mortgage lending. Congress had made this federal takeover possible when it deregulated the financial services industry in 1999. "If you want to know who is responsible for the subprime crisis, it's the Congress of the United States of America," inveighs Barnes. "They created preemption for state banks, federal banks, savings and loans. They prohibited states from passing consumer protection laws. It's the result of years of high-powered lobbying."

Governor Barnes has had to resign himself to warfare in the trenches. He had been there earlier in his career, when he sued Fleet Bank and Associates First Capital for alleged predatory lending practices and won multimillion-dollar settlements. After leaving office Barnes volunteered for six months with Atlanta Legal Aid, representing homeowners stuck with loans they couldn't pay. The former governor is now running his own consumer advocacy practice in Marietta, and he's finding that the line between predatory lending and mortgage fraud has grown increasingly blurry.

That's ultimately why fraud has been such a impossible target to shut down. The best way to get rid of mortgage fraud and its destructive consequences once and for all would be to make investors and fund managers pay dearly for it, and not just under doomsday scenarios. But lawmakers, at both the state and federal levels, have gone out of their way to shield investors from that kind of risk. Their objective is not entirely unreasonable: Subject those who provide the money to too much risk, and the mortgage market ceases to function. But the problem, in Atlanta and everywhere else, is that the risk is still very much there—it just gets offloaded onto borrowers, neighbors, and local officials, who lack protections that government has taken such care to bestow on professional investors.

One of Barnes's first clients was an elderly couple who were set to lose their home at the end of that week. She had had two strokes. He suffered from emphysema. Uninsured, they refinanced their house to cover medical bills, only to find that they couldn't keep up with the payments. With foreclosure looming, they were contacted by a company that promised to help them save their house; all they would have to do was sign over the deed for a while. The foreclosure rescue specialist, just out of prison for cocaine distribution, proceeded to take out $385,000 in mortgages on the house and disappear.

The only way for Barnes to fight the mortgage scams is after they've happened—long after the brokers and closing attorneys and fraud orchestrators have moved on. "All because a banker wants to buy a loan that he wouldn't make," the ex-governor marvels. "They were buying this paper and closing their eyes to whether the mortgage broker—did you inflate the income of the family, they told you $2,100 income, did you add $1,600 or $2,000 to that, instead of two bedrooms made four, knowing you would get your fee?"

Seven

HUFFING THE FUMES

Lee County, Florida, 2008

Q: What is the hottest time to buy in real estate,
in your opinion, or does it matter?
DT: Right now! I don't want to buy in a hot market.
I want to go into a dead shit market. This is the time to
start thinking about buying.

—DONALD TRUMP AND BILL ZANKER,
GET RICH AND KICK ASS, OCTOBER 2007

THERE IT WAS in the paper—the opportunity Brian Dunn had been looking for when he moved to Fort Myers, Florida. He planned to buy and run some kind of business once he and Sue got settled down. But this prospect looked a lot more promising. "What is the best way to make money in real estate? It's the most common question I'm asked in my real estate brokerage and as the author of this column," said the article by someone named Frank D'Alessandro. Every Sunday, D'Alessandro had the entire left third of the front page of the *News-Press* real estate section, prime space in a town—and at about forty-eight thousand people Fort Myers was still very much a town in 2002, with cows grazing in a pasture right in the middle of College Avenue—whose biggest business was selling pieces of itself.

Dunn himself had just arrived from Sterling Heights, Michigan, where his wife, Susan, up and quit her job at the gas company after twenty-two years. Unlike his dad, who had worked all his life fabricating stainless steel kitchen equipment in a factory, Brian Dunn could remodel homes anywhere. There wasn't much demand for what he was doing in the Detroit area. So why not Florida?

"The simple answer is it depends on what an investor is comfortable with," D'Alessandro continued, writing with the authority of a broker who was selling more real estate than anyone in Fort Myers. "Some investors choose to buy and hold properties as rentals, dealing with tenants. Others prefer to buy raw land, avoiding tenant issues. And some investors buy distressed properties, rehabilitate them and sell them. This type of speculative investing requires the most upfront work. But at least one Lee County company is taking a unique approach by providing investors the means to buy real estate and sell it at a profit."

Now, this is interesting, thought Dunn, who is tall and lean, with long arms, smooth blue eyes capped by severe eyebrows, and a demeanor that's at once intense and laconic. He didn't have money. What he did have was lots of experience remodeling homes. The guy who cleaned their pool out back on the lanai had asked Dunn if he had thought about investing in real estate. Yes, you could say that. Back in Michigan, Dunn had bought a bunch of books—*How to Buy Foreclosed Real Estate*; *Buy It, Fix It, Sell It*; *Flipping Properties: Generate Instant Cash Profits in Real Estate*; *Building Wealth One House at a Time*—which he kept on a shelf beneath Susan's set of old Nancy Drew editions.

What he didn't have was the financial know-how. Now D'Alessandro's column offered a solution. " 'We're helping people by teaching them how to effectively use equity as a tool to invest in real estate, and that ultimately helps the community develop a pride of homeownership,' explains Eric Herrholz, CEO and founder of Housing Redevelopment Inc."

Dunn wasn't quite sure what "equity" meant, but that week he looked up Herrholz and asked how he could join in. Herrholz agreed to take Dunn on for a rehab job and see what he could do. The entrepreneur liked what he saw—how couldn't he, since Dunn could turn a whole house around in less than three weeks.

They worked out a deal: on each place Dunn rehabbed, he would get 40 percent of the proceeds to Herrholz's 60. Herrholz would provide the money to buy the property. The funds (that would be the equity) to purchase and renovate the real estate came from D'Alessandro himself—immediate cash, at nearly 15 percent interest plus two "points," 2 percent up front on the total amount lent. D'Alessandro raised the money from his own private circles of investors, drawn from the Fort Myers elite: an eye surgeon, a dermatologist, an engineer who had become wealthy inventing optics for military use. Dunn's personal supplier of hard money would be a personal injury attorney whose brother was pals with D'Alessandro growing up in New Jersey.

Dunn was quickly learning what they wouldn't teach on *Flip This House* or *Flip That House*: The supposedly easy money via mortgage brokers, from the likes of Argent, New Century, and Countrywide, was nowhere easy enough for a real estate investor. Hard money was the only way to grab a place immediately, the moment Dunn got a call from his property wholesaler. He needed immediate cash to pay for what he needed from Home Depot and a work crew. If he didn't buy the house right then, it would be sold to someone else by noon.

No credit checks. No questions. D'Alessandro's appraiser would drive over—Dunn snaps his fingers twice in quick succession to demonstrate how fast—give a quick once-over, and green-light the job. Frank D'Alessandro didn't advertise this service. Nor did most hard-money lenders. Someone had to tell you about it—and Dunn was in.

He got to work, all over Fort Myers, with a crew of four, in the most disgusting places he and Susan had ever seen. Refrigerators full of food, unplugged in the Florida heat. Dog shit everywhere. Walls squirted with ketchup packages. Abandoned grow houses, sticky with the residue of the marijuana harvested there. Homes that had never been cleaned, ever. Once Brian had turned eyesores into upstanding pieces of real estate, neighbors thanked them for improving their streets.

And on his way to flipping thirty houses, Brian Dunn was making money, much more than he'd ever had in Michigan. That was 2003, and with the price of real estate rising like bamboo on HGH, his houses had no shortage of buyers—guys named Chen, Dong, Velazquez, Frey, in investor argot, "end users" looking for a place they could still afford to live in. Business was so good that when Herrholz didn't give Dunn his share of the proceeds, Dunn struck out on his own, borrowing large sums from D'Alessandro directly and getting tips on deals from real estate agents. In exchange, Dunn gave those brokers exclusive listings when he was done.

Dunn hates the flipping shows on TV. The financial calculus viewers see is often bogus, starting with the displayed prices the flippers allegedly bought their wrecks for—sometimes tens of thousands of dollars less than the actual purchase prices, with the result that viewers are led to believe the flip is much more profitable than it actually is. Basic expenses—Realtor fees, closing costs, carrying charges—are frequently omitted. But the misleading financial information doesn't bother Brian Dunn half as much as the fact that the flippers almost never do the reconstruction work themselves. Dunn handled plenty. He was part of the crew, ripping out rot, laying down tile, doing whatever needed his expert touch. He enjoyed it all tremendously, clearing about $20,000 on each house, doing what he knew best.

Still, as he shook off his boots at night and Susan cleaned up after him, the Dunns were coming to learn that there were more, and less physically exhausting, ways to make money in real estate. On the far side of I-75 lay Lehigh Acres—135,000 little lots of land reclaimed years before from swamps. It was a blank canvas for their aspirations.

The hundred square miles of Lehigh Acres tended to startle passengers landing at Southwest Florida International Airport. The place—it wasn't even incorporated as a town—resembled a mouth that had lost most of its teeth, with houses scattered one or two on a block amid expanses of sand and brush, but on a street grid as dense as Manhattan's and vaster still. On the ground, rough roads forded their way over canals dug to drain what had been swampland; the muddy ruts lowered the water table so far that wells were starting to run dry. There was nothing here but mile upon mile of lots, with little on them but spindly Australian melaleuca trees whose fecundity and appetite for water were killing all other vegetation.

With 90 percent of Lehigh Acres' lots still undeveloped, they sold for a couple of thousand dollars apiece, if they could sell at all. Many owners just gave the land to friends, charity, or back to the county, rather than pay a $10 tax bill. It used to be in Lee County that when someone wanted to dump a body, they'd do it in Lehigh Acres, because besides the rutted streets, there was nothing around.

In 2003, Lehigh Acres rumbled out of its slumber. By 2004, a lot would sell for nearly $25,000. Why? Don't ask—buy. With the guidance of a firm in Fort Myers that was advising hundreds of investors like her to do the same, Susan Dunn cleared out her IRA and put $75,000 into three lots in Lehigh Acres. With long bleached hair, in tight T-shirts and tiny button-fly cut-off jeans, she still looked like the Sue Dunn who used to go to Who concerts and help fellow fans who'd passed out, not the fifty-seven-year-old who might retire anytime soon.

She and Brian stood to make even more, they reasoned, with lots that had homes on them, and so they dug into their proceeds from the flips to put down a modest sum—just $2,100—for contracts on six more properties in Lehigh Acres, three in each of their Social Security numbers.

That was all they needed to do to spark construction on those lots. The developer, a local company called First Home Builders, arranged for them to borrow more than $800,000 from First Florida Bank, and got its construction crews to work, as fast as it could, anyway. So much building just like this was booming here and over in Cape Coral, on the other side of Fort Myers across the Caloosahatchee River, that work crews and materials were becoming scarce.

Those dusty lots eventually sprouted First Home's cozy "Belvedere" model, what Floridians call a 3/2/2: three bedrooms, two baths, and a two-car garage. The company advertised these HOMES FOR EVERYDAY HEROES on a billboard along I-75 featuring a sultry young firefighter caressing his helmet. At $240,000 or so each, a civil servant could almost afford to live here in Lehigh Acres, unlike pricey Naples or Fort Myers. Five of the Dunns' Belvederes sold, netting them $70,000 to $80,000 apiece.

While Brian and Susan were mining the eastern end of Lee County, a fellow investor they met in the Herrholz days beckoned them west to Cape Coral, a sprawling mass of lots ringed by canals that make a vague gesture toward Venice but were originally dug to drain otherwise useless swampland. Like Lehigh Acres, Cape Coral had been platted out in the late 1950s by northern pitchmen who mass-marketed land on installment plans using the same techniques as they did with the products that had made them successful, Charles Antell cosmetics (Cape Coral) and d-Con rat poison (Lehigh Acres).

During those same two mad years from 2003 to 2005, Cape Coral echoed Lehigh Acres' manic trajectory to a tenfold increase in land prices. Consider a lot in the middle of the woods at the northern edge of town, with no electricity, water, sewer, anything—a place that someone from Minnesota gave away in 1999. In 2003 the lucky recipient cashed in on the gift, for $7,500. A developer bought it a month later for $12,900 and then sold the land two months after that for $17,500. Finally, in early 2006 someone shook his retirement account upside down, using $75,000 to buy just one lot.

By then, hundreds of Lee County residents had, like Brian Dunn, cho-sen a business name—his was Sunrise Investment Company—put the let-ters "LLC" after it, duly registered in Tallahassee, and started looking for buyers. Remember, these were just vacant lots they were selling, offering little more than a Florida address. Schooled by an industry of real estate seminars, carefully tutored speculators from the Bronx to Mill Valley, Cali-fornia, made 2005 the year for Lee County, a place where property values still seemed remarkable bargains for those accustomed to the swollen prices back home. By the busload, thousands of eager investors visited Fort Myers and checked out builders' model homes prominently scattered, like three-dimensional billboards, at major intersections in Cape Coral and Lehigh Acres. Brokers put together complete packages for them: land, construction loan, builder.

Dunn knew Lee County real estate was becoming a treacherous business. He remembers the month everything stopped: "It was like someone turned a faucet off." That was October 2005. Nothing was selling. But, he thought then, how long could the slump last? "I was hoping, it can't be this bad for this long," he says with a stare, his eyebrows furrowing. "Oh, yeah? Bet me it can't be. Because it was." He took advantage of the lull in work to get a real estate broker's license. With his partner Lou, and using funds from hard-money lenders, heading into 2007 Dunn bought three Cape Coral foreclo-sures to flip, for the kind of prices you had to pay then. One lone three-thousand-square-footer, on a road that abuts a canal but like most in Cape Coral doesn't even have streetlights, cost him $310,000. He did his usual top-quality job, and built a huge amount of wiggle room into his fi-nancial calculations. For nothing. These houses just wouldn't sell at any price that could make him a profit. All over Cape Coral sat hundreds of empty homes. A lot of them were brand-new.

In retrospect Dunn realized his mistake. "You should always be selling to an average Joe Blow," he scolded himself.

But in Fort Myers and vicinity in those few astounding months, Joe Blow was nowhere to be found. Car wash owners, nurses, appliance repairmen, secretaries, firemen: all of them bought contracts, land, liens—anything that could get them a claim on a piece of southwestern Florida soil. Joe Blow had become Donald Trump.

Now the Dunns are flushing down a toilet, fast. Not only has their in-come evaporated, but they also have to make $6,500 in payments every month on four huge loans, none of which is for the home they actually live in. They've already spent everything that they made on the First Home deals on the mortgage payments for the places they can't sell. It's extremely unlikely that the houses will find buyers anytime soon, because Cape Coral, at the dawn of 2008, is the worst real estate market in the country, trapped in prices that are many times higher than anyone around here can afford to pay. The market is littered with thousands more homes than there are people to occupy them.

Dunn asks me to show him how my digital recorder works. He says he might get one like it for his own book he's thinking of writing, showing other contractors how to flip houses. Really, he wants to make sure the device is turned off. With that taken care of, the tone of the conversation turns alarmingly upbeat. Brian has spent the entire interview hunched in his easy chair on the far side of his spacious living room, barking, "What else do you want to ask me?" and "Next question" like he can't wait for the interrogation to be over. Now he's up close next to me in the kitchen while diminutive, deferential Susan sidles in from the other side. For the first time, she makes eye contact with me.

"Do they have MonaVie in New York?" Sue asks.

Mona what? I have no idea what she's talking about.

"Oh, I'm surprised! Cuz it's the biggest thing around here. You drink it, and it gives you incredible energy. The antioxidants help with all kinds of conditions." I hear about how Brian's eighty-seven-year-old arthritic father (he's still up in Michigan) wants to leave the house again; how the cultivation of the açaí berry helps protect the rain forest; how Brian was able to stop taking Prilosec; how they don't have to buy fruit anymore, since now they drink it all—eighteen different tropical fruits in one bottle of MonaVie! Susan proudly points to her kitchen counter, now barren of everything except a few decorative canisters.

"It's natural energy."

"*Natural* energy," Brian echoes on cue, raising his eyebrows meaningfully.

She dashes to the other room and comes back with a small stack of literature on MonaVie. No samples?

They have sat for hours, exposing their embarrassing story of aspiration, naïveté, and low-grade greed to a stranger because they hope that she just might buy, and in turn help them sell, as Brooklyn's own MonaVie sales representative, a $45 bottle of juice.

Frank D'Alessandro's body floated miles off Manasquan, New Jersey, bloated underneath his wet suit. His kayak had already washed ashore. He'd gone out five days before, after dinner with his mother, who had been ailing and glad to see Frank on a rare visit back to New Jersey. It was September 2007, and the new world D'Alessandro had helped build was already half dead; his own demise was only one more symptom.

In D'Alessandro's Fort Myers, buying and selling property for profit became a way of life, far more commonplace than going to work in a factory. In a span shorter than it takes to get a high school education, new homes pushed miles farther east and north, into swamp and woods, paid for with money borrowed by teachers, construction workers, nurses, policemen, and homemakers who expected someone else to live on these new frontiers.

Speculators didn't have to have Brian Dunn's construction know-how. Nor did they need much money; indeed, one couldn't properly call them investors, because they ventured almost no capital of their own. In D'Alessandro's most popular program, $1,000 bought a contract for a plot in Lehigh Acres and a construction loan that would put a new house from First Home Builders on the barren parcel, retailing for more than $200,000. You couldn't buy just one; participants were required to purchase two and, later, four at a time.

It was all spelled out in the PowerPoint that D'Alessandro's sales team first tested in Fort Myers and then took on the road in 2005, to the suburban fringes of Philadelphia, Boston, Columbus, D.C.—places cold enough that it seemed natural that money could grow in the Florida sun. Buyers would gross a 14 percent return, guaranteed, and wouldn't have to do anything after signing their names and handing over their deposits. His firm would fill the homes with tenants: customers who wandered into First Home's sales center on Colonial Boulevard, where eight model homes ringed a little brook with a bridge over it, but who couldn't qualify for a mortgage because of damaged credit. Through First Home's ministrations, this untapped mass of customers would become homeowners within a year. "It's just a matter of education," company president Pat Logue told a *News-Press* real estate reporter of these tenants, who couldn't even muster a down payment. "They still think there's cash out of pocket." Instead, First Home alerted the renters of southwestern Florida that they would apply their first year's rent toward buying their homes.

Heading the sales team was Lee County's perfect ambassador. Charming, strong-jawed, spiky-haired, a top Citadel graduate and not yet thirty, Samir Cabrera was married to one of Fort Myers's NBC news anchors and by extension her dad, the county manager. At his seminars Cabrera distributed a handy work sheet breaking down the revenue and expenses participants in the scheme should anticipate—real estate professionals call this a "pro forma," though Cabrera's was labeled a "Performa." Investors could expect net income of more than $1,500 on each house every year, plus $30,000 once the tenant made a year's payments on time and could therefore proceed to buy the home from the investor. "The refinance is possible because Sub-Prime lenders will allow a refinance on a property with 12 cancelled monthly checks for a lease payment," the prospectus promised.

From the packed hotel ballroom in King of Prussia, Pennsylvania, sheltered from the winter outside, Kelly Haegele thought that all sounded promising. She and her husband, Chuck, lived in Warrington, a respectable Philadelphia exurb of modestly paid professionals and small-businessmen, where they knew neighbors who were making money on these Florida investments. Her family of six needed that kind of income. Kelly stayed home with the kids. Chuck framed houses, which was a decent enough business but slowing down.

Tom Messina, over on Jericho Drive, was the first to get involved. He went from running an appliance repair service out of his house to establishing himself as Jericho Drive Investors, LLC, moving to Florida, and starting a property management service down there. Tom and his wife, Donna, were already getting rent payments from the houses that First Home built on their lots, which meant that the tenants were well on their way to qualifying for their own loans and buying those homes, bringing on a series of $30,000 paydays for the Messinas. That wasn't all that they were getting. For every investor he brought in, Tom Messina got another $10,000.

At the seminar, Kelly and Chuck learned about the booming economy in southwestern Florida—the population growing in double digits, the super-low unemployment, the small housing inventory that guaranteed demand would stay high. And sun and water, of course, if you were willing to drive eighteen miles for the latter. By the end of Cabrera's presentation, people were literally lined up out the meeting room door, waiting to sign up to buy homes and have First Home put tenants in them. Many of those queuing up were familiar faces to Kelly. The town of Chalfont, just down the road from Warrington, had barely more than a thousand families, and six of them ended up signing contracts with First Home. In Warrington, which wasn't much bigger, nine couples enlisted.

Diane Bannar, a registered nurse who lived in the house next to Tom and Donna Messina, took the plunge with her husband, William. So did Mariana and Jim Cliggett, who ran a flower shop and nursery, and the Curleys, and a chemical engineer named Raj Merchant, whose kids went to school with Kelly and Chuck's children. Merchant was encouraged to join by two other parents from Titus Elementary, John and Lisa Joyce.

Kelly and Chuck Haegele flew down to Fort Myers after signing their contracts, to check out the land that would yield them new prosperity. They didn't get to choose their lots—that was part of the deal. But when they were down there in the winter of 2005, they met with Cabrera over at the First Home sales center and asked him if he could take them to see their property. He looked at his watch. Sorry—another appointment. It was only later that they learned where their lots were, in the middle of next to nowhere. In Lehigh Acres, SW Twenty-sixth Street had just two houses on the entire block, which terminated in a canal that was more like a muddy ditch. The Cape Coral lots sat in what had been woods until they were bulldozed, miles from the center of town. The dirt landscape might as well have been on the moon.

The housewife and carpenter had borrowed close to $1 million in construction loans for four homes on four lots—two Ashfords, a Belvedere, and a St. Michael. All remained empty. While some investors managed to get tenants in the houses, few of those renters stuck around to buy. Why should a construction worker (for that was what many around here did for a living) keep paying $1,100 a month when he could rent an identical house for $800?

The money that Cabrera's Performa promised would come in started gushing back out instead. The houses themselves actually didn't cost that much to build; acrylic bathroom fixtures and laminate countertops were part of First Home's signature style. For the walk-throughs before closing, Kelly and Chuck had to hire someone local, who reported back, to their dismay, that the homes didn't yet all have their toilets or drywall.

What the Haegeles had paid dearly for in their package deal was the land. First Home bought one of the lots for $891. The Haegeles paid $45,900 for it. Over in Cape Coral, a lot way on the north end of the Cape cost First Home $1,500 in 2003; Kelly and Chuck got it for $65,900.

With Frank D'Alessandro brokering its purchases of land—most of it from widows, heirs, and men and women so old they had forgotten they'd ever bought a quarter acre on an installment plan—First Home bought and sold upward of three thousand lots this way in Lehigh Acres, and about as many in Cape Coral. That helped explain why property values were going kablooey in those two places: First Home was essentially making up prices as it went along, persuading the far-flung purchasers of these plots to look not at the debt they were taking on or the price of the land but how much money they were going to make. Selling more than half the lots in Lee County, First Home Builders of Florida wasn't following the market; it was fabricating it.

The Haegeles thought they'd be in and out in a little over a year, committed only to a few thousand dollars in deposits that they'd get back soon enough. By the end of 2006 it was clear that they owned not just one albatross, but a whole flock. Since they still owed First Home the balance of construction costs—expenses the renter-turned-buyer was supposed to ultimately pay—those new loans totaled tens of thousands of dollars more than they'd already borrowed.

Their first impulse was to make good on their commitments. Kelly and Chuck borrowed as much as they could against their own home, and from friends. As Christmas 2007 arrived, they'd spent more than $80,000 of their own money keeping all the Florida debts paid, and there was still no end in sight. With the new year Kelly decided to leave her kids on their own after school for the first time and go work as a part-time school aide (it was great to finally have health insurance, too).

Even if they sell the houses close to their asking price of $119,000—half of what they were supposed to retail for—the Haegeles will have to write a big check at closing. At this point, as interest rates inexorably reset and unpaid debt accumulates toward infinity, they'd be more than happy to do that. Investors, unlike homeowners, do not qualify for the government-sponsored program that Congress created in 2008 to help overcommitted borrowers refinance into less expensive loans.

"We followed other people. We trusted them," Kelly lamented before going back to the kitchen to make dinner for the family. The rite was a comfortable moment of normal. The kids have had to listen to their parents tangle in endless, vicious fights about who's to blame and what to do. The Lehigh Acres homes are scheduled for foreclosure sales, and it's only a matter of time before the Cape Coral ones follow.

Across town, Lisa Joyce is still trying to hold on. Avoiding foreclosure won't save her credit score, but it can buffer the damage to her pride and conscience she feels as one of the people responsible for dragging Bucks County, Pennsylvania, into Florida's real estate vortex. John and Lisa Joyce's backyard bumps up against the Messinas', and the couples installed a gate in the fence to make it easier for their kids to go back and forth. Tom and Donna are godparents to the Joyces' eldest son. The Florida real estate proposition Tom told them about sounded like a way to deepen his blessings to the family next door. John and Lisa expected that the proceeds from buying and selling eight First Home houses, four apiece, would let John fulfill his dream of quitting his marketing job at the cash register company NCR and opening a martial arts studio.

But more important than anything, it would buy higher education for their sons. For Lisa, it was just hard to say no to the promised double-digit returns. "I mean, where else do you get that?" she asks at her kitchen table in Warrington, while John and the boys spend their Saturday at a karate demonstration. "You don't get that in a bank; you don't get it in the stock market, or anywhere else."

Slender and focused, Lisa supervises billings for a crime lab. When Cabrera flew her and the Messinas down to woo them, she asked sharp questions and got answers that seemed convincing in the Florida sun. Cape Coral was sensationally popular, its population bulging with retiring boomers and those who serve them. There was no risk, since if a renter decided not to buy, the investor could always sell to someone else. Lisa went on Marketwatch.com not long before signing the deeds, and she saw that Cabrera's promises of a bright future for Lee County were true: Cape Coral now had the nation's fastest-growing job market. (Almost all of the new jobs, it would turn out, involved building, financing, or selling houses to speculators.) The local paper ran a report about how an expansion of the airport and Florida Gulf Coast University were providing further boosts to demand for real estate—written by, who else, Frank D'Alessandro.

Donna Messina still lives in Warrington while her husband looks after other people's empty investment properties down in Cape Coral. When Lisa Joyce goes to her backyard and Donna is there, the women won't look one another in the eye. Of all the friends and neighbors who joined them on their Florida escapade—"it was like an Amway Corporation kind of thing," says Lisa—only one is still talking to the Joyces, and that's testament to his forgiving nature. Ashamed of what his coworkers might think, he does not want his name published. Like the Joyces, their friend thought he'd found a way to send his kids to college; he was so entranced by Cabrera's presentations that he attended three of them. Instead he spent tens of thousands of dollars on mortgage payments for empty houses in Cape Coral, borrowing from family and friends, before coming to the conclusion that he'd be better off just losing the homes and incinerating his previously perfect credit. "I got creamed," he says. Like Kelly Haegele, he has closed his checkbook in defeat to mounting debts there's no longer any point in paying. He doesn't want to know when the foreclosure sale will happen.

Lisa isn't giving up yet on the two of her First Home houses that never sold. To refinance their expensive construction loans she and John sought mortgages with the cheapest monthly payments, and found them at a venture of General Motors called Homecomings Mortgage. As it happened, Homecomings was headquartered just down Easton Road from Warrington. Its parent company, ResCap, was one of the biggest issuers of securities made up of mortgages that were too big or too dubious for Fannie Mae or Freddie Mac to buy. (GM's mortgage operations, the company had just reported, earned the company $1.4 billion that previous year, even while the automaker itself lost many times that much.) Through a broker, in early 2006 this mutant hometown lender got the Joyces two mortgages, one for under $800 a month and the other for less than $600.

John and Lisa knew very well that these were negative-amortization loans, their initial payments artificially low because most of the interest owed was being added to the principal. Not only would they have to pay an adjustable rate—by the middle of 2007 their initial 1.5 percent interest rate would spike up to 8.5 percent—but they'd also be paying that higher interest on a growing amount of money owed. Like a lot of borrowers who turned to these neg am loans, the Joyces were hardly ignorant consumers who fell for an easy pitch. They were looking for a paddle big enough to navigate them out of financial disaster, buying just a little more time until they could locate someone, anyone, to purchase their houses.

Of course, that plan didn't work out so well, for the Joyces or most people in their position. Lisa has found a counselor who specializes in helping borrowers negotiate with mortgage billing companies to reduce loan payments, and she's been staying up late compiling proof of her family's economic hardship, a first step toward a workout with GMAC and other lenders. If the loss mitigators were in her house, they'd see it for themselves in the mold stains growing on the living room ceiling from a plumbing mishap they can't afford to replaster. They can see it in John's now-drained 401(k) account from NCR. (John lost much of that money on a subsequent land venture with Cabrera, who was later indicted for fraud for buying property cheap, flipping it to a phantom company, and then bringing some of his First Home investors in to buy shares at inflated prices.) The Joyces owe more than $500,000 and about $10,000 a month on four investment properties in Lee County. Lisa is working to whittle those numbers down and sell the houses and condos at a loss.

"We're professionals," says Lisa, mystified at where her family has landed, on a venture that seemed to have no downside. "Nobody thought it would end up this way."

Lisa Joyce's biggest regret? It's that she came in on the First Home program too late. John's first four houses sold at a profit. So did Tom Messina's. "The timing wasn't right," Lisa laments. For her the Florida storm wasn't a debacle. It was a missed opportunity.

It was only a matter of time before bigger money took interest in the gorgeous numbers emerging from Cape Coral and Lehigh Acres. In the summer of 2005, while Kelly and Chuck Haegele were still going to bed dreaming of checks, the publicly traded New Jersey–based homebuilder K. Hovnanian bought First Home. Hovnanian proceeded to claim, as federal judges started hearing stories like the Haegeles', that it wasn't responsible for whatever sins its acquisition might have committed to get where it was.

Lawsuits were the last thing Hovnanian needed to deal with in Florida. Of the nearly six thousand unsold houses the homebuilder had in its national inventory at the turn of 2008, more than a quarter of them sat dully in Cape Coral and Lehigh Acres. "We view Fort Myers as likely the worst housing market in the country," Hovnanian reported to shareholders, as if the company were an innocent bystander.

Hovnanian never suggested, however, that its management was unaware of First Home's unorthodox growth model. How could they be? Selling land on installment plans to dreaming Northerners was exactly what Lehigh Acres and Cape Coral had been built for.

In the early 1950s, a team of admen turned a sprawling ranch east of Fort Myers into a laboratory for a new formula in mass-marketing real estate. A Chicago entrepreneur named Lee Ratner had originally bought the eighteen-thousand-acre Lucky Lee Ranch to keep the IRS away from the millions he'd made turning d-Con into America's most popular rodent killer. His mail-order company was one of the nation's largest buyers of TV advertising. Besides d-Con, Ratner peddled a knife that'll slice a tomato every time, a gas tank pellet to increase your mileage—or your money back! That was Ratner's catchphrase.

Ratner was already such a sales legend that when he set up shop in Miami, a young adman named Gerald Gould introduced himself and asked if Ratner needed an agency. Ratner already had one, but he made a proposition to Gould: If you bring me a new product to sell, I'll bring you that account.

They launched a beauty products company together and became close friends. But meanwhile, Ratner's Lucky Lee Ranch, on the other side of the state, was fooling no one at the IRS—while Ratner liked to ride horses there in his custom cowboy hat and alligator boots, this was hardly a tax-deductible moneymaking venture. As Gould and Ratner rode together and Ratner vented about his dilemma, Gould asked him: Why not turn the Lucky Lee into a subdivision? That was what one of his agency's clients was doing up the coast in Warm Mineral Springs, selling lots through ads in northern newspapers.

Ratner liked the idea. He didn't want Gould, who was twenty-six, running the company on his own, but with the help of a couple of guys Ratner knew in Calfornia who had experience in finance, the men founded Lehigh Acres Corporation and began advertising Florida land for sale.

Gould and Ratner came up with the pitch on a flight to New York, writing it on a flattened-out barf bag: "For $10 down and $10 a month, you can own a lot in Florida." Back in Miami, Gould handed the bag to a colleague with instructions to turn the copy into an ad for the papers and TV. The campaign was successful way beyond their hopes or their capacity. Lehigh Acres sold twelve thousand lots that first year, 1954, to buyers from all over the country and above all, for some reason, Ohio. With sales continuing at a manic pace, they were running out of Ratner's ranch acres so fast that the corporation bought forty thousand more.

Getting all that land into passable shape to sell required drastic measures. Under orders from Ratner, his engineers took the street grid from the first of his subdivisions, along Leland Boulevard, and simply replicated it, over and over for miles around, without regard to the particulars of the landscape. As a result, many of the new roads drained uphill, while others plowed through wetlands. Crews dug more canals to dry the land, but that meant that most streets dead-ended at the trenches. Lehigh Acres lacked even a shopping center or a school, because the Lehigh Corporation had neglected to set aside land for them.

Did buyers care? The checks kept coming, along with notes describing visions of a sunny retirement. "I always dreamed of owning a piece of land where I would sit on the back porch and look at my land as far as the eye could see," wrote one who had just made his first payments on a half-acre lot. Another gentleman sent Gould a check for upward of $12,000 with a handwritten request: "I want you to build this house." Enclosed was a picture from the Lehigh Acres sales brochure. But that house didn't exist, at least not in Lehigh. While Gould was still working on finding a builder to erect a reasonable facsimile—he also quietly swapped the buyer's lot out on the fringes for one closer to the center of town—the man showed up with a truckload of furniture, asking to move in. The corporation put him up at a hotel in Fort Myers until the new house was ready.

While a few thousand retirees and entrepreneurs settled in to make Lehigh Acres' original subdivision into something roughly resembling a neighborhood—though a neighborhood where entertainment at the auditorium included Bing Crosby, Liberace, and an annual luau—from the beginning the tropical haven pictured in the beautiful brochures and sales force's spin was a chimera. Only about four out of ten of the buyers who signed contracts actually made all their payments and took title; the rest of the land went back to the company. While Lehigh Acres Corporation sold roughly 135,000 lots during its seventeen years of business, many of those were actually the same properties, over and over again.

By the early 1960s Lehigh Acres had big competition from another workingman's paradise across the Caloosahatchee River. Cape Coral was the creation of Leonard and Jack Rosen, brothers from Baltimore who got their start hawking coat hangers and other household items at carnivals and on the Atlantic City boardwalk. In New York, barkers herded audiences into a Times Square storefront to see Leonard do a half-hour pitch for lanolin hair cream ("Did you ever see a bald-headed sheep?"). He proceeded to take the show to the stage of the grand Roxy Theater and, as a founder with Jack of the Charles Antell cosmetics company, onto some of TV's first late-night infomercials.

Real estate hucksters had been selling Florida swampland to unsuspecting buyers as far back as 1914. But through their Gulf American Corporation, Leonard and Jack Rosen turned Florida land sales into a mass-marketing machine. Their crews sliced Cape Coral into a maze of navigable canals—A WATERFRONT WONDERLAND OF TRULY GRACIOUS LIVING, advertised the sign atop their first sales office—and moved fifty million cubic yards of earth to carve out hundreds of thousands of little lots.

Endorsements from Mickey Rooney and Philadelphia Athletics' owner Connie Mack, a computerized database, and a nationwide sales force beckoned millions of prospective buyers to Cape Coral: YOUR NEW WORLD FOR A BETTER TOMORROW. At grand sales banquets and house parties, guests received knife sets and other door prizes. International sales teams intercepted American tourists and servicemen in Germany and England, Tokyo and Rome. *The Price Is Right* gave away houses as prizes. Best of all were the free trips to Florida on Gulf American's own airline.

Alligators, cows, and mosquitoes gave way to a pool of porpoises, a massive Waltzing Waters fountain replicated from the Brussels World's Fair, and copies of the Iwo Jima statue and Mount Rushmore, part of a "Garden of Patriots" housed in the largest rose display in America.

Hundreds of thousands of visitors came for the attractions. Once prospects were in Cape Coral, the real sales job began, for lots that started at $20 down and $20 a month. The company planted bugs in the salesrooms so that supervisors could listen in on couples and advise salesmen on how to close the deals. Some separated husbands from wives until they agreed to sign papers. One salesman made his customers swear on the Bible that they would make at least six payments—the number he'd need to make his commission. Customers heard promises that they would double or triple their investment in the first year, or the company would buy the land back.

Such shenanigans, with Gulf American as the highest-profile offender out of many all over Florida, prompted Congress to pass a law regulating real estate investments. Cape Coral and Lehigh Acres just sat there, fallow, awaiting a future generation of Florida dreamers. The bulldozers had razed almost every oak, hickory, and palmetto. The canals brought in salt water and killed Cape Coral's once-spectacular fishing. There was little left but dirt and water, often combined.

By 1989, much of Lehigh Acres was the property of the U.S. government, after the Arizona savings and loan that bought Lee Ratner's company went kaput. The government-appointed caretaker of the S&L called Lehigh Acres "about as salable as a half-finished nuclear power plant"— fittingly, it turned out, since Minnesota's biggest public utility proceeded to buy the assets.

But most of Lehigh Acres remained harbored in safe deposit boxes and dresser drawers all over the country, and eventually another team of TV salesmen set out to liberate those yellowing deeds. National Recreational Properties, run by two high school buddies from Anaheim, got *CHIPs* star Erik Estrada to shoot late-night testimonials in English and Spanish, with an irresistible come-on: free junkets to Florida for prospective buyers. The company bought its first batch of Lee County lots for about $1,800 apiece in 1999, and it was as if time had restarted in Lehigh Acres, right where it had left off.

This time, the thousands of buyers writing out deposit checks for $895 were overwhelmingly Latino, many living in houses and apartments they didn't own themselves. At the end of their free trips they were buying the lots for $7,000, $10,000, eventually upward of $20,000. At $295 a month, they were effectively paying 15 percent interest, or more.

Scouring for new product to sell, Estrada's employers became the number one buyer of tax liens at the Lee County courthouse, bidding up lot prices to new heights. And then the craziest thing happened: The new buyers saw their fantasies come true. First Home and other builders came calling, paying $25,000 for lots they'd just bought for a few thousand.

Cape Coral attracted its own new generation of late-night TV viewers, as home to Whitney Information Network, founded in 1992 and better known to insomniacs as Millionaire University. Selling his stock over-the-counter under the symbol RUSS, founder and president Russ Whitney sent teams all over the country to present thousands of free seminars, advertised through infomercials, promising to teach the secrets of real estate investing at what the company internally referred to as "the 1590"—a three-day course, held at Gulf American's old headquarters on Cape Coral Parkway, that cost $1,590.

The first thing students learned, and heard throughout the three days, was that they needed to buy more courses from Whitney's Wealth Intelligence Academy, at nearly $5,000 each and at up to $40,000 for the full "platinum" package. Seminar leaders helpfully sat with each student in turn as they dialed their credit card companies, on speakerphone for the whole classroom to hear, and raised their credit limits. They'd hold a contest to see who could raise it the highest.

In between the sales pitches, Millionaire U. mostly taught the basic stuff of Brian Dunn's sweaty workdays: how to pick investment properties up for little money down, fix them up, rent them out, get them to "cash-flow" (invariably a verb).

Other seminar gurus had already marked this territory—such as Carleton Sheets, who sold millions of books and tapes through his own infomercials, offering advice that, not surprisingly, was often dubious. A classic no-money-down maneuver: have the seller advance you money for a down payment, but don't tell the bank.

Whitney just took the model to new heights of psychological conditioning, through a fawning regimen of positive reinforcement. Students who followed trainers' and mentors' directives received ever-escalating rewards of praise; the most compliant were honored at a Las Vegas conference with induction into the Wealth Intelligence Academy International Hall of Fame, "Where Only Eagles Fly."

But though Whitney Information Network was grossing upward of $100 million a year with the seminars, the money to be made selling real estate itself, in Whitney's own town, was getting too good to pass up. On the final day of their courses, Russ Whitney's seminar leaders escorted students around Cape Coral by bus, showed them a model home, and informed them that if they acted now, they could get one of a limited number of spots in a special investment program, which would not only earn them back all the money they'd spent on the courses but were such good deals that they could begin amassing capital to become successful real estate investors. Buyers would put just a little down to buy a lot, take out a construction loan, and sell the house before they'd ever have to take out a permanent loan. Or "houses," since students were encouraged to buy at least two packages. Whitney's partners even agreed to lease out and manage the properties if that was how the students wanted to cash-flow.

Hundreds hungrily seized the opportunity to put into practice everything they'd learned in the courses: above all, to trust in their Power Team of real estate agents, mortgage brokers, and other professionals. The students signed blank purchase agreements, which the development company later filled in with property addresses and other pertinent details, such as the price. Many of the homes turned out to be way out in the backwoods of Lehigh Acres.

Millionaire University was one of many wealth seminar operations flogging Cape Coral and Lehigh Acres, teaming up with local real estate agents (and builders, and lenders) who received substantial commissions on property sold to members. The Marshall Reddick Real Estate Network, with eighty thousand members in Southern California, brought its Florida agent (himself recently relocated from northern Michigan) in for a series of presentations from Orange County to the San Fernando Valley. Its AMAZING NEW 100% CONSTRUCTION-PERM OPPORTUNITY IN CAPE CORAL (translated: You pay $6,000 for the contracts; we'll build four houses for you; you'll rent them out and cash-flow) persuaded nearly five hundred buyers to sign up. In the Bay Area, International Capital Group had a similar arrangement, with $2,500 deposits for each lot. Much of the loan money for these deals came from, of all places, credit unions in Michigan, Alabama, and Colorado—little financial institutions whose membership is supposed to be limited to local civil servants. Two of those credit unions met their ruin in Cape Coral, and their federal regulator ended up stuck with $210 million in defaulted loans.

Southwestern Florida was just one of many places the seminars and wealth clubs promoted; at different times, Phoenix, Las Vegas, and Miami were the investors' darlings du jour. The ready availability of low-doc and no-money-down mortgages conjured heady opportunities in all those places for real estate flipping on a massive scale. But the sheer size of the Fort Myers supply, nearly half a million lots, made southwestern Florida the biggest feeding frenzy of them all.

For all that history repeated itself, echoing the Florida land craze of the 1950s and '60s, something profoundly different happened this time around. The seminar people, equipped with an open tap of money courtesy of the mortgage securities market, spawned an explosion of construction. Tens of thousands of new houses erupted one by one on hitherto empty streets. To growing ranks of locals who watched in bewilderment as home prices blasted to heights far beyond their incomes, it was like rainfall after a long drought.

For a brassy paralegal and weekend prep cook named Autumn Sturgis, who has lived in Fort Myers since she was nine, the new houses were a chance to get a little more space. And she'd heard the buzz that Lehigh Acres was hot. She's explaining this moments after bounding in the door, breathless and apologetic for being moments late, and untying the purple cape around her shoulders. Her chubby preteen daughter, Melissa, has quietly trailed in behind her, a nylon floral garland in her hair—they've just returned from a Renaissance fair, a welcome respite for Sturgis from her sixty-five-hour workweek.

"A very old man I used to work with at a car dealership told me: You can never go wrong with real estate," Sturgis recounts. She looks around her, at a house that she likes well enough and now can't hope to leave. She and her husband, Michael, bought it in 2006, for a little over $237,000, including a decent down payment from the sale of their old house. Michael had been forever renovating that place, hoping to increase its value; she was relieved to get rid of it.

Then her husband, a six-foot-seven cop, left her. Autumn got the house—and its $1,200-a-month mortgage bill. Her efforts to sell the home went nowhere, not with a flood of speculators' houses now on the market alongside hers. Autumn Sturgis's house happened to be the progeny of speculators Timothy and Diane Smith of Doylestown, Ohio, who bought three Lehigh Acres lots and managed to get only this one built on and sold.

Across the street, she tells me, her neighbors picked up and moved in the middle of the night, taking everything with them, even the kitchen cabinets. On one of the four bathrooms' mirrors, someone has written *Puta tu era a mi* (I was your whore) in lipstick. The Bank of New York now owns that house.

Sturgis earns $12.50 an hour, and that's at the better of her two jobs. If she was going to avoid her neighbors' fate, she would have to get creative. And so Melissa's dad, Jack Sturgis, came to live with them. It's worked out fairly well, considering that Jack and Autumn divorced nine years ago. His work in construction inspections is extremely slow now, so he's able to spend time at home with Melissa. He cooks a fine fettucine alfredo. "And he makes sure the place doesn't get robbed while I'm at work," adds Autumn.

Lehigh Acres has a rep, partly because of its growing Latino population, of being a dangerous place. But more than anything, crime here is a product of Lehigh's bizarre pattern of settlement: vast sprawl sprinkled with residences along dead ends, it's nearly impossible to police. This immense terrain, with its rapidly growing group of settlers, isn't incorporated. A couple of weeks after my visit, voters turned down the chance to make Lehigh Acres a real city, with services and the taxes that pay for them. And so Lee Ratner's ranch will likely forever be a place where inhabitants rely on wells in the back, and septic tanks under swells in the front yard. It's not clear how long that can go on. Lehigh Acres' aquifer is drying up and may be entirely tapped out by 2010, thanks to hundreds of new water hookups.

Like many houses in Lehigh Acres, Autumn Sturgis's is bordered by a patch of crunchy lawn that ends abruptly and gives way to raw dirt. After wildfires claimed dozens of homes in 2004, it's now customary to ring the grass with an expanse of pebbles as a barrier against the flames.

Jack's expert eye has identified endless little things wrong with the house, and many of them Autumn quickly discovered for herself, such as misdirected ventilation, gaping closet doors, a toilet that will never really flush. Those problems are perversely reassuring because they're fixable. The community they live in is a much less certain home. As the sun sets, Autumn, Melissa, and Jack stand in their driveway, one of three on their street, and wave good-bye in the descending darkness.

Twenty thousand arms, palms up, are raising the already very high roof at the Broward County Convention Center, where the hallway windows offer panoramic views of departing cruise liners as they pass shipping cranes unloading steel and cement destined to underpin Miami's rising forest of condo towers.

The arms are doing their part in the Money Dance. The Money Dance starts like the Macarena, except once your arms are out front the thumb and adjoining two fingers get to work, rubbing together like cricket legs. "I want money!! Lots and lots of money! I want the pie in the skyyy . . ." a pop soprano wails over an overamped sound system. And then the refrain, arms reaching for the heavens: "I wanna be RICH! Whoa-a-oh-oh . . ." A chorus line of college girls, in white tank tops that stretch the letters F-U-N across their breasts, leads the rally from the stage, in front of a thirty-foot-high collage image of skyline, Monopoly houses, and $20 bills.

Not for the last time on this Saturday afternoon, the throngs attending the 2007 Learning Annex Real Estate and Wealth Expo throw their bodies ecstatically into the possibility of a new state of being.

Emcee Michael Corbett, author of *Find It, Fix It, Flip It: Make Millions in Real Estate One House at a Time*, leads the Money Dance, warming up the frigid hall for the man who for the next two and a half hours will purée his standing-room-only audience into a frenzy of progressively lower inhibitions and a near-magical sense of purpose.

U2's "Vertigo"—*HELLO, HELLO*—pounds through the hall, and Tony Robbins bounds onto the stage and giant video screens even bigger than he is (six-foot-seven). He smacks one palm into the heel of another, again and again, revving the energy higher and higher, the cheers louder and louder.

"What does it take to get people to break through the fear?" Robbins demands to know via the wireless mic at his chin. The most famous motivational speaker on the planet promises to show the whole Broward Convention Center how to override the normal state of the human nervous system, which (we're told) conditions us to be passive.

Slides of Gandhi, Mother Teresa, and Nelson Mandela fade in one by one behind Robbins. These are the role models for future millionaires. "Resources are never the problem. It's always a question of *resourcefulness*. And emotions are the ultimate resource."

Robbins, who took just a few moments to seize control of a hundred rows of thumping hearts, has already proved that. Now he grows quieter, more serious. "Our brains are always looking for what's wrong," Robbins suggests. We have to let go of those inhibitions, he continues, and focus on what he calls Decisions of Destiny. Decision: meaning "to cut off."

"Many of you will come with the mechanics of what it will take to be financially independent. But most"—his voice grows even quieter here, and almost somber—"won't follow through."

This is a dare.

Up the escalators in the seminar rooms await opportunities to prove Robbins wrong. When he's done, following two and a half hours of mass hugging, jumping, tears, sing-alongs to the Monkees classic "I'm a Believer," and implorations to "increase your emotional intensity," hundreds of pumped and primed aspiring real estate investors will head to an overflowing session on Creative Financing. Gerald Martin, an instructor from an organization called the International Association of Investors, will spend another two hours teaching them how to "develop a wealth attitude."

Martin's bald head glistens as he touts the opportunity before them: $20,000 a month in "passive income," money that mints itself. "Do you think that right now in Florida is an opportunity?" Martin asks his crowd. "Yes?" He answers for them. "You'd better believe it!"

He bombards them with arguments sufficient to win a debate at a reasonably competitive high school. Not for the first time this weekend, the Learning Annex Expo will hear about data from Washington's esteemed Brookings Institution: Half of the national growth in population will occur in just eight states, lucky Florida among them. And all the homeowners out there who are having trouble paying their mortgages, now that it's the summer of 2007? An opportunity—if you act now.

"The door is closing!" Martin warns, pacing with an elegance he perfected as a champion gymnast at Ohio State. "You need to pick up a shopping cart and pick up as many foreclosures as you can. A few years from now, you're going to say, 'I wish I had picked up some of those properties.' "

Martin then plugs right in where Tony Robbins left off, though with a southern lilt. "You've got to make a *decision*. You've got to follow somebody" . . . or end up in the 87 percent of Americans who retire broke. Martin's hectoring grows relentless. "What did your parents teach you? To save money? Go to school, get a good job? Stop working, folks! Working doesn't work! People who work hard make the least money!"

Lynn Hutchison has already bought the product Martin is selling: a three-day seminar on how to Make a Fortune in Rehabbing Fixer-Uppers, from Martin's partner Don Burnham. In a plastic bag between her legs she's carrying a massive binder, which cost her $995. Burnham promised his audience earlier that day that investors who work with him will receive $5,000 for each deal they make, and that they'll get their first within thirty days, so the expense up front seemed entirely reasonable to Hutchison. Burnham and Martin say they're going to show how to make $40,000 on a deal; how to buy it ugly, sell it ugly; how to assign contracts, and never even take title to a property.

Standing next to a pair of massive bearded men in IATSE union jackets,

Hutchison explains why she's diving into real estate investing—and why the hell now, midburst of the bubble? "We've got to do something, because people are in trouble," says Hutchison, wearing baggy striped sweatpants and clogs, her hair pulled back plainly in a bright red scrunchie. "We have to help ourselves, because this country is going down." She's speaking from her own experience selling telecommunications services to businesses—work she's not getting much of anymore. She holds her right palm flat a couple of inches above her head. "We've been up here. And the rest of the world has been down here." She brings her left hand parallel to her waist. Then she floats her hands together until they're level at her chest.

The morning after Robbins's and Martin's performances, hundreds more will wait in a line snaking half the length of the convention center to commune with Armando Monteleongo, one of the stars of *Flip This House*—the first and still reigning reality TV program showing how to buy, fix, and resell decrepit real estate. One entrepreneur hands out flyers for her flippers' value-enhancement service: a colorful exterior paint job that, for just $1,000, will transform a hideous bungalow into a sure seller with the curb appeal of a hooker.

Monteleongo, who seems uncomfortable in front of the live crowd, relates how he flipped his own life from penury to astounding wealth—surviving his wife and baby's simultaneous stints in intensive care; begging a friend for a $1,000 loan so the family could relocate to San Antonio, $50,000 in debt, with a credit score so low it could be a tag number on a pair of Levi's, and on their last tank of gas. And then, the new Monteleongo as seen on TV: the one who claims the title of America's largest house flipper, confidently commanding his construction crew from the backseat of his SUV while buying and selling three hundred properties a year for profit.

He cautions his audience against the poisonous effects of thinking too much. In moments of struggle, they have to act fast—that's right, make a *decision*. You won't hear this on A&E. "Did you know there's a widening gap between rich and poor?" "Yes," comes the weary response from the room. "If you are not on the path to getting rich, you will be poor in the next ten years, or you can move to China, where the middle class is growing. You can go up, or you can go down. Because there's no middle class anymore." The rich, Monteleongo explains, educate themselves on how the system works, and the only way to figure it out is to actually take a leap and do it.

This stiff dose of the truth greases the way for the fantasy nonsense Monteleongo is here to sell.

Look at him: Right now he's buying houses for 30 cents on the dollar in California. (Or so he says; there's no evidence of this should anyone care to look for it in public records.) "Don't believe the popular myth of the media, where an economist who can't even make his rent and never flipped houses is saying that real estate is going down. We play to Middle America, the sweet spot of America. And that market is not going away."

As he talks, season three of *Flip This House* remains on the air. But Armando Monteleongo isn't doing nearly as well as Mando-Man, the real estate hero he plays on TV. Even as he urges his Florida crowd to buy his self-published series of books on how to "Flip and Grow Rich"—at $95, a bargain—two dozen of his houses in Texas have already been foreclosed on by his financier, midflip.

Monteleongo doesn't share this information. That would be contrary to the spirit and purpose of the Learning Annex Expo, which since 2004 has brought a caravan of model Midases, famous and obscure, all over North America to excite, entice, and convince the financially struggling that even if they don't have a penny in their pockets, they can make it as real estate investors.

The Learning Annex, founded in 1979 as a place where New Yorkers could learn the secrets of psychics, in 2005 signed Donald Trump to a three-year contract, for $1.5 million (plus expenses) a speech. Two years later, now former Federal Reserve chairman Alan Greenspan joined the show via satellite. How low will prices fall? Corbett asked Greenspan for the Learning Annex's New York audience that November as the mortgage securities market was imploding. "There is a possibility of prices flattening out in the spring," replied the man whose diet of low interest rates and pitifully thin regulations on the credit business was largely responsible for inflating the real estate bubble. At the Learning Annex, Greenspan's irrational exuberance lives on.

But Tony Robbins is the star of the Learning Annex's road show. The Robbins seminar experience is so intense that one student has claimed it induced psychosis. Using a vocabulary of intense body language—he pounds his chest, turns his chin with his eyes closed, and thrusts his fists forward—in Fort Lauderdale Robbins asks strangers to role-play that they're best friends who haven't seen each other in years. He tells them to jump up and down like they've just won the lottery. As his audience cheers and pumps their own fists into the air, he asks them to ask themselves: "In this state, what could you get yourself to do?!?!"

Courtney Smoot could feel the force field of motivation way in the back at the convention center, far from the VIP seats where she could have seen Robbins without the aid of enormous projection TVs. Courtney had risen at dawn and driven three hours through the Everglades to get to the Learning Annex summit, with her dad's girlfriend at her side. Courtney Smoot and Susan Tipton had never yet been especially close in the five years since Courtney had moved to Fort Myers as a refugee from Paradise, California. Courtney pulled out of her northern California marriage, fell straight into a Florida one, had a baby, and wondered what came next.

Then Courtney and Susan started finding things in common. They began complaining to one another that they didn't have female friends, just the men in their lives. And they shared their experiences as two women who'd racked up problematic mountains of debt, Courtney at Coconut Point and other malls of temptation. While working as an office manager for $40,000 a year, sparkly, redheaded Courtney had looked for ways out of the trap of spending that kept getting way ahead of her income.

Taking her cue from late-night television, she bought Carleton Sheets's real estate investors' coaching program, which gave her books, tapes, and a personal adviser. But Smoot stayed at her job and in her comfort zone.

When her daughter Hannah was born, though, she quit, and knew she needed to make a change. Her part-time job in a smoky bingo hall, working for tips, was not going to cut it. Smoot clicks her polished nails on a café table to mime the way her brain was churning, looking for a way to financial solvency. And so she set out with Susan for Fort Lauderdale that early June morning, to find their way into a life of independence from the weights that had been dragging them down. Soon Courtney would be carrying around an inspirational pebble in her pocket, polished, embedded with glitter, and inscribed with her new mantra: FREEDOM.

She had Tony Robbins to thank. "How fast can your life change? SNAP!" his hands smacked together. It was a turning point in her life.

"I feel like going out and hugging strangers now!" Courtney confided to Susan at the end of the Robbins marathon, high on the frenzy of love and trust echoing through the convention center. And that was just on day one. Courtney was so inspired she e-mailed a testimonial to the Learning Annex about what she'd learned from Trump on Sunday night (never lose your momentum; trust but verify; and when you have to, get even).

Courtney went back across Alligator Alley that night convinced that at age thirty-two, her life was moving in a new direction. "Boom!" Courtney cups her fists around her eyes and then thrusts out all ten fingers in a little explosion to illustrate what happened one night not long after that. She woke at four in the morning, with an idea of how she could make success happen for herself. "It sort of kicked things off," she says of the Wealth Expo. "I wanted to find creative ways not just to be a real estate investor, but to help other people."

To help other people. In the world of wealth-building, where one's job ultimately is to sell others the same product one has bought, this is the highest possible achievement. Her lime-green polo shirt sparkles with the name of the new enterprise she and Susan started after the Learning Annex Expo: $IMPLY $OLVED." Their job is to put their clients on the path to generating investment income. Step one is to clean up credit, using another company's service. While that's in the works, Courtney and Susan help them get the confidence they'll need to become real estate investors by playing the *Rich Dad/Poor Dad* board game "Cashflow" (subtitled "How to Get Out of the Rat Race"). Whitney Information Network is the exclusive distributor of the game and a growing family of *Rich Dad/Poor Dad* products.

The *Rich Dad/Poor Dad* books have sold so many copies that author Robert Kiyosaki says he stopped counting—he guesses twenty-seven million. Kiyosaki offers some sensible-sounding advice: Stop spending your money on things that don't make money and start buying things that do. In the worldview of Rich Dad, ownership of one's own house is a liability. Houses that other people live in, and pay for every month—those are the things to buy.

Rich Dad/Poor Dad players pull up cards: "4-plex available—forced sale. Owner behind on taxes. Good tenants. 56% ROI. Cost: $80,000. Mortgage: $64,000. DownPay: $16,000. Cash flow: $750." After two or three games of going for make-believe deals like this, one of Courtney's customers, a real estate agent in Fort Myers, decided she was ready to start investing herself. She paid $38,000 for a dead woman's house outside Pittsburgh and is now cash-flowing it.

Courtney is also selling the Financial Edge, which is where the

FREEDOM comes in. The seminar series bills itself as nothing less than a "Freedom from Debt Movement," as creator John Hyland explains to a roomful of unemployed mortgage brokers and real estate agents at the Comfort Inn meeting room in Sarasota.

"What do we know about debt?" asks Hyland, who's visiting from North Carolina and must have resembled Senator John Edwards before a car accident left Hyland's face scarred. A nervous young mortgage broker in blue jeans shouts "It sucks!" his knee jiggling so hard he spills coffee all over his lap.

"I'll teach you how to get rich when things go down next time," promises Hyland. But in the meantime he's enlisting conscripts to buy the product— the entry-level package costs $10,000—and then sell it to their colleagues. After all, this is a sales force already well trained in marketing pyramid schemes. Attend one real estate seminar, and chances are good that someone attending will try to sell you another. Whether the product is the Financial Edge, Fortunes from Foreclosures, or any of the hundreds of other wealth systems out there, indoctrination invokes the same phrases. As in a sermon, the trainer leads and asks those present to follow in unison.

I commit to taking action now to increase my wealth and happiness.

I work because I choose to, not because I have to.

Nothing feels better than when someone gives you the satisfaction of helping other people.

For Courtney Smoot, selling the Financial Edge is the short-term plan. Ultimately, she's looking to get enough money together so she can invest in real estate here in Florida. Smoot is excited to be getting in at the bottom of the market, where the opportunities are infinite.

Eight

TENANTS NO MORE

Brooklyn, 2007

IT'S BEEN HARD for Lisa Pines to explain to her seven-year-old son Graham why his neighbors have been disappearing while he's out at school, their possessions rolling out into moving trucks parked at the back gate. The common courtyard is quiet now. "There used to be a social life here—that's all gone," says Pines, glancing toward her front garden window. She tries to focus on the positives. "It's been very convenient to do the laundry, because the laundry room is empty."

There are buildings like this all over New York City, largely vacant, with a condominium sales office in a space where someone used to live. At the newly rechristened Court Street Lofts, the sales office is up on the tenth floor, in a pad with sweeping views of New York's skyline and the Statue of Liberty. Parents arrive with kids in their twenties, scoping out prospective investments. Empty nesters visit from New Jersey and Long Island looking to restart their engines in a newly safe and tidy city. Having owned houses since back when ordinary people could afford them, they've now built up enough equity to cash in for the new home of their choosing. More and more often these days, those new homes are old rental apartments.

Most visitors to the sales office take a pass on 505 Court Street. Two years after they first went on sale, fewer than half of the hundred apartments available had found owners. "How are the schools around here? 'Cause you know, the subway station, it looked a little . . . rough," a tightly wound apartment-hunter in her midforties interrogates the onsite sales agent as she waits for her own personal broker to show up. "Do you expect this neighborhood to, like, totally turn around?" The questioner doesn't get answers.

This Brooklyn factory building, on the far fringes of trendy Carroll

Gardens and colored by the roar of the Brooklyn-Queens Expressway, was carved up into 125 living spaces three decades ago as part of a government-financed scheme to create housing for the middle class. Even with new granite countertops and stainless steel appliances, the apartments remain vaguely funky, the kind of rough spaces that attracted two generations of artists and creative professionals to settle in the building. I know, because I used to live there.

Lisa, who's a stock-agency photographer, and her husband, Robert Hornsby, a former sculptor who heads PR for Columbia University, have lived at 505 Court Street for thirteen years. Why move? They have a two-bedroom apartment with twelve-foot-high ceilings, eight-foot windows, a small front yard and backyard, with a doorman, in a neighborhood with some of the best schools in Brooklyn. They are able to stay here with their sons, Graham and Henry, only through a twist of fate: They and a handful of their neighbors have guaranteed leases under New York State's rent regulations. They can keep living here for as long as they want, as long as they don't mind the Dumpsters of discarded drywall and old window frames that sit where the sandbox used to be.

A couple hundred of their old neighbors, myself included, weren't so fortunate. If we moved in after the mid-1990s, we were on our own. Our rent could go up to whatever the new owner thought she could get, and every lease could be the last one. That unlucky year arrived in 2006. Since 1997, when New York State rewrote its rent laws, roughly 173,000 apartments in New York City alone have lost their shield of security. While a dwindling number of protected tenants such as Pines and her family remain, there's less and less to stop owners of apartment buildings from kicking the rest out and selling off the flats one by one.

On Manhattan's East Side, a developer paid nearly $1.1 million per unit for a one-square-block complex of 583 apartments and evicted everyone he could—more than half the people who lived there. On the West Side, more than seven hundred renters had to leave another condominium-in-the-making. Those vagabond tenants crowd into an ever smaller number of apartments for rent, pushing rents up and driving anyone who can to buy, whatever the price.

New York City is rightly notorious for its most extreme real estate excesses. A single condo building on Central Park West sold $2 billion worth of apartments—average price above $10 million—to owners who include Sting,

Bob Costas, Denzel Washington, and retired Citigroup chief Sanford Weill, whose penthouse cost him more than $42 million. A twenty-three-room mansion on the East Side went for $45 million. And that's only the extraordinary, un-real estate. The average Manhattan apartment costs more than $1.3 million. Developers envisioned a rusty freight train track west of Chelsea as a new Gold Coast, sprouting starchitect fantasy condos for $2 million, $3 million, $4 million.

The pressures of those kinds of prices work their way all the way down the housing food chain, so Lower East Side tenement hovels built to house tubercular children sell for several hundred thousand dollars apiece. Buyers head farther and farther afield looking for a place they can afford, driving up prices as they go, until houses in what are still some of New York's poorest neighborhoods—places such as Harlem and Flatbush and Red Hook, where the typical family's income is little over $30,000 a year—go for well over $1 million.

This achievement, if it can be called that, would never have happened if those who make their money buying and selling real estate hadn't rewritten the rules New York and many other cities live by. Not long ago, almost everyone who lived in an apartment building here did so under a robust buffer of protections.

People who live outside New York, and even many in it, tend to misunderstand rent regulations. We think people like them because they keep the number on the check you send your landlord low, which of course they usually do. Yet their more important power is that those regulations give people who do not own their homes the only meaningful rights they have: to written leases, to sublet to someone else, even to get a new coat of paint. A hidden reason for the enormous increase in the cost of buying a home in recent years is that renters, here and across the country, no longer can count on any of those things.

New York wasn't the only state to cripple its rent regulations. California and Massachusetts, too, dismantled much or all of their systems in recent years. Out of the 21 million households in those three states, 9.2 million of them rented in 2006. In the rest of the nation, above all the parts of it where owners have greatly outnumbered tenants since World War II, most tenants never enjoyed protections in the first place.

Renters, one third of the nation's population, are second-class citizens. Many of them aspired to buy homes even as the cost of doing so grew

ridiculous not because of contagion of the American Dream, the sales
tricks of mortgage brokers, government homeownership campaigns, fantasies
of resale profits, or the allure of *Trading Spaces*, but simply because renting a
place in which to live as much as guarantees an uncertain and tentative existence. Even while deregulation of the banking industry shifted the ground
out from under homeowners, the movement to minimize government's role
in the economy was throwing renters into free-fall.

For Lisa Pines and Rob Hornsby, the price of owning Court Street Lofts
apartment 1E would be nearly $850,000, not counting $1,400 a month in
taxes and common charges. Had they accepted the deal the condo developer
offered, each month they would have to pay an amount more than triple their
current rent. They didn't buy.

Neither did Marissa O'Neill, who lives upstairs from them in 7S, offering price $997,000. She's done well in real estate herself with properties
she bought and sold in Brooklyn and Jersey City, and she recently started a
demolition company that guts worn-out Brooklyn homes for new buyers.
O'Neill knows a bad deal when she sees one, and she's not interested in
paying close to $800 a square foot for an apartment whose plaster façade is
crumbling underneath aluminum shields bracketing the mammoth window
frames. Since she wasn't protected by rent regulations, O'Neill has spent the
past two years fighting eviction from her penthouse.

Marissa is a thirty-two-year-old registered Republican. She drives a white
Explorer, and her coiffed hair is highlighted in platinum, evoking her origins
on Long Island, the regional capital of personal grooming. She's not who
you'd expect to roil in outrage over loopholes in obscure condo-conversion
laws, or outline bold plans to eliminate those loopholes by taking legal action
with a band of other outraged tenants. "We're going to get a ruling under
the Martin Act so tenants can't get evicted!" she exclaims giddily, hoisting a
happy hour beer at Old Town Bar, near Union Square in Manhattan, and
gesturing it to their future success. Through her demolition business,
Marissa is getting her own piece of the real estate boom's bounty. She has no
interest in tying up her capital in someone else's venture.

In the new New York, every tenant, no matter how financially secure or
politically conservative, is something of a radical, painfully aware of living
in a different, less privileged world from his or her property-owning neighbors. With each passing year, homeownership, a toehold in the tower, becomes a more and more distant fantasy.

Renters are torn between desire and anger, but Marissa is unusual in re-sisting at all. They tend to blame themselves for their plight and wax apolo-getic about their status as nonowners who should have bought back when.

Tenants shouldn't rue—they're being played. As recently as the 1980s, one in ten tenants nationwide was covered by some kind of rent control, and more than 170 cities—including New York, L.A., Boston, San Francisco, and Washington, D.C.—imposed rent laws.

As a nation, we've experienced two major waves of rent regulations, both brought on by crisis. World War II swept defense workers into hubs of pro-duction for ships and munitions, places (including New York) completely unprepared to house the onslaught of new arrivals. In 1942 the federal of-fice in charge of price controls put a freeze on rent hikes that lasted for five years.

That crisis eased as the FHA sowed new homes in freshly planted suburbs. But many of those left behind in cities festered in dilapidated apartments, a situation that couldn't be ignored anymore after the wave of urban riots in the mid-1960s. As the Kerner Commission concluded, terrible housing con-ditions, more than anything, prompted the fights and fires in cities such as Newark and Detroit. The Great Society proceeded to finance legal services and community programs that took on tenants' rights among their quiver of causes.

In the 1970s middle-class renters started feeling the heat, too, brought on by rising fuel costs, inflation, and condominium conversions. Tenant organi-zations sprouted all over the country, especially in radicalized college towns, and miraculous as it may seem now, in many places—Baltimore, Boston, more than a hundred municipalities in New Jersey, and thirteen California cities, including big swaths of the Bay Area and much of L.A.—city councils brought on regulations limiting rent increases, by popular demand. A quest to regulate rents was what prompted West Hollywood to incorporate as its own city in 1985.

Though ideologues on both sides have tried mightily, it's impossible to make a blanket case for or against rent control, any more than it's possible to say that police are always a force for good. A creature of local government and even more local real estate markets, their success or failure depends on gathering good information, exercising the political will to calibrate the an-noying details of administration, and taking leadership to reconcile conflicts when they do (inevitably) arise.

Places with rent laws have to figure out mechanisms to let landlords increase rents to cover their costs; otherwise, rent controls create slums. Inevitably, those cities also have to manage battles between landlords and tenants over the legitimacy of those increases.

Under good management and rules that are not overly restrictive, rent regulations do seem to have their intended effects. In 1981, when Los Angeles asked the RAND Corporation to tell it whether the city's three-year-old rent regulations were effective and should be extended, the answer was a qualified yes—yes, the regulations were likely to eventually put a dent in the production of new housing, but there was also no evidence that they had so far led to any shortage of supply or would in the long run strangle (or even excessively inconvenience) the real estate market.

Professional property owners and their trade groups lashed back, hard. By the time President Reagan and free-market ideology governed the land in the 1980s, most of those cities had gotten rid of rent regulation almost as quickly as they had imposed it. More than half of all states banned rent controls outright. The Reagan administration's own housing commission recommended that Congress do the same, nationally, for any apartments financed with federal funds.

Opponents of rent regulation built their case out of canards shading into outright lies about its perils. The landlord arguments often contradicted themselves. Rent regulations supposedly discouraged new construction that would add to a perpetually scarce supply. Even though the laws usually allowed owners to charge whatever they wanted to for newly built apartments, the low price of the old housing, in the landlord view, depressed demand for fresh product.

"When [developers] look at rent control, they see a policy that cuts deeply into the profitability of rental properties and discourages affluent tenants with rent discounts from shopping around for the new apartments that developers would build," decried Peter Salins of the Manhattan Institute, an urban planning professor turned leading critic of New York's rent laws, on the eve of their sterilization. Yet at the same time, rent control opponents claimed that the same limits on rents forced owners to maintain execrable conditions in their properties—never mind that most cities, including New York, allowed landlords to pass on the costs of most improvements to their tenants. Indeed, New York's rent hikes consistently rose higher than landlords' own expenses.

To believe the critics' reasoning, apartment dwellers were a race of scummy cheapskates who, left to their own devices, would choose to live in squalor; they would have to be forced, through the rigors of the marketplace, to aspire to better living quarters (and, of course, pay for them). An unregulated housing market, held the doctrine, would be much more effective than rent regulation at keeping rents affordable and apartments in good condition.

And so opponents sought not to improve rent regulations but to abolish them entirely. Politically, it would have been a catastrophe to lift protections overnight, and few elected officials embarked on that folly, not with more than two out of three New Yorkers believing that, in the words of a *New York Times* story on the poll numbers, "rent regulations were necessary to provide affordable housing and to prevent rents from soaring." The most expedient way to get rid of rent laws was to quietly let them drip away, as tenants died or moved out. Voilà—no dispossessed in the streets, just fresh product to rent or sell at whatever price the market would bear.

Landlord political action committees made generous contributions to state legislators to induce their cooperation in getting rid of rent regulations, in the face of organized popular opposition. In New York, the major landlord lobbying group, the Rent Stabilization Association, made contributions to the state legislature for the first time in its three decades of existence, nearly $750,000 in all, and spent hundreds of thousands more on radio ads. The money went not only to the Republican head of the state Senate, Joe Bruno, whose upstate, largely rural district was home to few tenants, but also to New York City Democrats in Harlem, the Bronx, and other districts for whose residents the rent laws made the difference between making ends meet and . . . well, who knew what they would do without them, since New York had had some form of rent regulation since 1920.

As the expiration date for the rent laws drew near, the hyperbole reached delirious heights. "An atom bomb would have created less of a problem, literally, in New York City to the real estate market than rent control has in forty-six years," insisted Bruno, who promised to "end rent regulation as we know it." A critic from the libertarian Cato Institute called rent control "a disease of the mind."

They had support from the editorial pages of every daily newspaper in town, including the *New York Times*, which, continuing the disease metaphor, asserted that rent regulation had "mutated into an entitlement for individual renters" and advised Governor George Pataki to "work quickly toward a compromise that will get as many units as possible out from under the rent regulation bureaucracy when their present tenants move out." In the *Times*'s view, the only fair solution was to get rid of rent regulation, as much as was politically feasible, anyway.

New York, in the end, did not abolish rent regulation. But for anyone looking for an apartment today, it might as well have. In 1997, the state legislature made it fairly easy for a building owner to take an apartment out of the regulated system once the place became vacant, and that is indeed what happened. After a significant decrease in the number of its rent-regulated apartments in the decade that followed, the median rent in New York City went up by 42 percent, and that's after being adjusted for inflation.

In other states, rent regulations didn't just get battered in the 1990s; they were fatally beaten. In Massachusetts, landlords got a measure onto the statewide ballot in 1994 prohibiting cities—that would be Boston, Brookline, and Cambridge, the only three places in the state that had managed to hold on to them by popular referendum—from imposing rent regulations. Landlords, including many from outside Massachusetts, spent more than $1 million on advertising promoting the measure. Tenants and labor unions raised little more than one tenth of that to oppose it. The rent-law ban passed with 51 percent of the vote.

California's landlords heaped even more money onto the cause, an estimated $50 million over twelve years. The result: The state legislature voted to override local rent regulations, so that any apartment that became vacant, and all new construction, would be unprotected.

Deregulation blew the ceiling off of where rents could go, and the value of the real estate itself. Once an apartment was in the free market, owners could move tenants in and out at will, or convert rentals to condos. Apartments in smaller buildings had never been regulated, but now their rents were skyrocketing, too, rising in lockstep with those of the deregulated apartments. Rent decontrol unleashed billions of dollars of value to be mined, literally sitting there on New York's streets.

Guess who descended to claim it. Wall Street investment banks hardly limited their business of packaging and reselling real estate debt to the humble realm of single-family homes, which, after all, represent less than two thirds of the nation's housing. Apartment buildings, inhabited by renters who mostly have never taken out a mortgage in their lives, became targets of opportunity for private equity funds that purchased the buildings and turned to the mortgage-backed securities marketplace to enhance their buying power. Just as shotgun shacks and McMansions were unlikely cohabitants among the thousands of loans bundled together in mortgage-backed securities pools based on single-family homes, their big-building counterparts combined loans on different kinds of property bought to generate income—malls, apartment buildings, hotels, casinos—and piled them together into one meaty investment, carved into cuts at different levels of profitability and risk.

A single $7.3 billion pool of commerical mortgage-backed securities issued by GE Capital in 2007, and sold by Citigroup, Bear Stearns, Deutsche Bank, Barclay's, and Banc of America Securities, combined loans on the Mall of America, ultraluxury New York office building 666 Fifth Avenue, a mobile home park in San Jose, a Residence Inn here and a Clarion there—and a bundle of thirty-six Harlem apartment buildings whose tenants were mostly paying a few hundred dollars a month for apartments that should, GE Capital promised investors, rent for more than double that. As the shareholders' prospectus detailed, "The sponsors plan on deregulating vacated units through the implementation of a significant capital improvement plan to enhance the profile of such units and raising rents." At the pace the plan promised, within ten years all the nearly eleven hundred apartments would be vacated and their rents hiked significantly.

Of course, tenants don't always leave voluntarily. To deliver on the shareholders' promised returns, the Harlem buildings' lead investor, the Praedium Group, had already gotten to work. Its hired management company sent eviction papers to occupants of five thousand out of the twenty-one thousand New York City apartments it owned, citing missed rent payments (even one or two) and any other technicality it could find.

Rudy Giuliani and his aggressive NYPD, *Sex and the City* and its siren call to cocktailistas everywhere, the destruction and trauma of 9/11—these events all transformed the city's landscape, but it took the real estate debt deluge to rearrange New Yorkers across the terrain of their city and remove them outside of it. As the rent laws faded away, investors could do far better with New York brick than they could with the stock market.

The Praedium Group, whose investment strategy is to invest in "undervalued and underperforming assets," has upward of $11 billion parked in New York City apartment buildings. Another of its recent projects is the former

Peaks Mason Mints factory, near the Brooklyn Bridge. In the 1970s, New York City sold a developer the vacant building for $55,000 and gave him a low-interest mortgage on the condition that he turn it into low-cost rentals for artists. Four years ago, the owner sold the building for $5.6 million to Praedium, which proceeded to evict all forty-two tenants. Praedium resold the property for $20 million, as a luxury condo conversion and construction site, where two-bedroom units went on sale in the summer of 2008 for $1,100 a square foot.

Another group of investors is plowing $426 million into a single rental building, the rambling Apthorp on Manhattan's Upper West Side, with plans to turn its 163 spacious apartments into condominiums. When they were regulated, each cost a few hundred dollars a month to rent. Unregulated, their leases go for up to $20,000 a month. The investors—including an Israeli diamond merchant who bought half the building—paid $2.4 million for each apartment, expecting to make a profit by reselling for at least twice as much as that.

These developers were not on crack, as far as anyone knows; they knew their market, and it came from overseas. Middlemen from Ireland, Korea, Brazil, and anywhere else investors were looking for bargains bought blocks of apartments, ten or twenty at a time, and resold them to their countrymen, who hold on to them to rent out or to alight there as pieds-à-terre. As the dollar has sunk among global currencies, our real estate has become dirt cheap internationally; about one third of New York condos are now sold to foreign investors. Briefly, real estate in Manhattan went for $500 per square foot—for the land, with nothing on it.

Under pressure from investors, New York is catapulting from a city where renters ruled into a place where one is valued by the property one owns. As recently as the 1990s, renting long term was a viable and accepted option for those who didn't want to buy into a thirty-year mortgage and the responsibilities it brings. By the mid-2000s, owning a home or co-op or condo—if you could afford it—had become the only reasonable choice.

One third of New Yorkers now own the places where they live, an all-time high. In the rest of the country, this would be a laughably tiny homeownership rate, but for New York, it's a sign of a revolution. In the three years starting in 2004, more than sixty thousand new condos came on the market, more than half of them in Manhattan. Upward of ten thousand more ex-rentals are being sold off as condos. Tens of thousands more apartments—

their buildings converted into co-ops in the 1980s—are trickling into buyers' hands as protected renters die off or move away or get caught with a second home in Woodstock.

You'd think that all this new product would have depressed sale prices. Instead, the appetite for buying prime pieces of New York City continued to grow even as other boom markets fell into a real estate coma. While prices have dipped as the Wall Street workforce loses jobs and, worse, bonus pay, the cost of buying property in New York remains far out of reach of anyone who isn't already in the game.

New York has paid a special price for being home to the workforce that packaged and sold the mortgages that made the housing market go-go-gonzo. By 2006, more than 174,000 professionals worked in the securities markets, earning an average salary of nearly $340,000—and that doesn't count the average $136,000 bonus each employee was estimated to make at the end of that year. As mortgage-backed securities reaped their fees and returns, the investment bankers who packaged these "fixed income" products saw themselves amply rewarded. Among the top five investment banks alone, fixed-income compensation tripled, to $60 million, in just six years. Even as mortgage-backed securities funding loans for homebuyers imploded, the part of the mortgage securities business that repackaged apartment buildings, shopping malls, and mobile home parks into tradable shares grew to record heights and brought commensurate year-end bonuses before it was done in by the fallout from the subprime crisis.

The 95 percent of New Yorkers not fortunate enough to have a Wall Street job have to cope in a housing market defined by the financial industry's grotesque compensation. Contrary to every prediction from free-market fundamentalists, the movement of hundreds of thousands of formerly regulated apartments to the open marketplace over the past decade has done everything but bring rents down; instead, it has been an invitation to push values into the stratosphere. The cycle is self-perpetuating. As prices rise, the old New York—the not-wealthy, the brown and black, the next generation of those who lived in the neighborhood when it was *el barrio* or just the 'hood—is locked out, to be displaced by new wealth that attracts its own, free of the messy diversity that complicates the valuation of property.

Native New Yorker Geoff Sheerar helps aspiring new buyers bust their way in. Lean, pale, shaggily blond, and driven, amid the café tables of Bryant Park at lunchtime he's poised to costar in some tourist's video as a

Manhattan creative—ex-Condé Nast impresario James Truman, perhaps, or a bistro chef-proprietor with the good sense not to sample too much of his own cuisine. Sheerar has his own artistic outlets; for one, he's among the growing army of graduates of the Upright Citizens Brigade's improv school in Chelsea, and does stand-up every now and then. But the job he took to support his creative habits has proven to offer even more fertile creative possibilities. Sheerar works as a mortgage broker, selling access to shelter in a city that has little to spare.

Sheerar held a seminar, "2007 New York City Real Estate Symposium, featuring Geoffrey Sheerar, Senior Mortgage Consultant, Apple Mortgage Corp." In a vaulted wood-paneled conference room at HSBC's New York headquarters across the street from Bryant Park, guests paid $15 apiece to learn about "the process and requirements of investing in NYC real estate" and "Various types of NYC property and which are the best investments now." Many brokers selling mortgages and property hold these kinds of seminars to acclimate their clients to the mind-set that it's perfectly sensible to borrow many times one's annual earnings, such as "Home Buying for Hipsters," which a Corcoran real estate broker holds at bars around Williamsburg and whose clients show their appreciation on the broker's MySpace page: "I'm sorry I didn't call you back last night AGAIN. I think I got drunk. Again."

Still dressed soberly for work, the fifteen or so attending Sheerar's evening gathering patiently endure his PowerPoint lecture on New York City's strange homebuying byways, most peculiarly co-op boards, which interrogate applicants with merciless financial inquiries but which also have served as New York City's great bulwark against wanton flipping and speculation, since buyers have to show serious income and assets and usually have to live in the places they own. Co-ops are rare elsewhere, because states' laws make them too complicated and expensive to be worth it. In New York, despite a new wave of condos, co-ops remain the gold standard—the place of choice for anyone who wants to control who moves in next door, which in the close quarters of Manhattan is of no small significance.

After an hour of sedulous review—of closing costs, the tax advantages of ownership, what it takes to apply for a mortgage, "amortize—do you know what that is?"—Sheerar opens the floor to questions. Sitting up in the hard gray seats, his paying guests pounce.

"Is there opportunity coming in the next year? Is it time to buy?" asks the dude leaning forward in his seat in the front row, with a Strokes-inspired haircut, designer-ripped jeans, and a girlfriend from Japan.

Sheerar takes a breath in the dim light next to the screen. "I used to work at Bloomberg News," he begins. "The numbers you see in journalism are misleading because they factor in everything. You either hear about this bubble or this mortgage crisis. What you don't hear is that people are happy and they're making money."

That's what those gathered here are dying to do.

"If I buy another property in New York City, can I say it's a second home?"

"Say someone's got seventy percent debt to income—will someone still make that loan?"

"Can I buy a co-op and rent it out?"

Sheerar offers almost as many arguments for buying as he has products to make it possible.

"People are waiting on the sidelines. People are willing to negotiate . . .

"This is something everyone will need, for its investment potential and building wealth in the future . . .

"There's a constant influx of people—college students, Europeans, Asians . . .

"There's not much more land to build on—Atlanta or Arizona can grow, but New York can't . . .

"Prices were too low for too long . . .

"New York City is not like Atlanta or Dallas. It's more like Paris or London. And really, there's nothing like it . . .

"The rate of appreciation will not continue, but prices will continue to appreciate . . ."

And then the universal advice, from anyone—Realtor, seller, or mortgage broker—whose earnings depend on the final price tag: "You always offer a little more than the asking price. It's someone else's money!"

The way to get as much of that someone else's money as possible is to pay it back as slowly as you can. Sheerar thus invariably recommends that borrowers use interest-only mortgages, where they get to decide how much or how little of the principal they pay every month, for the first ten or so years of a loan's life. Interest-only loans have become a necessity in high-priced places such as New York City, reducing monthly bills by 20 or 30 percent, preserving some of the benefits of homeownership (especially the mortgage interest deduction), but limiting how much of an ownership stake the buyer is actually building in the house in the long term.

By 2005, about one in every four homebuyers nationally was using an interest-only loan. Those borrowers were significantly more likely to fall behind on payments than others, suggesting that they're already stretched to their financial limits. Lax as they were as risky loans proliferated, federal bank regulators were so concerned about the escalating rate of foreclosure among interest-only loans that the following year they issued a special advisory asking lenders to make sure that they and their borrowers don't get in over their heads.

But as far as Sheerar is concerned, interest-only loans have been libel victims. These are not monsters, he says, but instruments of empowerment, letting buyers pick up apartments costing at least $50,000 or more than what they could have paid otherwise. They have special appeal for people who work on commission or as freelancers—among New York's creative professionals, that's pretty much everyone—and therefore see big fluctuations in income. As Sheerar always tells borrowers, an interest-only loan is what he chose to get for himself, when he bought his co-op in Brooklyn for upward of $400,000 in the summer of 2005 ("the most idiotic time to buy a place"). "It's like a credit card—there's more flexibility. You can choose to renovate your kitchen, build a college fund, go to Vegas."

Not long ago, borrowing too much, for too long, was the path only for those backed into desperate corners—those easy, poor victims who, in the 1990s, got sucked into predatory lenders' maws. Looking back from this decade, those days seem almost as distant as newsreels from the Lower East Side of the 1910s, a world of suffering unique to its bedraggled inhabitants.

Today it isn't just the financially desperate who turn to real estate debt for their survival. It's anyone buying a home for the first time, in any part of the country that offers reasonable economic opportunity, and no place more than in New York. Middle-class and affluent buyers are hardly spared. If they want to maintain their accustomed standard of living, they'd better be prepared to borrow big, and accept the risks that come with the obligation.

The total amount of home mortgage debt in the country more than doubled during the George W. Bush years. Partly, that's because more people took out home mortgages, in a population that grew and kept splintering into smaller and smaller households. But each borrower in turn took out a much bigger loan than he or she had in the past. The higher the borrower's income, the greater the leap in the size of the mortgage; for all but the wealthiest, the amount of money being borrowed escalated far more than any gains in income. In 1991, Americans borrowed about $370 billion to buy homes. By 2004, we were taking out $1.2 trillion. (These figures don't count another few hundred billion a year in home equity borrowing and refinancing.) In 2005, about one quarter of all new home loans were "jumbo"—that is, they exceeded the $417,000 limit on the size of the mortgages that Fannie Mae and Freddie Mac were legally able to buy at the time. Closer to half of New Yorkers who bought in recent years went jumbo. It turns out we're all living in borrowed space, renting our homes from the banks we cadge from.

"The purchase price is somewhat irrelevant, as weird as that sounds," Sheerar earnestly explains during our lunch in the park, the newly sheathed skeleton of the still-rising Bank of America headquarters looming above us (twenty-four hours earlier, it showered glass onto the sidewalk below and the unfortunate pedestrians who happened to be walking there). His chicken fajita panini sits with only a couple of bites taken out of it as he lays out the path to a New York City apartment. "At the end of the day, it's like: How much do you pay out of pocket? Can I get assets together right now to pull it off? I think a lot of people don't realize how easy it is in some ways. It's like, easy legitimately."

In 2007, the typical Manhattan apartment sold for $800,000. That's quadruple what it cost in 1996, the year before New York State's legislature strangled rent regulations and left them to die.

I grew up in a New York City virtually unrecognizable today. In the 1970s and '80s, my family lived in a rent-controlled apartment on the Upper East Side—two bedrooms of solid, elevator-man brick for a few hundred dollars a month. Dad was a writer and documentary filmmaker, Mom worked as a state bureaucrat; and for us, owning property made about as much sense as acquiring a tractor. Yes, this place had been built as luxury housing, in the 1920s mania that's the only thing close to our recent boom experience. Profit was, and remains, the only incentive to build anything this nice. But for almost all of its dignified life, 229 East Seventy-ninth Street and rent regulations had coexisted without too many misgivings. The plumbing worked; heat went on in winter, even during the 1970s oil crises; and a crew of elevator operators, including one who once tried to hypnotize my father, shuttled us to the street and back.

When I came back to the city after college, I knew the game: find a regulated apartment, and get on with my life. But fifteen years on, that way of being had become quaintly obsolete. I'd relocated to Brooklyn for the cheaper rent and did my best to tune out the roar of the Brooklyn-Queens Expressway outside my windows. One day, a note with my rent bill informed me that my loft building, a warren of creative professionals like me, had a new owner. And that owner had no intention of holding on to the property for long. Within a year we—Lisa Pines, Marissa O'Neill, and more than two hundred other neighbors—were embroiled in a condominium conversion. Sure, we could buy our own apartments—for a monthly bill more than double what we were paying in rent. And renters, of course, would no longer be welcome.

As the editor of a magazine investigating New York City's neighborhoods and the issues that vex them, I'd come to think of tenant strife as something that happened to people with no other options—who put up with the ceiling falling in because they couldn't afford to pay even for a moving truck to get their stuff out; poor people; or suckers living in doomed places already bleeding, whose bones were exposed for picking. Such travails were not, and never had been, surely, the experiences of the middle class.

So why were we all sitting in the living rooms of each others' apartments with thick prospectus books on our laps, informing us of the price of our cooperation? One of us helped run an art show on the piers in Red Hook. Another did the IT for the vaguely mobbish organization that runs New York's Columbus Day Parade. An editor at *Details*; the chief graphic designer for the Sundance Channel; one of the top wedding photographers in New York: These were the people who made the city what it is, by being willing to put up with a loud, smelly, grim, and fringey neighborhood.

These were also people who had rarely encountered a problem they couldn't solve by reaching for their checkbooks. Suddenly we were faced with a much trickier choice. This wasn't just a matter of spending hundreds of thousands of dollars to keep one's home. The more appalling prospect was indentureship, for individuals and couples whose lives were built around freedom, enterprise, and creativity. We knew our building, and we knew—most of us did, anyway—that no one was going to come out ahead by flipping one of these overpriced pads. There was nothing in this transaction for us except a chance to keep our homes.

As someone with passable credentials as a housing expert and the patience to explain tenants' rights to them (you have none, and your eighty-two-year-old mother doesn't either, as I informed the tearful daughter of one elderly tenant), I found myself serving as president of our newly formed tenants' association, prepared to wield whatever meager power we could muster. We pooled together dues and hired a tenant lawyer to hold a seminar in the basement of our local Mexican restaurant, telling us how to fight the eviction notices we were about to receive. (The office of the community development corporation downstairs from us—the nonprofit that had turned these industrial lofts into affordable housing in the first place—was off-limits as a meeting place once we learned that the son of its founder was the head of Brooklyn marketing for Corcoran, the mega-real estate agency that would be selling the apartments.) We called contacts in the city housing agency to see if all the government money they used to rehab this place in the 1980s dictated that the building had to remain affordable (no one there was sure, either). If nothing else, surely we had some muscle, collectively, as prospective purchasers.

With Vice President Lisa Pines, I sat down across a table from the condo's sponsors in their lawyer's cloud-level Wall Street conference room, angling for a deal—a package discount, a halt on impending evictions until the apartments started actually selling, anything.

These developers were not happy people. One looked like she hadn't been out of her car in a month. Her partner had either just come off a bender or needed the services of a top dermatologist; he stayed silent and glared at me and Lisa through narrow eyes. I knew their numbers—what they'd paid for our building, what it would cost to keep it habitable—and knew that they couldn't afford to sell these apartments for anything less than more money than I'd make in ten years. No wonder they looked sleepless. While it was a long shot that we'd be able to stay in our homes, I was also thankful that I sat in my seat and not theirs.

The experience finally snapped me out of my reverie. I didn't own property, therefore I had no power—to determine where I lived, at what price, on what terms. Maybe I'd been naïve. But what would I be now? My monthly mortgage bill reminds me: $221,013.02 in debt. My husband and I bailed out of 505 Court Street and bought a co-op miles deeper into Brooklyn, far from anyone we knew or anyplace we worked but at a price that would keep our monthly housing costs the same and deliver security, I hoped, in the bargain. I had just quit my job to take a one-year fellowship paying $23,000. Based on my credit score, generous down payment, New York City address, and best wishes for my future prospects, Wells Fargo handed me nearly $250,000.

By daring to move off the map, we got off easy. I've gotten into the habit of PropertySharking my friends and colleagues: the magazine editor who took out $900,000 on the house I'd envied; the historian friend with the mystery inheritance, the beautiful brownstone, and a mortgage payment that stuck its tongue out at gravity.

Across the river and battered by half a century of crime and neglect, Brooklyn had been a haven of relative affordability from the out-of-control prices in Manhattan. But lately Brooklyn, too, has been the scene of unabated real estate inflation. Brooklyn house prices have gone up by double digits every year since 1998, and they've never looked back.

A mile uphill from Court Street Lofts, in Park Slope, Valerie and Simon Hymas paid $2,400 a month to rent 850 square feet on the ground floor of a brownstone, with a shared garden. Like a lot of bottom-floor dwellers who help their landlord (that would be the historian) pay their mortgage, they were dying to buy. Their upstairs neighbors bought the place for a little over $1.1 million five years ago. Today it would sell for closer to $2 million.

Surely a tech manager for the advertising colossus Ogilvy & Mather and the administrator for Fulbright grants in Europe could find their own place to buy. But the condos Valerie and Simon saw for $600,000 and $700,000 were icky—cramped and cheaply built. Then, on a gander, Valerie dragged Simon to an open house for a $2.3 million brownstone up the hill near the park. As Valerie experienced a shudder of schadenfreude when she looked at the tiny backyard, the seller's real estate agent mentioned what they could expect to earn from the downstairs rental abutting the little lawn, and a lightbulb went off—Valerie and Simon could, like their own landlords, rely on their neighbors to help pay the mortgage.

So with a mélange of panic and giddiness they started looking at *homes*, places that, with their rain gutters and front steps, and above all their backyards, reminded Valerie of the place where she grew up in rural Pennsylvania. Valerie and Simon soon became used to a routine of disappointment: a broker would usher them to a lovely façade, harboring a house of horrors inside. When they saw the disaster of crumbling concrete stairs, rusted steel security doors, and not-quite-complete siding on Fourteenth Street, they thought they had met another loser. But inside, the renovation looked passable. This house was listed at $1.275 million.

In these parts, that's a bargain. At least it was renovated—not like the warren of drywalled living-cubbies on the market nearby for $1.4 million, or the $1.6 million brownstone with an asbestos-coated basement preserved pristinely from 1898.

At first they thought there was no way they'd even make the down payment. Then Simon's dad surprised them. He lives in the United Kingdom, and he's still kicking himself for not getting in on London's housing boom when he could have. In the land where Margaret Thatcher put public housing for sale on the open market, London property prices multiplied almost tenfold in the twenty-five years that followed. Hymas Sr. wanted in, an investment that would shield his earnings from U.K. taxes. He gave Valerie and Simon the extra cash they needed, and they went into contract for $1.15 million.

"When we got the contract, I said to my coworkers, We're one step closer to bankruptcy," Valerie only half-jokes. Like all New Yorkers buying a house for more than $1 million, they also had to pay a 1 percent "mansion tax" on the purchase price.

But this was no mansion, or even a detailed brownstone like their old rental. Their prospective new home, whose first occupant back in 1879 was a humble plasterer, is an aging three-story wood frame stripped of historic anything, and it needed serious work—rebricking on the foundation, a new interior staircase, redone siding where the previous owner had left a wide-open patch when he'd run out of money.

Oh, and the squirrels. They'd burrowed into the walls, chewing through wires and multiplying. The trick to getting rid of squirrels is luring them out and sealing off their point of entry. But the exterminator inadvertently left a litter of babies behind. The tenants upstairs were unpleasantly surprised when one of the little rodents burst through the drywall and into their bedroom.

As Valerie and Simon settled in, the house kept revealing more stories.

They began hearing from the neighbors about debris buried under the backyard, detritus from the era when this building was a rooming house with a dozen-odd occupants. Renovations that looked okay weren't—the skylights were just panes of window glass slapped on holes in the ceiling, which caused the roof to leak. Simon came to conclude, "This is what you get from someone who says he knows what he's doing."

They knew none of this when they started. And anyway, this place was the best they could do for what their mortgage broker could get them within their spending limit: two loans, one for 80 percent and the other for the rest of the million-plus dollars they've borrowed. They'll have to pay interest only for ten years—a cheaper way in, but one that will delay their reckoning with the principal. Even though their loans both have fixed rates, their monthly payments will jump by several hundred dollars once the interest-only period ends. If they stay here into middle age, make the minimum payments, and hold on to that mortgage, they'll end up spending more on the interest than on the house itself.

That's not their plan. Valerie speaks of their future financial agenda with the self-affirming grit of someone who has just signed up for a gym membership. They're giving their interest-only mortgage two years. At that point, she vows, they're going to start paying toward the principal voluntarily. "We are committed"—Valerie pauses for an involuntary laugh—"to making sure that in ten years we're not facing a huge payment, but have knocked off a good chunk of the principal."

For now, their mortgage bill is about $5,700 a month, or about 40 percent of their income. They initially reckoned on charging their tenants in the duplex upstairs up to $3,300 in rent, a hefty hike from the $2,500 the family had been paying to the previous owner. The people living in that rental apartment make a guest appearance in Valerie's Flickr photo gallery showing off her house-to-be, in a photo titled "Rental Unit Living Room." We see a stylish woman's back as she changes the TV channel, her infant on her left hip. A blond five-year-old looks on vacantly from the couch, which, like all the rest of the furniture and toys here, is wooden and vaguely Danish. Their dad, Kyle Kramb, edits TV commercials for a living—Ziploc, Taco Bell, Dr Pepper, Chex. The Hymases and the Krambs ended up with a compromise on the rent: $3,000 a month.

Valerie and Simon needed the tenants there. To begin with, the bank would only lend them all the money they need for the purchase if they already have someone paying rent upstairs. "I keep thinking we're taking a big risk," Valerie remarked just after they'd closed on the house, before they had the big talk with the Krambs. "Like, what if we can't get the rental income?"

Now that the Hymases are settled in, they are dealing with a myriad of certainties. On the day we meet she has to take a break to confer with the electrician troubleshooting their nonfunctional new range hood; in the afternoon they'll be heading out to pick up glass minitiles for the kitchen backsplash. Simon and Valerie are also experiencing a vigorous bout of déjà vu: Just as in their rental apartment, they live under the pounding of their upstairs neighbors' feet. Actually, with two small children living upstairs, it's much worse here. "The house—it shakes," Valerie says with a shudder, gazing upward.

The renters' payments cover more than half of the current mortgage bill. But what if their tenants' place—or theirs, for that matter—needs repairs? A new boiler? What if their tenant loses his job? What if Simon has a stroke?

Actually, that last one happened, between the time the Hymases signed the contract and closed on the house—a painful headache that exploded in his brain. Several weeks of rehab brought him back to functional form, and with Valerie he took a cab straight from the facility to Queens for the closing on the house. Since Simon wasn't yet able to hold a pen, Valerie signed all the ownership papers as his proxy.

Like a patient without health insurance, Valerie and Simon now just have to pray that they, and their building, stay sound. "That's the hope," she says, "that the roof doesn't fall in."

It once did, not so long ago. New York City's housing agency had literally given away this house twenty years earlier, after its owner failed to pay taxes. The subsequent owners, William and Carmen Vega, had bought the property in 1999 for $187,000, under an FHA loan program to buy and fix up run-down buildings.

The federal government had handed the Vegas a cash machine. In their first year, they were so broke that their fuel company took them to court for overdue bills. But in the years that followed, as neighborhood property values appreciated and they moved forward with renovations, banks gave them huge loans on their white-sided pile of wood: a second mortgage for $200,000 and a third for $150,000. With a refinancing they borrowed $705,000. That didn't count a revolving line of credit of $16,000.

The aluminum-sided house on Fourteenth Street is far from a unique monument to what has happened, in New York and across the country, when the federal government has tried to encourage urban homebuying. In 1994, the Clinton administration decided that it could help revitalize inner-city neighborhoods by making it much easier to borrow money to buy and fix up real estate. HUD secretary Andrew Cuomo, now New York State's attorney general, boasted that his agency's newly amped up 203(k) FHA loan program would "create affordable housing opportunities throughout the country."

The idea behind these programs was that homeowners like William Vega, willing to pick up a hammer and drip some sweat, could lead the way to revive decaying inner city neighborhoods. In Vega's case, the loan succeeded in helping improve what had been a shabby house on a marginal street. The problem is that the government put money in without limiting what buyers could take out. All over New York City, houses that were rebuilt with those government loans just a few years ago are selling for almost unfathomable amounts of money.

A slender structure, just seventeen feet wide, on West 126th Street in Harlem used to be a rooming house—a place where eight people shared a single bathroom, but at least had a home. It's boarded up now, much more useful at earning speculators money than it is in actually providing a place to live. Back in 1999 a real estate investor from Long Island paid $130,000 for the building. The next day he resold it for $262,000 to a Brooklyn ministry—a nonprofit organization that qualified to get the same federal loans the Vegas did. Six months later, the nonprofit sold it back to the investor for $401,375, who then resold it to a new speculator in early 2002, for $520,000. Its latest buyer, on board since 2005, has borrowed $850,000 to buy and fix up this empty shell. If the loose roof cornice doesn't whack some unlucky pedestrian first, the developer should be able to sell this place for more than $1 million.

Like its private counterparts, and as in its earliest days in the late 1960s, HUD did little to scrutinize whether properties like this were worth anything close to what investors claimed they were. Cuomo has been trying, belatedly, to make up for his past enabling of runaway home appraisals at HUD. As New York State's attorney general, he sued the country's biggest real estate appraisal, title, and research firm, First American Corporation, for inflating appraisals to meet the demands of Washington Mutual, which in

2006 stopped using its own appraisers and began to rely on First American's appraisal service.

The suit's allegations, backed up by damning e-mails, made official what New York appraisers had complained about all along: The prices set for New York homes and apartments were in large part fictions, engineered through the collusion of sellers, financers, and appraisers. Lenders and the Wall Street banks that funded them clearly knew that the appraisals justifying their loans were concocted, but hid behind legal disclaimers that put all the responsibility on the appraiser—the nobody who like a handyman had to show up at the house for a fee of a few hundred dollars but made it possible for the lenders to net far more.

As Cuomo began hurling subpoenas at appraisal firms, New York appraiser-blogger Jonathan Miller offered a dismal assessment to the *New York Observer*: Perhaps one out of every four or five appraisers works the way they're supposed to, independent of influence from the mortgage companies who employ them. The rest he called "order-takers."

"It's a joke—the system is a joke," Miller told the *Observer*. "There is very little independent analysis of what collateral is really worth."

New York's history offers a surprising rejoinder to the standard wisdom—the idea behind the Clinton-era loan programs—that homeownership makes a neighborhood more stable, and owners more invested in their communities. A co-op craze in the late 1920s crashed hard. In the 1980s, landlords looking for quick money converted nearly 350,000 regulated rental apartments into co-ops, but until the late '90s many of those foundered so badly that apartment buyers couldn't even get banks to give them mortgages. New York's most elegant, prestigious, and expensive buildings today—internationally known names such as Dakota and Apthorp and Ansonia—were built to be rented out.

Some of the very neighborhoods that best weathered the years of the city's decline in the 1950s and '60s and '70s, when hundreds of thousands fled for the suburbs, were those where most people rented, such as Manhattan's East and West sides. Areas with lots of homeowners—the boroughs outside Manhattan are full of them—were extremely vulnerable to maneuverings by real estate speculators.

Swaths of Brooklyn went haywire in the late 1950s as blockbusters moved black families into white neighborhoods, looking to panic white homeowners into selling their houses cheaply. Within a couple of years, entire neighborhoods moved out to the suburbs. Just as in Chicago and all over the country, banks generally refused to lend to new black residents, so if they wanted to buy a home they had to borrow from the blockbusters who sold them the property, at usurious rates. New York, too, saw speculators in the 1970s use HUD loans to flip houses in Queens and Brooklyn. Entire blocks in neighborhoods such as Sunset Park and Jamaica ended up boarded up.

Now that the pendulum has swung to the other extreme, New Yorkers find themselves pitted against one another once again. When they pay hundreds of dollars a square foot, new apartment buyers are as possessive of turf as the Jets and the Sharks of *West Side Story* ever were, angling to rank the neighborhoods where they've invested high within a merciless and ever-shifting hierarchy of property values. Some areas—the West Village, Brooklyn Heights—are unassailably blue-chip. But most others, especially if they involve a subway commute to Manhattan or more than a minority of immigrants or black people, have inspired new buyers to swarm to the Internet, to shill for their new neighborhoods, hoping to raise their own stock or lower the competitions'.

On an ever-growing array of neighborhood and real estate blogs, property owners promote their own communities and denigrate others. The blog Kensington (Brooklyn) bills itself thus: "One of the last affordable (and safe!) areas within reasonable commuting distance to Manhattan. Currently, seeing a resurgence of young apartment and home buyers." "Young" is code for "college graduates"; "safe" for "white," which the neighborhoods to the east are not. Kensington, in the 1960s, was a hot spot for blockbusters, but in recent years prices have quadrupled.

"Why Borders are Important," one entry instructs visitors: "In the last week two crimes have been associated w Kensington that were clearly outside our borders. The first from the NY Times about a guy on East 21st who killed his wife then himself." Not here, please note—ten blocks east. "Differentiation of borders are important in cases like this because it associates crime to the area which consequently brings bad press."

On the blogs posters like these are known as "boosters," a term that applies equally to one's love for one's neighborhood and one's property values. Generally, although not always, booster is a term of derision, a determination that self-interest renders a poster less than truthful about the facts on the ground (crime, transit, schools, the reliability of pad thai delivery).

AMENITIES AND CHARM SPAT LEADS TO BLOODSHED IN BROOKLYN
Nov. 16, 2007

An alleged argument between two Brooklynites over whose neighborhood was better for amenities and charm ended in bloodshed Wednesday night. The conflict reportedly began online at a popular real estate website called "Brownstoner" where a forum topic over the relative merits and pecking order of Brooklyn's posh brownstone neighborhoods raised tempers among discussion participants. Two participants, whose identities police are currently withholding but whom post under the handles "parksloper" and "clintonhillguy", proposed to meet offline to settle their disagreements via a knife fight at midnight.

Thus began an anonymous comment on Brownstoner, the most bodacious real estate blog of them all. Its founder, Jonathan Butler, is a native Manhattanite and NYU MBA who at the end of 2004 bought a brownstone in Clinton Hill—a Brooklyn neighborhood where delicious brownstones cohabit with housing projects and everyone commiserates equally over terrible transit service—and documented its meticulous restoration to historical form. He bought the place for $965,000, managing, on the strength of the Wall Street job he held at the time, to borrow nearly $1.1 million for its purchase and restoration. It was at the time a single-room-occupancy residence, set up to house ten or more people who shared bathrooms and cooked on hot plates.

After agreeing to an interview for this book, Butler cut off contact following my suggestion that the meeting take place in his beloved home. But the site continues to speak, with a dignified but unrestrained enthusiasm, to (Butler asserts) a hundred thousand or so real estate obsessives. Brownstoner serves as their Dow Jones, their futures market, their therapist, social science graduate school, architectural workshop, and village green. Butler is trying to support his family full-time via the Web site, with the help of ads from condo developers and real estate brokerages, all of whom, like Butler, have placed heavy and not unreasonable bets on the transformation of Clinton Hill and other areas nearby from ghetto to fabulous.

"We recently met the former owner of the next-door house who gave us a colorful description of the cast of characters who lived in our place until they were cleared out over the past two years by the woman who sold us the house," Butler wrote in the winter of 2005, in his fourth entry in his own blog-within-a-blog chronicling the restoration of his brownstone. Butler did the writing and photos, but the eight-month renovation was carried out by a hired crew under the direction of him and his architect father, who's based in Connecticut. The workers are never pictured on the blog.

He pauses to note the graffiti he found in the closets, and what it tells us about who lived here. "It sounds like it was mostly drug dealers—in fact the neighbor was held up at gunpoint by the drug dealer who used to inhabit the front room on the parlor floor."

Then Brownstoner moves to the real action: the marble fireplaces, plaster moldings (when the electricians manage not to break them), inlaid wood floors, the "music room" for his thousands of vinyl albums. Along the way, Butler steeps his readers in a vocabulary of obsessive possession.

"Here's a detail of the existing wallpaper in the front hall. It's in pretty bad shape and several portions are destroyed, but we still feel a little regretful about removing it, especially because there is lincrusta under much of it. In fact, not restoring the lincrusta is arguably the biggest crime against preservation that we're committing in the whole renovation." And then, he reassures us, "We are preserving a well-preserved section of the lincrusta in the staircase from the basement to the parlor floor." Lincrusta, it turns out, was a mass-produced product from the inventor of linoleum. Shaped into bumpy flourishes, it provided decorative filigree on plaster walls and looks like, well, decorative plaster. The object's value lies in its very ordinariness, in a past in which homes were unique possessions.

In today's new construction, of course, such architectural details are nowhere to be found. Almost all new homes and condos are designed to be bought and sold to the widest range of tastes possible; they arrive almost completely unadorned, and buyers take care not to build in any touches that might turn off a future buyer.

On another Web site, Curbed, part of the same blogpire as the celebrity-media gossip machine Gawker, such design offenses go into stockades in a regular feature called "That's Rather Hideous."

More often, Curbed dresses up adulation—barely, like in a thong—in a costume of derision. "The Pierre Has Closets for its Closets," Curbed snarked of a landmark hotel where a new three-bedroom condo offers twenty-two of them in all, all for $29.5 million. "Why did it take so long to sell? Probably because the buyer had to figure out what he was going to stick in all those closets. . . . Makes you wonder how many clothes cubbies that $70 million penthouse—743 days on the market!—is rocking."

That's rather hideous, but it's also hard not to watch. Its barely grammatical language complemented by fish-eyed digital photos reappropriated from the Web sites of real estate brokers, real estate porn has become New York's literary form of the moment, as much as beat poetry was in the 1950s or the society novel in the 1880s. Just 6 percent of New Yorkers could afford the typical home sold here in 2006. The rest of us, lusting after something so out of reach and yet so primal as home, can go online as long as we've got a place to store the laptop for the night.

Next to Manhattan's fantasias, Brooklyn's homes feel downright attainable, and Brownstoner takes on a suitably pragmatic tone of a guide through bumpy terrain—more *Cook's Illustrated* than *Wallpaper*. Each Friday, Butler posts new brownstones on the market via brokers' Web sites, and anonymous commenters rush to pore over the listings. Is that North Slope rehab worth the $2 million, or more? Can the painted oak trim be saved? What's with that revolting kitchen?

Just as important as the inside of one home is the cityscape beyond it. Is Red Hook for real? Can you survive a move to the other side of the park? Q train or F? It's a deep consumer mind-set, imported from the suburbs: through self-interest in one's own property values, one builds a better community, for those with the means to gain entry. Online, one can feel reassured, twenty-four hours a day, that like-minded neighbors are out there, preserving their lincrusta and building their ranks.

Brownstoner thrives on its bizarre and often creative contradictions: It's a celebration of commerce and community development; Jane Jacobs and Barbara Corcoran; enlightened urban planning and scary economic determinism, in which those with financial means are entitled to evict, displace, and say good-bye to the lesser classes. It was big news on Brownstoner when a bunch of neighborhood teenagers threw a metal café chair through the plate glass window of a local bistro. The kids who grew up around here have no door into the brownstone dream, or even the cut-rate speculators' version of it. Brownstoner rightly condemns the cancer of cheap "Fedders buildings," new brick condos so-called because of the brand-name air conditioner sleeves beneath their windows, but for renters around here these architectural offenses, bought with a subprime mortgage, are likely the only shot they'll have at buying a home in their hometown.

Epilogue

RETURNING HOME

*T*HIS IS ABOUT THE WAY *we live as a people and what kind of society we're going to have.*

President Clinton was right, more than he knew, when he made that promise. The phrase has entered history, not as infamously or bloodily as "We will be greeted as liberators," but resulting in the familiar pain of dismal results born from grandiose ambitions. The U.S. government and its business partners marched the nation into a delusion.

In hindsight, the scheme was mind-blowingly naïve—a vestige of a more innocent time not long ago when it was possible to believe that the fixed-income managers of Lehman Brothers and cashiers who couldn't even save for a down payment would both profit by doing business together—on terms set by one side, infinitely wealthier and more powerful than its partner.

The enterprise foundered on a contradiction. It's just not possible to transmit wealth to tens of millions of homeowners when the transaction depends on enriching investors and their fund managers to the fullest extent possible, with few boundaries. That much is confirmed by the scholarship on financial engineering and its fruits. Numerous studies have shown that pooling mortgages and then reselling their fragments results in greater earnings for investors than they enjoyed back in the dark ages, before Congress let Salomon Brothers and the rest of Wall Street make salami out of home loans.

But what about borrowers? Few experts felt the need to ask, since finance theory on "marketplace efficiency" indicated that homeowners would see benefits, too, in the form of lower interest rates, just as Lewis Ranieri of Salomon Brothers had promised Congress back in 1983. But a few decided to peek anyway. They've found that it's quite likely securitizing mortgages does not lower their interest rates. A 2001 study coauthored by a Federal Reserve economist as much as predicted what was about to happen in the five years to come: the exact inverse.

First the Fed lowered interest rates, in an effort to stimulate the economy after the dot-com bust and 9/11. The vastly increased potential for gain greased the securities-making machinery into gear, churning out thousands of new offerings. Investment bankers then faced a curious problem: more money seeking their high-yielding products, coming from all over the world, than they had raw material—mortgages—to sell. Their quest for new customers led to the astonishing deterioration of standards, and suspension of rational judgment, in deciding who and what would qualify for the mortgages they were financing. An armor of disclaimers and caveats, which accounted for much of the bulk of prospectuses that ran to hundreds of pages, provided them the illusion of a defense against any temptation the companies selling the mortgages to the public might have to tart up their loans' profiles before sending them off to the securitization mill.

Homeowners didn't just end up with bills they couldn't pay. The debt boom has realigned the American economy into two nations, one of creditors and another of perpetual debtors. The two decades following investment bankers' 1980s takeover of housing finance have borne a decline in wealth—that is, their total worth, of assets minus liabilities—for the bottom four fifths of all American households. The top fifth has had its wealth jump sharply, both in sheer dollars and in comparison to the typical American.

There are a lot of reasons for that troubling trend—a tax system newly rigged in favor of the rich; the ebbing power of labor unions; rising immigration—but in all that it's clear that enabling the majority of people to borrow vast amounts of money against property not even plausibly worth as much not only failed to counter the emergence of the wealth gap, but also helped to pry it open. In New York City, where the (then) seven big U.S. investment banks were headquartered, the average securities industry *bonus* in 2006 was nearly $190,000, or nearly triple what it had been four years earlier. Bankers made that money by putting households' balance sheets deep into the red.

The homeownership crusade strewed $13.2 trillion onto the streets of America, with remarkably few safeguards. Its architects assumed that grown-ups would be keeping order—above all, Fannie Mae and Freddie Mac, with their public service missions, government oversight, and sensitive interventions such as obligatory counseling for borrowers. They hadn't counted on the pummeling those institutions would receive from conservatives hostile to the very idea of government involvement in the finance system, or the lawlessness that increasingly prevailed on the front lines of the mortgage industry, with brokers and salesmen rewarded again and again for delivering loans no matter how dubious and the firms that financed the loans willfully ignorant of how the money was made. As the Fed dropped interest rates to almost nothing, and as opportunities for investment firms to create lucrative derivatives from subprime loans appeared almost limitless, the best business strategy was to ask as few questions of debtors as possible.

By now you've had the opportunity to meet many borrowers who were happy to help—whose greed, recklessness, ignorance, desperation, criminal intentions, aspirations, ovine temperament, or magical thinking led them to the other side of those transactions. But even the most cautious homeowners and purchasers were hard-pressed to exercise sound financial judgment. With idealistic ambitions, in 1966 President Johnson prodded Congress to pass a law detailing what borrowers had to know about the loans they took out, above all how much they would have to pay every month. What we have more than forty years later is a mush of unintelligible legal code. In 2007, the Federal Trade Commission reported that of hundreds of borrowers it surveyed, nine out of ten could not identify the total charges on their loan paperwork. Half couldn't discern the total loan amount, and one in five couldn't even figure out what their monthly payment was, or whether it included property taxes.

For the financially skilled and illiterate alike, taking on extreme debt became, in many instances, a rational act. At first the troops selling debt were greeted as liberators—because they sure looked like it. In the decade that began with President Clinton's second term, Americans, on the whole, were prosperous as they've never been before, making more money and buying more things, no small thanks to the larger economic force of the debt surge itself. At the boom's peak, home equity loans alone pumped up the gross domestic product by more than 2 percent.

But in the real world, that new wealth was proving illusory. Just try to send kids to a competitive college on $54,000 a year, the income of the typical

American family. See if you can find a good school district, career, and home in the same place (without a PhD or an MBA). And pray that you don't have to deal with a serious illness, with or without health insurance.

Americans coped with increasingly extravagant but necessary expenses through trillions in borrowing against rising property values. In 2004, the nation's homes were collectively worth $19 trillion, $12.5 trillion of which was home equity yet to be tapped. That year, homeowners took out another $1 trillion in home equity loans and credit lines, and spent most of the money to pay off other debts.

Why did so many borrow so much? There's no one answer, of course, except perhaps an economic habit that has united a culturally disparate nation for generations. Second only to oil, the U.S. economy runs on anxiety—on the gambles of more than three hundred million people scrambling for security.

Ever since Herbert Hoover's homeownership campaign of the 1920s, Americans have been consistently rewarded for leaping into a financial commitment that in the light of sanity might look downright un-American. What kind of free people choose to shackle themselves with debt, and with it to a bank and one's employer? On what basis should anyone expect those lending money to help their customers profit, instead of the other way around? And why, why did so many buyers (and lenders) assume that prices would keep rising?

Government has used more than propaganda to advance the cause. Most of us can't expect aid to secure higher education, or more than a pittance when we're retired or unemployed. But between 2006 and 2010, Congress's economists calculate, the home mortgage interest income tax deduction will grant more than $400 billion to the nation's homeowners.

The home mortgage interest deduction, which is as old as the income tax itself and by all accounts one of history's goofy accidents, might as well have been designed to promote excessive and risky borrowing. Borrowers can take the deduction on mortgages of up to $1 million. They can claim it on vacation homes. The deduction encourages homeowners to take out interest-only mortgages, which after all are 100 percent tax-deductible. Interest on home equity loans qualifies, too, which is why millions switched their credit card debt to home equity lines—loans that are now putting homeowners at peril of foreclosure.

The home mortgage interest deduction doesn't produce more homeowners. What it does do is make the rich richer, and keep real estate prices higher than they'd otherwise be—15 percent higher, asserts the National Association of Realtors in defense of the giveaway. More than half of the $400 billion goes to the small minority of households earning more than $100,000 a year. Silicon Valley's homeowners, who overwhelmingly turned to interest-only loans to get a foothold on some of the most expensive real estate in the nation, get more federal aid than anyone, an average deduction of nearly $35,000 each. In 2005, a presidential panel recommended eliminating the tax break, advice that was promptly shouted down by the National Association of Realtors, whose political action committee contributes more to Congress than any other organization. Instead of eliminating the deduction, President Barack Obama has committed to render a mortgage interest credit automatic for all homeowning taxpayers; until now, the deduction has been available only to those who itemize their taxes. That will be fairer—except, of course, to renters.

Each year, the federal government spends more on the mortgage interest deduction than on the entire U.S. Department of Housing and Urban Development, the agency that (among much else) helps millions of Americans who couldn't otherwise afford their housing have a decent place to live. Even as it promoted homeownership and juiced up the mortgage industry through deregulation, the federal government allowed the owners of more than three hundred thousand apartments built starting in the 1960s with public subsidies—on the proviso that they rent to the poor—to instead rent or sell to anyone, at any price.

Congress and the Reagan administration eliminated funding for new public housing; today all that's left of a New Deal–era commitment to shelter the poor is a corporate tax credit that supports the construction of about sixty-five thousand apartments every year—not bad, except that the tax break, and its requirement that the housing has to be affordable, expires after fifteen years. (It amounts to less than 1 percent of what the IRS gives away through the mortgage interest deduction.) Under a program championed by the first George Bush and then Bill Clinton, public housing authorities across the country have demolished housing projects and replaced them with homes for rent or sale at much higher prices. George W. Bush's administration and Congress embarked on a brutal agenda of budget cutbacks for the public housing that's left, leading the projects to literally rot. The generations between FDR and Reagan barely knew what homelessness was; now, nearly seven hundred thousand Americans, most of them hardly stereotypical street people, have no place to live at all.

So what have we bought with the boom's trillions, and with the inestimable power of government to shape the financial marketplace? Above all, the public and private sectors have joined to make it more and more costly to find a place to live. Shelter, whether to own or to rent, remains in most of the country far more expensive than it has been at any point in modern history, and it isn't just the poor who are feeling the pain. An early 2008 Zogby poll found that 43 percent of Americans were spending more than 30 percent of their income on housing—which put them above HUD's recommended maximum—and that nearly one quarter would lose their home if they lost a job even briefly. One out of every nine working families is now spending more than half its income on their rent or mortgage. Americans are devoting more of their income to housing now than they have at any point since interest rates rocketed north of 15 percent in the early 1980s—the very crisis that persuaded Congress to unleash the mortgage securities market to do whatever it would. In other words, we're right back where we started, except in far deeper debt.

Payment-option mortgages—used by an astonishing three fourths of California borrowers in 2005—provided a brief illusion of power to purchase. As you'll recall, these are loans with minimum required payments, just like on credit cards, amounting to far less than even the interest owed. That excess unpaid debt gets added to the principal, and minimum monthly payments automatically hike when that amount exceeds 15 percent or so of the amount of the original loan. Lenders loved payment-option mortgages (option ARMs are a subspecies) because even when they just collected the minimum amount due they could, legally, claim on their balance sheets that they'd received the full amount of principal and interest owed for that month. At Washington Mutual, half of all new mortgages in 2005 were payment-option loans. Most borrowers have only made the lowest possible payments, so a new wave of foreclosures is due in 2009, as substantially higher bills kick in.

What payment-option and interest-only mortgages really did was heave home prices even farther upward by lowering monthly payments, and in the scheme of things values still haven't come down all that much. In L.A., following a nearly one-third drop in real estate prices, the typical home still costs nine times a typical family's income. In New York, it's seven years of income (in Queens, twelve years). Oh, you can still find a city that lives by the old limits of sane borrowing, three times a family's annual earnings: Kansas City.

The Case-Shiller Index tracks the rise and fall of real estate values over time based on the resale prices of existing homes in twenty metropolitan areas, combining mansions, ranches, shacks, and any other freestanding home into one giant snapshot of housing prices. In 2000, Case-Shiller set the index at 100 points. In the fall of 2008 it stood at almost 155 points, after peaking near 190. The index has been tracking some cities since 1987. Working back from the 2000 baseline, Chicago started out at 55; in 2008, a decline had brought the index there down to—horrors—150. Boston rose from 70 to 162 (peak was 182); Seattle from 58 to 175, following a high point of 192. In all three cities in the fall of 2008, prices were dipping, not imploding, despite buyers' persisting difficulties in qualifying for mortgages.

Numbers from the National Association of Realtors show the same thing: In the summer of 2008, just one third or fewer of Californians could afford to buy an entry-level home in L.A. or Oakland, never mind in the more exclusive parts of the state. At the boom's peak, home prices there leaped upward by 20 to 30 percent every *year*, yet a 30 percent drop between 2007 and 2008 was decried—mostly by those who build, sell, or finance homes, and were seeking government intervention to support the real estate market—as a calamity.

The areas that have seen outright price collapses were mostly brand-new bubble towns, some of which you've gotten to know in this book. To Cape Coral, Sacramento, and Phoenix add Las Vegas and California's Inland Empire and Stockton. At the other extreme stumbled rickety neighborhoods in Cleveland, Atlanta, Pittsburgh, and elsewhere whose no longer desirable bungalows, the Norma Desmonds of real estate, served as mere conduits for mortgage-flipping schemes. Most other neighborhoods and parts of the country have settled into far less precipitous declines in home values, a threat only to those who bought or refinanced near the peak, and borrowed most or all of the home's alleged value.

Granted, that's a whole lot of people swimming "underwater," owing more than their homes are worth—some twenty million borrowers. Based on trends at the end of 2008, analysts at Crédit Suisse predict an astonishing eight million foreclosures, or one in six of all homes with mortgages—most of them not financed with subprime loans. At the same time, even the most alarmist predictions of home price declines have them returning to levels well above where they were before the insanity started, and still far in excess of most families' budgets. In early 2009 home prices are back at their levels from mid-2004—that moment just before lenders went truly loony.

One would be forgiven for the impression that matters are much, much worse. They are—from the point of view of the financial markets. Gussied-up mortgage loans infected their securities pools, then the collateralized debt obligations made up of the riskiest parts of the pools, and from there a ganglia of derivative financial instruments and insurance funds, reaching through all these channels into the financial markets in every part of the world. A multitrillion-dollar industry sprang up that essentially made bets, through devices called credit default swaps, on how well mortgage securities would perform. The reason the entire construction ultimately collapsed in the fall of 2008 was actually quite straightforward: in tandem with higher than expected rates of foreclosure, the value of the collateral backing these transactions—the homes that you and I live in—was falling. That meant that the financial foundation that all of these credit deals relied on was melting as surely as a glacier in Antarctica.

This is why pleas from homeowners for more help avoiding foreclosure went nowhere in Washington, at least in the anxious months before President Obama entered the White House. Congress, the White House, and the banking and building industries instead united to do whatever they could to prop up the price of real estate—the best way to guarantee that the mortgage-based investment portfolios would maintain their value. Assuming that the strategies work, some underwater homeowners would benefit if a halt to the slide in home prices makes it possible once again for them to sell or refinance their homes.

The problem is that every intervention Congress has cooked up so far is doomed to make the problem worse, by turning to forces that led to the crisis in the first place: excessively huge loans backed by an insurance program that as much as invites the same old schemes to peddle unworthy real estate under dubious circumstances. The same objective remains: Encourage as many financial transactions, of every kind, as possible. Buy a home, refinance, trade up, repeat. For the painful hangover that followed the multitrillion-dollar debt binge, Congress anointed a hair-of-the-dog cure. At its behest, the FHA now insures home loans of $700,000, $1 million, and more, more than double what it previously permitted. Fannie Mae and Freddie Mac are being asked to purchase mortgages of similar heft.

To be fair, the dilemma is a doozy. If government doesn't act to prop up home prices, a collapse and resulting foreclosures will claim millions more victims and their neighborhoods. But if officials do successfully intervene to keep prices high—and so far, that is exactly what has happened—the cycle of extreme debt continues, and deepens. The unprecedentedly high price of real estate consigns future generations to the same trap, huffing on a treadmill of debt, or alternatively to a cure by inflation that hikes the price of everything else. In 1950, all the home mortgages in the nation amounted to 10 percent of the gross domestic product. It's now closer to 70 percent. The solution to the obscene amount of debt has been still more debt, in huge quantities.

But the even bigger challenge is one that hasn't seriously come up for discussion yet, because it lies beyond the interest groups, alliances, and habits of thinking that the real estate boom has forged so powerfully over time. And that is this: If Congress, the Treasury, and the Fed just attack the problem of the nation's debt addiction, they will have failed. Limiting the fallout from plummeting home prices and frozen credit markets simply stops the bleeding. It has nothing to do with setting a course for a saner future.

After all, the future is exactly what borrowing money is about building in the first place. The more freely the money flows, the grander the scale on which that new world can rise—and the more spectacularly it can fail. The idea that the private market can build a better world on its own met its end once homebuilders erected houses no one wants, needs, or can pay for, in swamps, farms, towers, and deserts; now that the streets of midwestern cities have been stripped of copper, wealth, and hope; now that the economic growth of the past decade has been revealed to be built in no small part on organized crime.

We owe it to ourselves to ask a very basic question:

Where do we want to live?

The next time treasuries and bankers toss trillions into the air, what kind of world should that money build?

Once upon a time, a president posed exactly that challenge. The answer was the right one for his era long ago, and perilously wrong for this one.

By the time it was possible to utter the words "President Obama" it was already a cliché to invoke President Franklin Delano Roosevelt as a model for action in our own troubled times. But if anything, it's important to look more deeply into why the New Deal's response to the mortgage crisis of its moment proved so successful. The Home Owners' Loan Corporation and its million-home refinancing project were just the beginning. Roosevelt's New Deal brain trust didn't just remake the nation's financial system; their Federal Housing Administration also literally transformed the American landscape.

Invariably, the subdivisions insured by the FHA were built on fields outside cities, and not just because the land was cheap and available. The good bureaucrats of the FHA, intent on protecting their insurance fund—the risky lending and then mass foreclosures of the Great Depression were very much on their minds—developed a vast array of rules, regulations, guidelines, and suggestions that dictated the way most Americans would live for the next hundred years. The head of the FHA's team of land planners compared it to a life insurer deciding whether a customer was robust enough to cover.

Those same guidelines encouraged the FHA's appraisers to refuse to authorize loans in many city neighborhoods, until Congress opened the floodgates in 1968. But the FHA's rules for what it *would* insure turned out to be even more enduringly influential. As a condition of its support, the FHA kept a keen eye on every aspect of how the new houses were built, and more than anything else where they were built and what those places looked like.

Curvy streets and culs-de-sac, without sidewalks, on flat plains; houses located apart from places to shop or work, on lots at least fifty feet wide; easy access to highways; the careful placement of oaks, maples, and elms—the U.S. government deemed all of these features and much more desirable assets for the new American suburb, as spelled out in a series of pamphlets distributed to builders hoping to qualify for its financial backing. Federal planners insisted on zoning codes, still a novelty in much of the country, and deed restrictions—above all, "No building shall be erected on a lot except one detached single family dwelling and a one- or two-car garage."

Private industry built the suburbs, but it did it on terms dictated by the U.S. government. Three-quarters of a century later, developers who think of FDR as a figure a few inches to the right of Fidel Castro continue to build their subdivisions by the rules set by government planners from the 1930s, not because they are still required to but because the resulting landscape became so familiar that it is now hard for Americans to imagine living differently.

In the twenty-first century, we're still following the same script that a team of car salesmen, real estate appraisers, and social workers wrote decades ago in response to circumstances utterly different from our own now. Then, slums were the urgent housing problem facing much of the nation—too many people crammed into too little space, and unable to afford to live better. The majority of Americans were renters and lived in cities, too often under unacceptable circumstances. Today, the success of the New Deal's response has left no choice but to deal with its consequences, as suburbia sprawls beyond sustainable limits.

If there's a place to begin to redeem something positive from the mortgage crisis and its fallout in the financial markets, it's that the American people again have the power, for the first time in generations, to make sure the places where we live meet our needs, now and into the future. After all, we the taxpayers are now direct stakeholders in the mortgage machine. In the process of seeking a fair and safe return on investment, that money should work for some greater good, too.

In the fall of 2008, the federal government took over Fannie Mae and Freddie Mac after declining home prices and shareholder panic rapidly drained the two organizations of billions in assets and put them at risk of insolvency. With the collapse of the private mortgage financing market, the feds also expanded the FHA and gave it a mandate to refinance mortgage loans for homeowners behind on their payments. And of course the U.S. Treasury reluctantly committed to feed hundreds of billions of dollars into the nation's biggest financial institutions, to keep the lending business alive.

Those moves put a heady lot of power in the hands of the White House and members of Congress. Before another day of reckoning comes, they had better stage an intervention, and ask what the FHA's appraisers did back in the 1930s. What makes a place work? How do we know a home in that location will still be worth something in year twenty of a thirty-year mortgage? Will that little town really be able to run a sewer line all the way out there? Build that school it promised? Who the hell would live *there*?

Buyers in newly built communities (what people used to call subdivisions) imagined a better future there, based on CGI renderings and the power of hope. Those who packaged and rated the mortgage securities looked only cursorily at *where*, literally, the loans they were buying were coming from— and even then, just to make sure they didn't include too many properties from any one state.

Midmeltdown, former Fed chair Alan Greenspan articulated that place-blind sense of the world as he sat in his Washington office, "his desk, couch, coffee table and conference table . . . strewn with printouts of spreadsheets and multicolored charts of housing starts, foreclosures and population trends siphoned from government and trade association sources," reported *Washington Post* columnist David Wessel. (Greenspan frequently pored over such documents in his bathtub.) No wonder, then, that Greenspan, predicting a turnaround for real estate prices in the coming year, compared housing to copper and other commodities. "The grain markets can have a huge excess of corn or wheat, but the price never goes to zero," explained the maestro. "It'll stabilize at some level of prices where people are willing to hold the excess inventory. We have little history, but the same thing is surely true in housing as well."

Excess inventory? Willing to hold? Surely Greenspan has never seen for himself just how many of those hundreds of thousands of unwanted houses are spurned for good reasons, like rotten ears of corn. Never mind that most people possess one and only one house, which they will have to sell when better job opportunities beckon. Or that the value of that house has everything to do with that of its neighbors' and relatively little to do with those from the next town or county over. The man who freed the mortgage securities market to its wildest tendencies looks at housing as an interchangeable commodity unmoored from where it sits—a fatally erroneous assumption, and one that his commodity-trader mind never let go of.

But the rest of us have to. Simply to protect their own financial interests, the guardians of the public mortgage funds—the FHA, Fannie Mae, Freddie Mac, the IRS—will have to find ways to encourage building and settlement that's sustainable in the long term, not just next year or the one after that. After all these years of making universal homeownership a national cause, government policies have to come full circle and once again build places worth living in.

That means favoring areas that have already been developed, have the potential for public transportation, have nearby shops and schools. If a study sponsored by the Federal Transit Administration is correct, building homes in areas like this will actually be less expensive than in sprawly twentieth-century suburbs. Any developer is free to build wherever he wants—but don't expect taxpayers to help make it happen. This one maneuver, far more than any refinancing program, will protect American homeowners and their property values in the long run.

For three decades doctrine held that government has to get out of the way of private business. But the legacy of the FHA shows that targeted nudges and a helpful hand can yield enormous benefits—for business most of all. Ironically, that's a source of our current troubles. After enjoying massive government support for the past seventy-five years, the industries that build, finance, and sell homes are not about to alter a winning formula.

Real estate interests constitute the most generous lobby in Washington. Four out of the ten biggest political action committees contributing to Congress build, sell, or fund homes. The finance and real estate industries together spent nearly $2 billion lobbying Congress in the decade that began in 1998 (with almost $300 million of that in 2007 alone). Since 1990 they've given nearly as much in congressional campaign contributions.

The real estate industry's lobbyists have helped create a climate in which the very possibility of government policies that might set reasonable limits on lending have been rendered unthinkable—a threat to recovery and the economy as a whole. The Federal Reserve's financial support of Bear Stearns's burial and other bailouts of 2008 only made official what had already become a standard expectation—that the role of government in real estate is to amplify the private sector as much as possible, through tax breaks and other financial backing, and, of course, ridiculously cheap money.

As President Obama and a strong Democratic congressional majority settle in, it's fair to hope for smart, strategic—heck, adult—boundaries on the financial services industry and on mortgage-making. They're starting against the current: Treasury's $700 billion bailout of major banks paddles in exactly the opposite direction by subsidizing economic activity at any cost, the same old formula that caused the crisis in the first place. As long as such lunatic corporate socialism continues, so will the insanity we've endured over the past decade—bogus appraisals, supersized houses, debt that's more available than jobs to pay it off.

It's simply not shocking that businesses would do anything within the moral order, and sometimes outside of it, to compete and to get what they want. That is the nature of what they do. Technology made it possible to disseminate the incentives out far from the seats of power, an infection spreading through networks of brokers, agents, appraisers, and so many others. What is astounding is that our own government not only allowed them to exercise their most atavistic tendencies, but in fact encouraged them, based on the childish belief that any excesses would correct themselves.

If there's a place to start rebuilding from, it lies in that vast well of entrepreneurial energy that the makers of the boom so effectively tapped. The securities markets were able to mobilize trillions of dollars to advance one of the worthiest of human ventures—creating comfortable places to live. Had the Reagan administration, Congress, and Wall Street not made mortgage securities such an excessively rewarding investment, much of that money would have gone into other parts of the economy to build many things the nation needs, such as businesses that employ people, bridges that stand strong, and retrofitting buildings to limit how much fuel they consume. Instead of constantly shuffling people around to bigger, better abodes on new frontiers, like it's perpetually 1950, the economy could give a boost to enterprises that make places worth remaining in.

As usual, Gale Cincotta came to that conclusion years before almost anyone else did, steered by her unshakable faith in experience and common sense. She spent her final years making increasingly pitched warnings against reckless and destructive mortgage lending, but by her fifty-fifth time testifying to Congress since the day she first described Austin's foreclosure agonies, she had much more to say than that.

At a 1996 hearing on Fannie Mae and Freddie Mac, she listened with some annoyance as other speakers called for the agencies to do even more lending to poor buyers and those who could not make down payments. That should have been exactly what Cincotta wanted to hear—after all, her group pushed for quotas in the first place. But turning every American into a homeowner or spouse or child of one was never the point. The objective was always making great places to live, where one could make a decent living, too.

Cincotta came to the Rayburn House Office Building, year after year, to sit next to men who seemed to only want to make numbers, even if that meant tearing down old places to build up new ones. She wanted to forge neighborhoods, where people had jobs, and lives, and shops, and families, and stayed and built ties far stronger than bricks.

When it was finally her turn to talk, after Larry Summers from Treasury and Nicolas Retsinas from HUD had finished praising the contributions of Fannie Mae and Freddie Mac—Retsinas also urged members of Congress to push them harder to reincarnate still more renters as homeowners—Cincotta shared her own vision of home. She described her family's two-flat on Meade Street, where four generations lived together—two in the apartment upstairs, and two down. The street was lined as far as the eye could see with homes just like hers, distinguished only by subtle stonework at the cornices. Cincotta always made sure to live in corner houses, so on the Wabansia Avenue side, rows of windows let in abundant light.

She wondered aloud why those in the room with her, leaders from government and from business, gathered again and again supposedly to talk about improving the places where people live, but always in the end worked to make homes and neighborhoods like hers expendable—to tear them down in a never-ending quest for more and more "housing starts" and all the economic activity that act represented. Construction, finance, sales, marketing—add them all together and real estate would come to employ one in every ten working Americans. "Maybe the reason we all meet so often on housing," she ventured, "is that it is a kind of a cover for what is really going on: We have to have the secondary market, 'too big to fail,' because the housing jobs are what we are operating on in this country." And she asked the men with her in the Rayburn House Office Building: Could Americans also make the best cars, the best refrigerators, the best switches?

The answer, now as then, is no. Year by year, hearing after hearing, willful acts of government had made the buying and selling of the places where we live so intensely rewarding that it would have been folly for anyone—banker, fund manager, family—to put their dollars in anything else. Like rats granted cocaine for pushing a lever, they had this one reward center stimulated so hard, and so often, that in the end, and as with any addiction, no other activities were possible. Even those necessary for survival.

Acknowledgments

Reconstituting decades of obscure and convoluted history into a single readable—dare I hope enjoyable?—story is a task for an obsessive, but even obsessives need a lot of help, and I got plenty. Many of those I interviewed are named in this book, but many others are not. I owe an otherwise unacknowledged debt to, among many others, Gordon Mayer, Gail Parson, Dan Immergluck, Calvin Bradford, Alicia Sheppard, Alan White, Kevin Byers, Rachel Glass Bratt, Kathleen Engel, Patricia McCoy, Gerald Gould, Irv Ackelsberg, Ellen Seidman, Joe Weisbord, Naomi Bayer, Richard Cincotta, Jeff Tumbarello, "Max" of SacRealStats, Alan Sokolow, Kathleen Keest, Susan Jaffe, Andrea Simakis, Ron Heckman, Clark Broida, Jean Gunner, Rochelle Nawrocki Gorey, Mike Hudson, Shel Trapp, David Mogavero, Mark Seifert, Dick Weiss, Ira Rheingold, Madeline Talbot, Mike Swain, Bruce Dorpalen, Mike Shea, Jane D'Arista, Steven Todd, Paula Miller, William J. Brennan Jr., the 30310 Mortgage Fraud Task Force, St. Marlo Fraud Coalition, Barbara Nelan, Dean Prigmore, Danny Pearlstein, David Goldberg, Scott Sommer, Allen Fishbein, Robert Kuttner, the staff of the Jimmy Carter Presidential Library, Susan Meiklejohn-Turner, Rex Bloomfield, Ray Pianka, Lucas Lechuga, Elizabeth Lee, Jared Beck, Paul Whalen, Peter Zalewski, Greg Paquin, Miroslava Chavez-Garcia, and Frank McKenna. An especially deep appreciation goes to the late Doris Dungey, aka "Tanta" of the blog Calculated Risk, who through her hilarious, literate, and mordant tutorials taught me and many others intricate and frightening truths about the mortgage business.

Anne Meyers gave me a home, office, and homemade applesauce in the Cleveland snow, while Sasha Abramsky, Julie Sze, and family opened the door in Sacramento. Fran and Bill Swirsky were gracious hosts, as always, in Florida. Sandra Strome and Toby Tate generously let me hole up in their basement to finish the book.

I could not have even begun this project without my amazing colleagues at *City Limits* magazine, above all Kemba Johnson, whose extraordinary exposé of fraud in HUD's 203(k) loan program first led me, as her editor, to examine the wild world of the mortgage business. Matt Pacenza read a draft of this book and provided invaluable feedback. Kat McGowan, Annia Ciezadlo, Kim Nauer, Kai Wright, and Debbie Nathan all challenged me to be the reporter I never knew I was.

Monika Bauerlein at *Mother Jones* had the foresight in 2005 to assign an article that became chapter 4 of this book.

My colleagues at the New York University Arthur L. Carter Journalism Institute were exceptionally supportive of this project, which brought me into the office far more often than my teaching commitments warranted. Special thanks are due to Brooke Kroeger, Susie Linfield, Rob Boynton, Cathleen Dullahan, and Pete Hamill. Besides encouragement, advice, and stories of life in the old Park Slope, Pete gave me that most precious gift, a place to write. Additional appreciation goes to the staff of the Bobst Library and Jack Brause Real Estate Library.

This book germinated during my year at Columbia University as a 2005–2006 Charles H. Revson fellow. Sudhir Venkatesh, Karen Vrostos, and my fellow fellows pushed me to learn from others' experiences as much as from books (and to chill out, always the hardest part). The proposal for *Our Lot* originated in Sam Freedman's excellent book seminar at the Columbia Graduate School of Journalism, where I learned how to be a better teacher as well as a better writer. Fellow seminarians Mable Haddock and Loren Fox provided especially helpful input on the proposal's development.

Brad Lander, Jessalee Landfried, Peg Fox, Janelle Farris, Vicki Weiner, and Madelaine Burkert at the Pratt Center for Community Development proved remarkably patient with my travel and writing schedule. This organization of urban planners and architects does kick-ass work to help New Yorkers influence planning and development for the betterment of their neighborhoods, and it's a privilege to work with and learn from such gifted and committed practitioners.

When I met my agent, Larry Weissman, I immediately knew I wanted to work with him, and not just because of his fantastic client list. Larry loves books and injecting them into the world of action and ideas. He and his partner in life and work, Sascha Alper, have been thoughtful readers and persistent instigators.

At Bloomsbury, an immense thank you to Kathy Belden for sharp and sensitive editing and to Colin Dickerman and Karen Rinaldi for their enthusiastic commitment to this project.

My mom and stepdad, Helen and Daniel Rothstein, have been extraordinarily encouraging, supportive, and faithful, even when Dan, a savings and loan executive, has disagreed with my views on the worthiness of mortgage-backed securities. My late father, Ephraim Katz, taught me how to prevail as a writer committed to getting the story right.

More than anyone, my husband, Bryan Swirsky, has been there for me and for this book. Our daughter, Thalia, was born just before I embarked, and I've watched book and child grow up together. Bryan's patience, flexibility, compassion, knife-edged views on human behavior, and willingness to set limits were all essential ingredients in this book.

GLOSSARY

Adjustable-rate mortgage (ARM): A home mortgage whose interest rate rises or falls at predetermined intervals. The amount of increase or decrease upon *reset* depends on financial market conditions and is calculated based on a formula that differs from mortgage to mortgage. Many ARMs' interest rates reset at six-month intervals and are tied to the interest rate at which financial institutions borrow from one another.

Alt-A: Short for "Alternative-A," Alt-A *mortgage* loans were made to borrowers whose *credit scores* qualified them for *prime* mortgages, but under much less stringent application standards. With most mortgages, applicants have to prove that they have the ability to make their monthly payments. In the case of Alt-As, borrowers did not have to provide complete proof, or in some cases any; they could also borrow much more than they otherwise might be able to. Depending on the mortgage, they did not have to document their income, could avoid down payments by taking out multiple loans amounting to the entire appraised value of the mortgaged property (see *piggyback loans*), or could have sizable other debts they were obligated to pay off.

Amortization: The calculus by which a mortgage is paid off over a period of time—most commonly thirty years, but sometimes in as many as forty or fifty or as few as ten years. Amortization can take many forms, but typically mortgageholders pay off loans in monthly intervals, with early payments consisting largely of interest (to guarantee those payments regardless of whether the loan eventually goes into *default*) and later ones consisting primarily of principal. See also *negative amortization.*

Appraisal: The process through which the value of a piece of real estate is determined. Appraisals determine the putative worth of the *collateral* on which lenders make home loans, and therefore the amount of money that can be borrowed and the underlying value of *mortgage-backed securities* made up of those loans.

Appraiser: Appraisals are conducted by these specialists, who are supposed to have extensive knowledge of local real estate markets. However, qualifications for entering the field vary from state to state and can be quite lax. Appraisers depend on *mortgage brokers* and lenders for work and frequently feel pressure to give inordinately high *appraisals* as a condition of receiving future jobs. High appraisals make a property appear more valuable than it really is, which allows borrowers to qualify for loans and properties they otherwise might not be able to obtain.

ARM: See *adjustable-rate mortgage.*

B&C lending: Every lender dealing in *subprime* loans developed its own grading system, and most assigned them a variation of the letter "B" or "C," in contrast with "A," *prime* loans. Some less risky subprime loans were also classified "A-minus."

Collateral: The property against which a *mortgage* is made. In the event a borrower cannot pay a mortgage, the lender is entitled to file for *foreclosure* and may obtain the proceeds from an auction or other resale of the collateral.

Collateralized debt obligation (CDO): A security made up of pieces of other securities composed of loans, including home mortgages, credit card debt, and car loans. CDOs frequently included *tranches* of *mortgage-backed securities* that posed high risks of nonpayment; insurance on the CDOs made it possible for these packages of toxic loans to receive high grades from the *ratings agencies.*

Community Reinvestment Act (CRA): A law passed by Congress in 1977 that requires federally regulated financial institutions to meet the credit needs of the communities in which they hold deposits. CRA did not, however, require banks to make loans to unqualified customers.

Conforming loan: A *mortgage* whose characteristics qualify it for purchase by *Fannie Mae* or *Freddie Mac.*

Conventional loan: See *conforming loan.* Generally refers to a fixed-rate mortgage paid off over thirty years, made with a 20 percent *down payment* and not backed by *Federal Housing Administration* or Veterans Administration insurance.

Credit score: A number reflecting an assessment of a consumer's reliability in paying back debt, following a system propagated by Fair Isaac Company, or FICO. A FICO credit score reflects payment histories on many kinds of debt, including credit cards and auto loans as well as home mortgages. To qualify for a *prime* home mortgage in the mid-2000s, borrowers typically needed a FICO score of at least 620 (in many cases higher), on a scale of 300 to 850.

Deed: The legal certification of ownership of a property.

Default: The ultimate failure to pay one's loan obligations.

Delinquency: The failure to pay one's *mortgage.* Typically mortgages are determined to be delinquent if a borrower is thirty days behind on payment. After payment is sixty or ninety days late a lender will then send a "notice of default," indicating the terms a borrower must meet to prevent a *foreclosure* filing.

Down payment: The amount of cash contributed by a property's buyer toward its purchase. From World War II until the 1990s, down payments of at least 20 percent were standard. Home purchasers who put down less than 20 percent usually must buy *private mortgage insurance* to compensate for the greater risk of losses to the lender. The *Federal Housing Administration* insurance program allows down payments as low as 3 percent.

Equity: The portion of a property's value owned outright by the holder of its deed. Through a *home equity loan* an owner may obtain cash based on this value.

Fannie Mae (Federal National Mortgage Association): A *government-sponsored enterprise* that purchases *mortgages* from lenders, with the objective of ensuring that funding is consistently available for home loans across the United States. Beginning in the 1980s, Fannie Mae also packaged and sold *mortgage-backed securities* based on the mortgages it buys. Created by the U.S. government in 1938, Fannie Mae was sold to private shareholders in 1968. Forty years later, declining property values (which decimated the value of the mortgages it owned) combined with the collapse of *mortgage-backed securities* Fannie Mae had purchased in great quantity from other *issuers* left the company at risk of insolvency. In 2008 Fannie Mae's government regulator took over its operations, along with those of *Freddie Mac.*

Federal Housing Administration (FHA): A division of the *U.S. Department of Housing and Urban Development* (HUD) that insures home mortgages under a special program that makes mortgages available to those who might otherwise not be able to obtain them, usually at favorable interest rates. The Veterans Administration (VA) runs a similar program for those who have served in the military.

FHA: See *Federal Housing Administration.*

Flipping: The practice of buying real estate cheaply and reselling quickly at significant gain, typically with the aid of inflated *appraisals* and *mortgages* requiring minimal documentation (see *no-doc loan* and *low-doc loan*). In many flipping schemes the buyer—known as the "straw man"—is paid a fee for submitting a mortgage application using his name and Social Security number.

Foreclosure: The legal proceeding through which a creditor with a claim on a property goes about repossessing it from the holder of the *deed.* In states with "judicial foreclosure," a court must be involved in the transaction. In states with "nonjudicial foreclosure," no court involvement is necessary and the process typically happens much more quickly.

Freddie Mac (Federal Home Loan Mortgage Corporation): A *government-sponsored enterprise* created soon after the federal government's sale of *Fannie*

Mae to private shareholders, Freddie Mac was originally charged with buying mortgages from *savings and loan* institutions but came to rival Fannie Mae in its scope of operations. In the 1990s Freddie Mac was more open than Fannie Mae to experimenting with *subprime* lending. Like Fannie Mae, Freddie Mac was taken over by its regulators at the new Federal Housing Finance Agency, a division of *HUD*, in 2008.

Ginnie Mae (Government National Mortgage Association): A division of the U.S. Department of Housing and Urban Development, Ginnie Mae is in effect the remaining portion of *Fannie Mae* that was not sold to private shareholders. It is charged with buying loans generated through the *Federal Housing Administration* mortgage insurance program, and it advanced the use of *mortgage-backed securities* to finance mortgages for single-family homes.

Government-sponsored enterprise (GSE): A term describing Fannie Mae (and later, Freddie Mac) following its privatization in 1968, and describing its unique status as a profit-making company, regulated by the federal government, operating under a charter requiring it to make mortgages available "for low- and moderate-income families." The GSEs benefit from unique access to low-cost funds from the U.S. Treasury.

Home equity loan: A personal loan that relies on a home's value as *collateral*, and typically amounts to a modest portion of the property's appraised value. A home equity line of credit works on a similar principle, but instead of a lump sum provides access to loan funds as needed up to a specified amount. See also *second mortgage*.

Home Mortgage Disclosure Act (HMDA): A 1975 federal law that obligates all home lenders to publicly report basic information on their mortgages, including the size of the loans, locations of the properties, and demographic information about borrowers.

Homeowners Equity Protection Act (HOEPA): A 1994 federal law that sought to protect consumers from exploitative loans, including those with high interest rates and excessive fees. HOEPA gave the Federal Reserve extensive new power to regulate mortgage lending, which the Fed neglected to exercise.

Home Owners' Loan Corporation (HOLC): A federal agency established in 1933 to provide long-term, low-interest home *mortgages* to homeowners facing *foreclosure*. HOLC ultimately *refinanced* more than one million loans, about 10 percent of which ended up in foreclosure despite the aid.

HUD: See *U.S. Department of Housing and Urban Development.*

Interest-only mortgage: A home *mortgage* that for a specified period of time—often ten years—requires repayments of interest but not principal. After that period expires the mortgage *recasts* and the borrower must pay back principal as well as interest. Many interest-only mortgages are also *ARMs.*

Issuer: Any entity that packages a bond or a security for sale, including *mortgage-backed securities.* The securities may be issued by a *government-sponsored enterprise*, investment bank, *mortgage lender*, or other financial institution.

Jumbo mortgage: A *mortgage* in excess of the maximum size that Fannie Mae or Freddie Mac is legally permitted to purchase, $417,000 (as of early 2009).

Lien: A legal claim against a property. Typically the primary lien belongs to the mortgage lender, meaning that in case the borrower *defaults* the lender is entitled to begin *foreclosure* proceedings.

Low-doc loan: A *mortgage* made based on limited documentation from a borrower. Depending on what a lender permits, applicants might omit information about their total amount of debt, their employment, or earnings, or savings, or other details that might reveal their ability to repay the mortgage.

Mortgage: A pledge of property by a borrower to a lender, to secure a promise of repayment of a loan. Most homes are purchased with the aid of a mortgage, typically paid over a period of thirty years, though mortgages of fifteen and forty years also are common. The term derives from a combination of French and Germanic origins—*mort*, meaning death, and *gage*, a pledge.

Mortgage-backed security: An agglomeration of *mortgages* purchased and packaged for resale to investors. Known in the financial industry as "MBS," the pool of mortgages is structured into *tranches* of varying levels of risk and return, with investors in the top, low-risk tranches fully paid first, and those holding stakes in the lowest, high-risk tranches last. The highest-risk tranches were frequently repackaged into *collateralized debt obligations.*

Mortgage broker: A salesperson who sells home *mortgages* in exchange for a fee on each transaction (see *yield spread premium*). Most brokers sell mortgages from multiple lenders and bear little responsibility in the event a mortgage they sell *defaults*. Because they are paid for each loan they close, brokers have an incentive to sell loans that a borrower may not be able to repay.

Mortgage lender: A generic term for a company—distinct from institutions such as banks or *savings and loans* that hold deposits from customers—that creates and markets home loan products under one or more brand names. Mortgage lenders sell their loans through their own sales representatives, *mortgage brokers*, or both. Mortgage lenders obtain funds by reselling their loans to investors, to the *government-sponsored enterprises Fannie Mae* or *Freddie Mac,* or to a private *issuer* of *mortgage-backed security* pools.

Negative amortization: The condition of having the total amount owed on a mortgage grow over time instead of shrink. Many mortgage products that offered initial low payments set up borrowers for negative amortization; see *option ARM.*

Negative equity: A homeowner with negative equity owes more than a property is worth. An owner in a state of negative equity cannot refinance a *mortgage* or sell a home without adding cash of their own to the transaction. Colloquially, they are known as "underwater." A homeowner with negative equity in a state of *negative amortization* is at extreme risk of going into *default.*

NINJA loans: "No income, no job, (no) assets" describes an exceptionally risky *Alt-A* mortgage.

No-doc loan: A mortgage that requires no documentation from a borrower reflecting income, existing debts, or other information vital to assessing the likelihood that he or she will be able to repay the loan.

Option ARM: Also known as a "pick a payment" mortgage, this is an *adjustable-rate mortgage* that gives borrowers the option of making a minimum monthly payment, much like that on a credit card bill, amounting to far less than the actual amount of interest and principal owed for that month. If the minimum payment is less than even the interest owed, the loan enters *negative amortization.*

Piggyback loans: Mortgages taken out for the sole purpose of covering down payment costs for purchasing a property. See also *silent second.*

Predatory lending: A broadly defined term encompassing loans, usually *subprime,* whose terms or sales tactics set up borrowers for *default.* Common characteristics of predatory loans include excessively high interest rates, large up-front fees, *prepayment penalties* that make it prohibitively expensive to refinance into a more affordable loan, and substantial "balloon payments" due several years into the mortgage.

Prepayment penalty: A charge, usually amounting to several thousand dollars, to a borrower who sells a property or refinances a loan before its term is up. Prepayment penalties were a common feature of *subprime* mortgages and made it difficult for borrowers to secure new loans with lower interest rates.

Prime mortgage: See *conventional loan.*

Private mortgage insurance (PMI): An insurance policy that must be purchased by most borrowers who make low *down payments* and are therefore more likely than others to *default* (because they have little money of their own at stake) or achieve *negative equity.* The insurance compensates the lender in case of default.

Ratings agency: A firm that evaluates the soundness of bonds and "fixed income" securities—including *mortgage-backed securities* and *collateralized debt obligations*—for sale to investors. Moody's, Standard & Poor's, and

Fitch Ratings are the three major ratings agencies. Each uses a slightly different scale, but AAA generally refers to a top-rated security or *tranche.*

Recast: A change in payment obligations for *interest-only, negative-amortization,* and other mortgages in which initial payments cover less than the average actual monthly cost of a loan over its scheduled lifetime. At a predetermined interval (for interest-only mortgages), or once the amount of unpaid principal has accumulated to a predetermined fraction of the total amount owed (for *option ARM* mortgages), the minimum monthly payment "recasts" to a higher amount, putting the borrower back on pace to pay off the loan in full.

Refinancing: Also known as a "refi," refinancing is the transaction in which a borrower who already has a mortgage on a property obtains a new mortgage to replace the first loan, usually because the new mortgage has a lower interest rate than the old one. Many consumers took advantage of "cash out" refinancings that tapped home *equity;* by simply signing up for refinancing and paying associated fees, they could obtain a check for tens of thousands of dollars.

Reset: A scheduled change in interest rate on an *adjustable-rate mortgage.*

Savings and loans (S&Ls): Local financial institutions that traditionally have accepted deposits from individuals and small businesses and lent out those funds to area homebuyers seeking home *mortgages.* Until the early 1980s, S&Ls made the majority of home *mortgages* in the United States.

Second mortgage: A homeowner whose property is valued at a much higher level than his or her *mortgage* can take out an additional mortgage on the property, often at a higher interest rate, reflecting the greater risk that the second lender is taking on (since it is typically in line behind the first mortgage to get paid back in the event of *foreclosure*). Many homeowners have used second mortgages for home improvement. A *home equity loan* is a type of second mortgage.

Secondary Mortgage Market Enhancement Act: A 1984 federal law that facilitated the creation and sale of *mortgage-backed securities* by private financial firms. Congress permitted the use of *ratings agencies* to grade *tranches* of *mortgage-backed securities* offered for sale.

Section 8: The former (and still frequently used) name for *HUD* Housing Choice Vouchers, used by hundreds of thousands of low-income tenants to help pay rent. In urban areas, many real estate investors hoped to attract Section 8 tenants, whose vouchers enable them to pay much higher rents than other renters. HUD encouraged Section 8 voucher holders to purchase homes.

Short sale: A real estate transaction in which a lender agrees to allow a property owner to sell a home for less than the amount owed on the *mortgage.* A lender may agree to a short sale if it is clear that the property is destined for *foreclosure* and is worth much less than the amount owed.

Silent second: A *second mortgage*, usually taken out in lieu of a down payment, and of which the lender on the primary loan is unaware. (See also *piggyback loans.*)

Stated-income loan: A form of *low-doc loan* or *no-doc loan*, a stated-income mortgage is based on a borrower's assertions regarding past and present earnings.

Subprime: A term loosely encompassing mortgages that are demonstrably too risky to qualify for purchase by Fannie Mae or Freddie Mac and whose interest rates and fees are usually higher than those for *prime* loans. While subprime mortgages were typically made to borrowers with relatively low credit scores, the term applies to the loans, not the borrowers.

Teaser rate: An interest rate on a home mortgage that starts out at a relatively low level for two or three years but is then scheduled to jump sharply upward for the duration of the loan, often at an *adjustable rate.* The most common teaser rate loans were known as "2-28"s and "3-27"s for their years of duration—two or three years of low interest followed by twenty-eight or twenty-seven years of high interest. Borrowers were frequently (mis)informed by mortgage brokers that they would be able to refinance into a new low-interest loan before the interest rate *reset.*

Tranche: A segment of a *mortgage-backed security* packaged to be sold at a specified rating and rate of return. Tranches are arranged on a hierarchical list; those nearest to the top receive higher ratings from *ratings agencies* and relatively low rates of return and are paid back first, while the lowest have lower ratings and higher rates of return, reflecting the fact that they are last in line to be paid (and may not be paid in full).

U.S. Department of Housing and Urban Development (HUD): The federal agency that governs and runs programs facilitating access to housing and homeownership, including the *Federal Housing Administration.* HUD also is the overseer (and currently conservator) of *government-sponsored enterprises Fannie Mae* and *Freddie Mac* and administers assistance to renters, including *Section 8* vouchers and subsidies for public housing.

Yield spread premium: An additional payment granted to *mortgage brokers* who succeed in selling a *mortgage* with a higher interest rate than the borrower in fact qualifies for. While critics and some courts have maintained that yield spread premiums are improper kickbacks to brokers who exploit clients' ignorance, they remain a legal and prevalent form of compensation to mortgage brokers.

NOTES

CHAPTER 1: ALMOST LIKE A CONSPIRACY

1   *Huddling in the dorm room*: Shel Trapp, *Dynamics of Organizing: Building Power by Developing the Human Spirit* (Chicago: self-published, 2005), p. 51; Trapp interview.

1   *She always brought two bottles to organizing meetings*: Trapp, *Dynamics of Organizing,* p. 27; Trapp interview.

2   *vowed to crack down on the mortgage companies*: George Bliss and Chuck Neubauer, "FHA Scandal Enmeshed in Red Tape," *Chicago Tribune,* June 23, 1975.

3   *"may change the very physical, mental and moral fibre"*: "The Home as an Investment," Better Homes for America, Plan Book for Demonstration Week October 9 to 14, 1922.

3   *hundreds of thousands of copies of a book*: John M. Gries and James S. Taylor, *How to Own Your Home: A Handbook for Prospective Home Owners* (Washington, D.C.: U.S. Government Printing Office, 1923).

4   *a vast marketplace*: The securities consisted mostly of loans for constructing apartment buildings. In 1933, the multibillion-dollar market in mortgage-backed securities collapsed, leaving hundreds of thousands of investors, many of them of modest means, wiped out.

4   *real estate prices hurled upward*: William W. Bartlett, *Mortgage-Backed Securities: Products, Analysis, Trading* (New York: New York Institute of Finance, 1989), p. 5.

4   *GM started its own loan company*: Lendol G. Calder, *Financing the American Dream: A Cultural History of Consumer Credit* (Princeton, N.J.: Princeton University Press, 1999), p. 192.

5   *could sell almost anything on installment*: Julian Goldman, *Prosperity and Consumer Credit* (New York: Harper & Brothers, 1930), p. 10.

5   *consumers were $7 billion in the hole*: Roland I. Robinson, "The Downward Course of Consumer Credit," *Journal of Marketing* 7, no. 4 (April 1943): 346.

5   *$30 billion in mortgage debt*: Leo Grebler, David M. Blank, and Louis Winnick, *Capital Formation in Residential Real Estate: Trends and Prospects* (Princeton, N.J.: National Bureau of Economic Research, Princeton University Press, 1956).

5   *Most just refused*: Henry Beaman, Survey of Foreclosure Operations, Home Owners' Loan Corporation, 1937.

6   *Roosevelt administration called for private financiers*: Warren B. Farb, Douglas L. Bendt, and Robert A. Eprile, "The Role of the Federal National Mortgage Association in the Secondary Mortgage Market" (Congressional Research Service, 1976).

7   *Real Estate Appraisers' manual*: *Real Estate Appraisal: Basic Principles, Methods, and Techniques* (American Institute of Real Estate Appraisers, 1971).

7   *"not social or welfare agencies"*: Statement of William B. O'Connell on behalf of the U.S. League of Savings Associations, to the Senate Committee on Banking, Housing, and Urban Affairs, May 7, 1975.

7   *fewer than 3 percent of all the FHA-insured loans*: Correspondence of HUD secretary George Romney to the House Committee on Banking and Currency, July 31, 1970.

7   *Chicago Freedom Movement staged demonstrations*: Alexander von Hoffman, "Like Fleas on a Tiger? A History of the Open Housing Movement" (Cambridge, Mass.: Joint Center for Housing Studies, Harvard University, 1998), pp. 33–34.

8   *"We must create and fortify a new spirit"*: Charles H. Percy, "A New Dawn for Our Cities," as published in the *Congressional Record*, October 17, 1966, pp. 27258–27260.

8   *"the Conservative Answer to Public Housing"*: William F. Buckley Jr., "The Percy Plan," *Washington Daily News*, October 12, 1966.

8   *he was running against Richard Nixon*: Tom Wicker, "In the Nation: Counting Votes Before They Hatch," *New York Times*, March 16, 1967; see also "The Soul of the Elephant," ibid., April 30, 1967.

8   *unanimous Republican front*: Remarks by Senator Charles Percy, *Congressional Record*, April 29, 1975.

9   *Johnson administration insisted*: Hearings of Subcommittee on Housing and Urban Affairs, March 1968.

9   *if it was literally falling down*: Philip N. Brownstein, assistant secretary-commissioner, Federal Housing Administration, "Memo to All Approved Mortgagees," August 2, 1968. For the previous year, this exemption from the appraisal rules had applied only "in areas where riots or other civil disorders have occurred." In the Housing and Urban Development Act of 1968, the law that created HUD, the exemption widened to "all older, declining areas without regard to riots or disorders."

9   *agents made sure homeowners got the message*: Trapp, pp. 16–17.

10   *FHA's staff of real estate appraisers*: HUD employees were well represented among the more than 470 participants eventually convicted nationwide in connection with the

FHA insurance scandal; they included appraisers, inspectors, managers, and section chiefs. U.S. Department of Justice report, July 10, 1975, cited in remarks by Senator Adlai Stevenson, hearing of the Senate Committee on Banking, Housing, and Urban Affairs, July 14, 1975.

10 *the government agency was pooling FHA-insured mortgages:* Bartlett, *Mortgage-Backed Securities,* p. 12.

10 *They hounded real estate agents:* Amanda I. Seligman, *Block by Block: Neighborhoods and Public Policy on Chicago's West Side* (Chicago: University of Chicago Press, 2005), p. 197.

11 *"It's a plan":* Perry L. Weed, "Urban Activism: The Fight to Stem the Blight," *Chicago Tribune,* April 23, 1972.

12 *These "thrifts" had originally emerged:* David Mason, *From Building and Loans to Bail Outs: A History of the American Savings and Loan Industry, 1831–1995* (New York: Cambridge University Press, 2004), p. 214.

12 *Researchers from Northwestern University:* Darel E. Grothaus in collaboration with Roger Dennis, Keith Gordon, and Mike Romansky, "Disinvestment by Savings and Loan Associations and the Branching Policies of the Federal Home Loan Bank Board," Urban-Suburban Investment Study Group, Center for Urban Affairs, Northwestern University. See also "Mortgage Patterns in Chicago," National People's Action on Housing, exhibit in testimony of Gale Cincotta to the U.S. Senate Committee on Banking, Housing, and Urban Affairs.

12 *"We are not asking for handouts":* Home Mortgage Disclosure Act of 1975, Hearings Before the Senate Committee on Banking, Housing, and Urban Affairs, May 5–8, 1975.

14 *sold FNMA to shareholders for $216 million:* Harry R. Bivens, *Background and History of the Federal National Mortgage Association* (Washington, D.C.: Federal National Mortgage Association, 1969).

14 *Fannie Mae still wasn't . . . buying:* Statement of Darel Grothaus, staff director, Mayor's Reinvestment Task Force, Seattle, to the Senate Subcommittee on Banking, Housing, and Urban Affairs, December 9, 1976. Grothaus noted that Fannie Mae continued to use 1930s-era standards for determining the risks of urban home loans, guidelines premised on the explicit assumption that all neighborhoods will eventually deteriorate and become economically worthless.

15 *looking to increase its volume: Secondary Market Reporter,* November 16, 1976. When it privatized Fannie Mae, Congress required home lenders that sold mortgages to the company to purchase its stock, with the result that the majority of shares were held by banks, savings and loans, and other financial institutions.

15 *earnings had been doubling and tripling:* Statement of Lorraine Legg, Boise Cascade, to the Senate Subcommittee on Banking, Housing, and Urban Affairs, December 9, 1976.

16 *"Lewie had this spiel about building homes":* Michael Lewis, *Liar's Poker: Rising Through the Wreckage of Salomon Brothers* (New York: W.W. Norton, 1989), p. 113.

16   *turning them into a security*: Lewis Ranieri, "The Origins of Securitization, Sources of Growth, and Future Potential," in *A Primer on Securitization*, ed. Leon T. Kendall (Cambridge, Mass.: MIT Press, 1986), p. 31.

17   *Salomon's biggest moneymaker by far*: Lewis, *Liar's Poker*, p. 109.

17   *pump vast sums of new money*: Laura Mulcahy, "White House Pushing Private Sector's Banking Role," *American Banker*, May 1, 1983.

18   *should become entirely private corporations*: "The Report of the President's Commission on Housing" (Washington, D. C.: President's Commission on Housing, 1982).

18   *He met with the President's Commission*: "The Whiz Kid of Wall Street's Home Mortgage Boom," *BusinessWeek*, June 11, 1984.

18   *carving up the pools into numerous slices*: S&Ls were hungry for short-term commitments, insulated from fluctuations in interest rates and other unpredictable future events that posed undesirable risks to their balance sheets. The longer-term parts of the pool would be marketed to pension funds and life insurance companies—almost entirely untapped sources of new money for home loans. Reagan hadn't even been in office two weeks when his Department of Labor declared that retirement funds were free for the first time to invest in mortgage-backed securities.

19   *Ranieri set about putting together*: Ranieri, "Origins of Securitization," p. 37.

19   *no longer would the U.S. government exclusively manage the market*: In 1974, as Ginnie Mae entered its fourth year of packaging FHA-insured mortgages as securities, Congress authorized the agency to also make securities out of other mortgages. Wall Street investment banks, including Salomon Brothers, sold these thirty-year securities to investors.

19   *save borrowers half a percent*: Testimony of Lewis Ranieri, Secondary Mortgage Market Enhancement Act of 1983, Hearings Before the Subcommittee on Housing and Urban Affairs of the Committee on Housing, Banking, and Urban Affairs, September 21 and 22, 1983.

20   *made more money for the firm than anyone*: Lewis, *Liar's Poker*, p. 90.

20   *capture the savings for themselves*: "Either CMO creation has not reduced mortgage originators' lending costs," posited Loyola University business professor Steven Todd, "or mortgage originators have not passed the savings on to consumers." Steven Todd, "The Effects of Securitization on Consumer Mortgage Costs," *Real Estate Economics* 29, no. 1 (2001): 29–54. See also James W. Kolari et al., "The Effects of Securitization on Mortgage Market Yields," *Real Estate Economics* 26, no. 4 (1998): 677–693.

20   *"Just because a few people abuse"*: Evelyn Wallace, "Ranieri Looks in Dismay at Mortgage-Backed Market," *Bond Buyer*, May 5, 1988.

21   *had advocated to exclude Fannie and Freddie*: Kenneth Lore, *Mortgage Backed Securities Special Update: REMICS* (New York: Clark Boardman, 1987).

21   *toughening up lending standards*: Fannie Mae Annual Report, 1988.

22   *stories of ghetto economics*: Bruce Dorpalen, ACORN, interview.

24   *raise the national homeownership rate*: Peter Linneman, Isaac F. Megbolugbe, Susan
      M. Wachter, and Man Cho, "Do Borrowing Constraints Change U.S. Homeowner-
      ship Rates?," *Journal of Housing Economics* 6, no.4 (1997): 318–333.

24   *"demonstrate the soundness of mortgages"*: Tom Schraw, "NPA Wins New Home Lend-
      ing Program," *Disclosure* (July–August 1989).

25   *Fannie and its sibling Freddie Mac*: The federal government established Freddie Mac,
      short for the Federal Home Loan Mortgage Corporation, shortly after privatizing
      Fannie Mae, and gave it the mission of buying loans from savings and loan institu-
      tions.

25   *it was time to force*: Allen J. Fishbein, "Filling the Half-Empty Glass: The Role of
      Community Advocacy in Redefining the Public Responsibilities of Government-
      Sponsored Housing Enterprises," in *Organizing Access to Capital*, ed. Gregory D.
      Squires (Philadelphia: Temple University Press, 2003), pp. 102–118.

25   *Their project got major backup*: Bill Dedman, "Atlanta Banks Losing in Home Loans
      Scramble: Banks Favor White Areas by 5–1 Margin," *Atlanta Journal-Constitution*,
      May 1, 1988.

25   *"Secondary market purchases"*: Submitted testimony of Gale Cincotta, Subcommittee
      on Consumer and Regulatory Affairs of the Senate Committee on Banking, Housing,
      and Urban Affairs, February 28, 1991.

Chapter 2: The Rising Tide

29   *immense economic agenda*: Elizabeth Drew, *On the Edge: The Clinton Presidency* (New
      York: Simon & Schuster, 1994).

31   *tap new borrowers*: "State of the Nation's Housing, 1998," Joint Center for Housing
      Studies, Harvard University; Michael Stegman interview.

31   *another Apollo Project*: Memorandum from HUD secretary Henry G. Cisneros to
      Robert E. Rubin, assistant to the president for economic policy, re homeownership
      strategy, August 17, 1994 (draft).

32   *"The National Homeownership Strategy"*: Emphasis in the original. National Home-
      ownership Strategy, U.S. Department of Housing and Urban Development, 1995.

33   *Community Empowerment Agenda*: The Clinton Administration's National Urban
      Policy Report (draft), U.S. Department of Housing and Urban Development, Of-
      fice of Policy Development and Research, July 25, 1995.

33   *"An expanding economic pie"*: Michael Sherraden, *Assets and the Poor: A New Ameri-
      can Welfare Policy* (Armonk, N.Y.: M. E. Sharpe, 1991), p. 9.

34   *a brighter tomorrow*: "Proclamation 6807—National Homeownership Day, 1995
      June 2," *Weekly Compilation of Presidential Documents* 31, iss. 23 (1995): 968.

34   *carry on for generations*: Sherraden, *Assets and the Poor*, p. 167.

35   *"more than money and sticks"*: Aron Kahn, "Clinton Touts Homeownership Goal to Housing Pros," *St. Paul Pioneer Press*, June 6, 1995.

35   *where no mortgage lender had gone before*: David Listokin, Elvin K. Wyly, Larry Keating, Kristopher M. Rengert, and Barbara Listokin, "Making New Mortgage Markets: Case Studies of Institutions, Home Buyers, and Communities," Fannie Mae Foundation, 2000.

36   *"going to be riskier"*: Snigdha Pradash, "Clinton's Homeownership Program: A 2-Edged Sword for Lenders," *American Banker*, June 7, 1995.

37   *"powerful engine of economic growth"*: John D. McClain, "U.S. Homeownership Hits Record 66.1 Million," Associated Press, July 23, 1996.

37   *"how many refrigerators"*: Oversight of the Federal National Mortgage Association (Fannie Mae) and Federal Home Loan Mortgage Corporation (Freddie Mac), House Subcommittee on Capital Markets, Securities, and Government-Sponsored Enterprises, Committee on Banking and Financial Services, July 24, 1996.

39   *renters still couldn't afford to buy*: David Listokin, Elvin K. Wyly, Brian Schmitt, and Ioan Voicu, "The Potential and Limitations of Mortgage Innovation in Fostering Homeownership in the United States," *Housing Policy Debate* 12, iss. 3 (2001): 465–513.

40   *less committed to "neighboring"*: William M. Rohe and Michael Stegman, "The Impact of Home Ownership on the Social and Political Involvement of Low-Income People," *Urban Affairs Quarterly* 30, no. 1 (September 1994): 152–172.

40   *the worst neighborhoods*: Anne B. Shlay, "Low Income Homeownership: American Dream or Delusion?" *Urban Studies* 43, no. 3 (2006): 511–531.

40   *Yale School of Management professors*: William N. Goetzmann and Matthew Spiegel, "Policy Implications of Portfolio Choice in Underserved Mortgage Markets," in *Low Income Homeownership: Examining the Unexamined Goal*, ed. Nicolas P. Retsinas (Washington, D.C.: Brookings Institution Press, 2002), pp. 257–274.

41   *sell public housing*: *Moving Up to the American Dream*, U.S. Department of Housing and Urban Development, 1996.

42   *nearly went bankrupt*: "Business Notes," *Time*, June 18, 1990.

43   *"The evidence now is so overwhelming that there is discrimination"*: Phil Roosevelt, "Fannie Mae's Johnson Pressing Social Agenda," *American Banker*, November 6, 1992.

43   *receiving guidance from Countrywide*: Listokin et al., "Making New Mortgage Markets," p. 118.

43   *lower-income and minority buyers*: Abby Schultz, "Fannie Mae Pools to Include Low-Income Loans," Dow Jones Newswires, October 27, 1993.

44   *"a dialogue with every renter"*: H. Jane Lehman, "Fannie Mae Targets Renters as Owners; Mortgage Buyer Pledges $1 Trillion for Program Until the Year 2000," *Washington Post*, March 19, 1994.

44   *"People like me don't get mortgages"*: James A. Johnson, *Showing America a New Way Home* (San Francisco: Jossey-Bass, 1996), p. 101.

44   *"consumer information crusade"*: ibid.

45   *"biggest political campaign"*: John Buckley interview.

45   *increasing scrutiny on Capitol Hill*: In 1996, the Congressional Budget Office estimated the cash value of Fannie Mae and Freddie Mac's government support at $6.5 billion a year. "Assessing the Public Costs and Benefits of Fannie Mae and Freddie Mac," Congressional Budget Office, May 1996. Two years later a group of financial institutions, including Chase and Wells Fargo, formed a lobbying group called FM Watch, with the objective of limiting the agencies' business.

46   *Ford spent its $51 million*: Ford Foundation Annual Report, 1998.

46   *borrow more and pay less*: David W. Berson and Eileen Neely, "Homeownership in the United States: Where We've Been, Where We're Going," *Business Economics* 32, no. 3 (1997): 7–11.

47   *calculating the amount of debt*: Fannie Mae Announcement No. 94-17, November 2, 1994, "Expanding Home Ownership Opportunities: More Low Down Payment Mortgages, Revised Mortgage Insurance Requirements, Changes to Community Lending Models, and Negotiated Refinance Transactions."

47   *Buyers who lacked credit scores*: Fannie Mae Announcement No. 95-14, July 17, 1995, "Nontraditional Mortgage Credit Reports."

47   *inspect just the outside*: Memorandum to All Fannie Mae Sellers, September 26, 1996, "LL07-96: Desktop Underwriter™ Appraisal Report Forms."

47   *"automated underwriting system"*: William Kelvie, "Fannie Mae's New Realm," *Mortgage Banking*, November 1994.

48   *people in the bottom rungs*: Johnson speech, National Press Club newsmakers luncheon, November 23, 1998; Harold L. Bunce and Randall M. Scheessele, "The GSEs' Funding of Affordable Loans," Working Paper No. HF-001, Office of Policy Development and Research, U.S. Department of Housing and Urban Development, 1996.

48   *doubling during Johnson's tenure*: Mark Duda and Eric Belsky, "The Anatomy of the Low-Income Homeownership Boom in the 1990s," Joint Center for Housing Studies, Harvard University, 2001.

48   *taking on vast debt*: Matt Fellowes and Mia Mabanta, "Borrowing to Get Ahead, and Behind: The Credit Boom and Bust in Lower-Income Markets," Brookings Institution, Metropolitan Policy Program, May 2007.

49   *outperformed the market*: Jim Collins, *Good to Great* (New York: HarperCollins, 2001), p. 7.

49   *A dollar invested in Fannie*: ibid, p. 64. Collins identifies Fannie Mae's "turning point year" as 1984, crediting the company's success to its management practices and "its vital role in democratizing home ownership." Collins neglects to mention the regulatory changes that made Fannie's freakishly fast growth possible.

49   *"record earnings clip"*: "Under Johnson Fannie Goes from 'Good' to 'Great,'" *National Mortgage News*, January 29, 1996.

49   *"drive to push the homeownership rate"*: National Press Club newsmakers luncheon, November 23, 1998.

50   *"simply outside the reach"*: James A. Johnson speech, Council for Excellence in Government, John C. Whitehead Forum, January 6, 1998, reprinted in *Why Homeownership Matters: Lessons Learned from a Decade in Housing Finance* (Fannie Mae, 1998).

50   *"product is going to take off"*: "Bankers Find Options in B/C Loans," *Thrift Accountant*, November 8, 1993.

50   *fewer than seventy thousand borrowers*: State of the Nation's Housing 2000, Joint Center for Housing Studies, Harvard University, appendix, table 11: Total and Subprime Lending, 1993–1998.

51   *more than $316 billion*: Diana Henriques and Lowell Bergman, "Mortgaged Lives," *New York Times*, March 15, 2000.

51   *totaling $160 billion*: "Curbing Predatory Home Mortgage Lending: A Joint Report," U.S. Department of the Treasury and U.S. Department of Housing and Urban Development, June 2000, p. 2.

51   *risk of default and foreclosure*: Fitch Investors, as reported in Mary McGarity, "Hot Product or Hot Potato?" *Mortgage Banking*, October 1994.

52   *loans that stole homes*: Mike Hudson, "Stealing Home," *Washington Monthly*, June 1992.

52   *Annie Diggs of Georgia*: Testimony of Annie Diggs to the Senate Committee on Banking, Housing, and Urban Affairs, February 17, 1993.

53   *"never had a prayer"*: Opening statement of John Kerry, Senate Banking Committee, February 17, 1993.

Chapter 3: Subprime Time

56   *commissions for every loan*: Long Beach Financial Corp. prospectus, April 29, 1997.

57   *federal judge in Virginia*: Mentecki v. Saxon Mortgage, U.S. District Court for the Eastern District of Virginia, 96-1629-A.

57   *imminent foreclosure proceedings*: Prospectus Supplement, Asset-Backed Floating Rate Certificates, Series 1996-LB1, Salomon Brothers, Registration No. 33-84924.

58   *mass downsizing of corporate employees*: Jeanne Burke, "With Refis Out, B&C Loans May Fill the Gap," *Mortgage Marketplace*, May 23, 1994.

59   *didn't have to prove their income*: Prospectus Supplement, Amresco Residential Securities Corporation Mortgage Loan Trust 1996-3.

61   *one of the nation's biggest players*: The FDIC determined that Long Beach Savings &

Loan had brokered nearly $15 million to renegade S&Ls, less than Salomon Brothers but more than Morgan Stanley. Testimony of FDIC chair William M. Isaac to the House Banking Committee, Subcommittee on General Oversight and Investigations, August 19, 1985.

63   *ratings on the mortgage-backed securities*: "S&P Raises, Affirms Ratings on Greenwich Capital Acceptance Inc.'s Mortgage Pass-Through Certificates," PR Newswire, October 26, 2001.

63   *reselling the foreclosed homes*: Salomon Brothers Mortgage Securities, Asset-Backed Certificates, Series 1997-LB6, p. 101.

63   *lawsuit against Palazzo*: Long Beach Mortgage Co. v. Palazzo, Manuel, et al., Civil Case 773458, Orange County, California, Superior Court.

63   *Arnall took 10 percent*: Arnall v. Arnall, Los Angeles Superior Court, BD261011.

64   *1993 congressional hearings*: Office of Thrift Supervision, 65 Fed. Reg. at 81441.

64   *rigid rule started slipping*: "Room for More? Competition Heats Up in B and C Mortgage Lending," *Asset Sales Report*, May 9, 1994.

64   *lenders had to find homeowners*: "More Subprime Lenders Topping Equity Market," *National Mortgage News*, March 11, 1996.

64   *refinanced their conventional loans*: Anthony Pennington-Cross, Anthony Yezer, and Joseph Nichols, "Credit Risk and Mortgage Lending: Who Uses Subprime and Why?" Research Institute for Housing America, 2000.

64   *million homeowners a year*: Allen Fishbein and Harold Bunce, "Subprime Market Growth and Predatory Lending," in *Housing Policy in the New Millennium*, ed. Susan M. Wachter and R. Leo Penne, U.S. Department of Housing and Urban Development, 2000.

65   *"someone who's a chronic delinquent"*: Mary McGarity, "Hot Product or Hot Potato?" *Mortgage Banking*, October 1, 1994.

65   *Long Beach vice president promised*: "Home Equity: Products Multiply in Bid for Securitizable Loans," *American Banker*, October 8, 1997.

65   *"valuable social function"*: Morton Dear and Len Blum, "Introduction to the B&C Home-Equity Loan Market," in *Asset-Backed Securities*, ed. Anand K. Bhattacharya (New York: Frank J. Fabozzi Associates, 1996).

65   *homeowner Janice Demarchi*: "Lending a Hand to Credit Risks," *Cleveland Plain Dealer*, February 13, 1994.

65   *"Our innovative industry has found a great way to expand homeownership"*: John Handley, "Easy Loans May Not Be Wise," *Chicago Tribune* wire service, February 1, 1998.

66   *late on their loan payments*: National Delinquency Survey, Mortgage Bankers Association, Second Quarter 2005, Chart 1: Total Loans Past Due By Loan Type (1998–2004).

66   *subprimes were failing at triple the rate*: Bonnie Sinnock, "Recent MBS Pools Show 'Alarming' Delinquency Levels," *National Mortgage News*, May 20, 1996.

67   *judge refused to put the law to work*: *Newton v. United Companies*, CV 97-5400, U.S. District Court for the Eastern District of Pennsylvania, Findings of Fact and Conclusions of Law.

67   *Fed, under Alan Greenspan, had never weighed in*: Fishbein and Bunce, "Subprime Market Growth."

68   *"not clear to me we would have found anything"*: Greg Ip, "Did Greenspan Add to Subprime Woes?" *Wall Street Journal*, June 9, 2007.

68   *Freddie Mac ran data*: "Fannie, Freddie Entry May Tighten Subprime Margins," *American Banker*, July 28, 1998.

68   *half of all subprime customers could qualify*: Kathleen Day, "Fannie Mae Vows More Minority Lending," *Washington Post*, March 16, 2000.

69   *"aberrant behaviors"*: "Economic Challenges in the New Century," speech by Federal Reserve chairman Alan Greenspan to the National Community Reinvestment Coalition, Washington, D.C., March 22, 2000.

69   *Nine out of ten of them had refinanced*: Alan M. White and Cathy Lesser Mansfield, "Subprime Mortgage Foreclosures: Mounting Defaults Draining Home Ownership," May 12, 2000. White and Mansfield reviewed SEC filings of the top sixteen subprime loan servicers, which handled about half of the outstanding loans, and calculated about seventy thousand borrowers in default or foreclosure.

69   *In Atlanta*: Debbie Gruenstein and Christopher E. Herbert, "Analyzing Trends in Subprime Originations and Foreclosures: A Case Study of the Atlanta Area," Abt Associates, 2000.

69   *More than a third of the fourteen hundred Chicago foreclosures*: "Preying on Neighborhoods: Subprime Mortgage Lending and Chicagoland Foreclosures," National Training and Information Center, 1999.

69   *Fannie Mae's market research*: Barry Zigas interview.

69   *stopped investing in the riskiest parts*: Kenneth Temkin, Jennifer E. H. Johnson, and Diane Levy, "Subprime Markets, the Role of GSEs, and Risk-Based Pricing," Urban Institute, for the U.S. Department of Housing and Urban Development, Office of Policy Development and Research, 2002.

70   *"rogue originators have created a problem"*: Angelo Mozilo, "Making Our Voices Heard in the 'Predatory Lending' Debate," *Mortgage Banking*, April 2000.

72   *HUD raised that requirement to half*: The move was strongly advocated by FM Watch, a lobbying group of major banks openly seeking to limit the reach of Fannie Mae and Freddie Mac; it wrote a letter to Cuomo supporting the higher quotas. "Fear of Fannie and Freddie: Other Lenders Sound Alarm, Claiming Market Incursions," *Washington Post*, June 18, 1999. FM Watch spent more than $1.5 million lobbying Congress that year.

72   *poor enough to qualify for a government-subsidized rental*: Households earning less than 60 percent of area median income qualify for rentals from the Low-Income Housing

Tax Credit and other federal housing programs. While Fannie Mae and Freddie Mac operated extensive and effective programs to finance affordable housing for renters, the housing these created did not count toward the agencies' federal obligations to finance housing for low-income people; only loans to homeowners did.

72   *committed to finance $1.1 trillion*: "Blueprint for the American Dream," U.S. Department of Housing and Urban Development, June 2003. Departing Clinton Treasury secretary Larry Summers had warned that the rapid growth of Fannie Mae and Freddie Mac posed "systemic risks" to the U.S. economy, but investigators concluded, "The risk of either company causing a systemic disruption is highly unlikely." "Systemic Risk: Fannie Mae, Freddie Mac, and the Role of OFHEO," Office of Federal Housing Enterprise Oversight, February 2003.

73   *"Operation Noriega"*: Bethany McLean, "The Fall of Fannie Mae," *Fortune*, January 24, 2005. For the first time, Treasury and HUD set up a plan for taking Fannie Mae and Freddie Mac into receivership in the event of their bankruptcy, a move that signaled to shareholders that the agencies were not stable. The White House and conservative think tanks also launched a media campaign questioning the agencies' purpose and benefits.

75   *"No tienes que estar nervioso"*: Librada Martínez, *"Sorprendido hispano que entrevistó Bush," Prensa Hispana* (Phoenix), March 31–April 6, 2004.

76   *more than 8 percent of all homeowners in Avondale:* Michael M. Phillips and Bobby White, "Housing-Crisis Grants Force Cities to Make Tough Choices," *Wall Street Journal,* December 5, 2008.

Chapter 4: Into Oblivion

81   *for every foreclosure within the surrounding block*: Dan Immergluck and Geoff Smith, "The External Costs of Foreclosure: The Impact of Single-Family Mortgage Foreclosures on Property Values," *Housing Policy Debate* 17, iss. 1 (2006): 57–79.

83   *more than four out of every five home loans*: Michael Hirsh, "Mortgages and Madness," *Newsweek,* June 2, 2008.

86   *mortgage debt surpassed $11 trillion*: Flow of Funds Accounts of the United States, Board of Governors of the Federal Reserve, L.217, "Total Mortgages."

87   *5 percent of all the mortgages in Ohio*: Mortgage Bankers Association, "National Delinquency Survey," Second Quarter 2005.

87   *Lehman Brothers and Bear Stearns, generated more than $200 billion*: "U.S. Mortgage Backed Securities," Dow Jones Capital Markets Report, December 31, 2007, via Thomson Financial.

88   *Citigroup's volume of subprime loan business*: Citigroup Mortgage Loan Trust 2007 AMC-3, Prospectus Supplement, April 27, 2007, p. 37.

88 *required little to no documentation*: The MarketPulse, LoanPerformance, March 2007 data.

89 *employing more than 418,000 people*: Wholesale Access Mortgage Research and Consulting, "Mortgage Brokers 2004," July 28, 2005.

89 *accounted for 43 percent of their business*: Ibid.

89 *rate at which mortgage companies denied loan applications*: Edward Gramlich, *Subprime Lending: America's Latest Boom and Bust* (Washington, D.C.: Brookings Institution, 2007), p. 4.

89 *agencies such as Moody's helpfully sat down*: Jack Milligan, "The Model Meltdown," *Mortgage Banking*, April 1, 2008.

89 *could not be held legally responsible*: Kathleen C. Engel and Patricia A. McCoy, "Turning a Blind Eye: Wall Street Finance of Predatory Lending," *Fordham Law Review* 75, no. 4 (2007): 2039–2103.

91 *worked on laptops from their homes*: *Wayne A. Lee v. Ameriquest Capital Corporation*, Superior Court of California, Orange County, 07CC02258, Deposition of Wayne Lee, former CEO, ACC Capital Holdings.

92 *Argent rejected just one in six applicants*: Home Mortgage Disclosure Act data, 2003 through mid-2006.

92 *were paid on commission*: Deposition of Wayne Lee, *Wayne Lee v. Ameriquest*.

92 *Argent didn't do much to screen the brokers*: Ibid.

92 *"This number would bear no relationship"*: *Landa v. Ameriquest*, U.S. District Court, Northern District of California, C-03-0405, Declaration of Joseph Khaliq.

93 *Sales agents had to follow scripts*: *Ricci v. Ameriquest*, U.S. District Court, Northern District of Minnesota, Declaration of Mark Bomchill.

93 *sales teams' supervisors also oversaw Ameriquest's staff of loan processors*: Deposition of Wayne Lee, *Wayne Lee v. Ameriquest*.

94 *More than half of those loans were refinances*: Ameriquest Mortgage Securities, Inc., Asset-Backed Securities Series 2003-5, Term Sheet.

95 *"almost like an insanity"*: "Predatory Lending Practices," Hearing of the House Committee on Banking and Financial Services, May 24, 2000.

97 *HUD gave cities a choice*: Center on Budget and Policy Priorities, "Local Consequences of HUD's Fiscal Year 2004 Voucher Funding Policy," August 16, 2004, available at http://www.cbpp.org/7-15-04hous-survey.htm.

Chapter 5: Reaching the Limits

102 *most lucrative assembly line*: The percent of gross domestic product (GDP) generated by housing development peaked at more than 6 percent in early 2006. According to the CIA's *Factbook*, military spending accounts for 4.06 of GDP.

104 *preserve profit margins*: Standard & Poor's, "Industry Survey: Homebuilding," January 3, 2008.

106 *Lennar remained a rarity*: Ivy Schneider, "What Investors Look for in Home Builders," *Housing Economics* 44,iss. 4 (April 1996).

106 *fewer than five thousand houses a year*: Donaldson, Lufkin and Jenrette, Lennar Corporation—Company Report, March 18, 1994.

106 *nearly sixty other pop-and-son homebuilders*: Stephen Melman, "Publicly Traded Residential Builders," *Housing Economics* 44, iss. 1 (January 1999).

107 *forty-two thousand development sites in California*: Remarks by Lennar chief financial officer Bruce Gross, Donaldson, Lufkin & Jenrette Homebuilding/Building Products Conference, 1998.

107 *Half of the company's business*: Ina Paiva Cordle, "Strategic Land Purchases, Expansion Boost Miami Home Builder Lennar," *Knight-Ridder Business News,* August 30, 1999.

108 *Miller himself has been known*: Wainwright & Co., Equity Research, Lennar Corp., January 10, 2002.

110 *wanted a home in the "outlying suburbs"*: Another 30 percent indicated a preference for close-in suburbs. National Association of Home Builders, Consumer Preferences presentation at International Builders Show, February 14, 2008.

110 *more than doubled the amount of space*: Behjat Hojjati and Stephanie J. Battles, "Two Decades of U.S. Household Trends in Energy-Intensity Indicators: A Look at the Underlying Factors," Energy Information Administration, 2005.

110 *number of miles we collectively drive*: Bureau of Transportation Statistics, "National Transportation Statistics 2007."

111 *more than 140,000 new houses*: The Gregory Group, "Sacramento Housing Update," February 2008.

111 *one in eight or nine buyers purchases virgin property*: Standard & Poor's, "Industry Survey: Homebuilding."

111 *options to buy the property*: John Caulfield, "The Long and Winding Road," *Builder*, August 1, 2006.

111 *Tsakopoulos directed them*: Mary Lynne Vellinga and Stuart Leavenworth, "Stakes High as Developers Pressure Growth Boundaries," *Sacramento Bee*, April 9, 2000.

112 *Chertoff was moved to castigate*: States News Service, "Remarks by Homeland Security Secretary Michael Chertoff at Harvard University," February 6, 2008.

112 *Lennar teamed up with Tsakopoulos*: "N. Natomas Sprouting New Homes; Lennar Communities Starts Work on Two Projects That Will Add 4,000 Units," *Sacramento Bee*, July 18, 2002.

114 *Reynen still owed $47 million*: *In Re John D. Reynen and Judith Reynen*, U.S. Bankruptcy Court, Eastern District of California, 08-25145.

115 *built by a shareholder-owned company:* The Gregory Group, "Developer Market Share: Sacramento PMSA/Yolo PMSA/Yuba MSA," spreadsheet prepared by Greg Paquin.

115   *Lennar anticipated reaping $800 million*: David Reilly, "Lennar's $800 Million Tax Refund," *Wall Street Journal*, February 6, 2008.

116   *sixth-least-affordable real estate market*: California Association of Realtors Housing Affordability Index, 2003–2008.

116   *admitted that they did not intend to live in the house*: Home Mortgage Disclosure Act data.

117   *fastest-growing suburb*: "America's Fastest-Growing Suburbs," *Forbes*, July 16, 2007.

118   *bulldozer with teeth eight feet long*: Interview with Dean Prigmore, former planner, Placer County.

120   *spend nearly $6 million a year*: City of Lincoln Community Facilities District No. 2003-1 (Lincoln Crossing Project), Special Tax Bonds Series 2003A, Prospectus; Lincoln Public Financing Authority, Twelve Bridges Limited Obligation Bonds, Series 1999, Prospectus.

126   *spend two to three times that on options*: Sherry Glewald, "Homebuilders' Design Centers Capture Customers—and Dollars," *Housing Giants*, October 2007.

127   *Lennar's in-house lender, Universal Mortgage, made piggyback loans*: Home Mortgage Disclosure Act filings and interviews.

127   *half of its loans were exotic products*: The most common negative amortization loans are "option ARMs," so called because borrowers can choose how much to pay toward the mortgage each month; if the payment is smaller than the amount of interest owed, the unpaid interest gets added to the total amount owed.

127   *buyers paid interest only*: First American LoanPerformance data.

CHAPTER 6: CRIME SPREE

130   *dangerous drug-industry operative*: Don Plummer and Ben Smith, "Authorities Apprehend Final Slaying Suspect in DeKalb Shootout," *Atlanta Journal-Constitution*, April 13, 2001.

132   *taken away by the Secret Service*: Nancy Smallwood, "Local Man Arrested by Secret Service," *Forsyth Herald*, December 11, 2003.

132   *front half of a cat*: "Cruelty to Cat Under Investigation," *Forsyth Herald*, August 25, 2005.

132   *mayor of Barnegat, New Jersey*: *United States of America v. Ammons et al.*, 1:05-cr-00316-BBM-ECS.

134   *Gold's Gym across the street*: Caroline Wilbert and Henry Unger, "A Deal Maker's Trail of Chaos," *Atlanta Journal-Constitution*, April 22, 2002.

135   *McGill agreed to borrow $586,500*: *In re William N. McGill*, U.S. Bankruptcy Court, Northern District of Georgia, 02-80309, Statement of Financial Affairs.

136 *"a well-known social figure"*: McGill v. Hill et al., Fulton County Superior Court, 2002CV50048, Complaint.

136 *Ted Tagalakis worked . . . for a mortgage company*: USA v. Alcindor et al., U.S. District Court for the Northern District of Georgia, 1:05-cr-00269, Testimony of Theodore Tagalakis.

139 *serving a twenty-eight-year sentence*: Department of Justice, U.S. Attorney for the Northern District of Georgia news release, January 26, 2006.

139 *aide who lived down the hall*: Federal Bureau of Prisons Inmate Directory.

141 *premised on lies*: Federal Bureau of Investigaton, 2007 Mortgage Report.

141 *two thirds were based on misrepresentations*: BasePoint Analytics, "Early Payment Default—Links to Fraud and Impact on Mortgage Lenders and Investment Banks," 2007.

141 *pension funds stepped up*: See *City of Ann Arbor Employees Retirement Fund v. Citigroup*, Eastern District of New York, 2:08-cv-01418; *Plumbers' Union Local No. 12 Pension Fund v. Nomura*, Superior Court of Massachusetts, 08-0544.

142 *sale of the Yazoo lands*: For an account of the Yazoo land rush and other early real estate crazes, see Aaron M. Sakolski, *The Great American Land Bubble* (New York: Harper & Brothers, 1932).

144 *stalking perps like a parole officer*: Bill Montgomery, "5 Arrested in Mortgage Fraud Scheme," *Atlanta Journal-Constitution*, August 12, 2006.

153 *Banking industry contributions*: Glenn Simpson, "Lender Lobbying Blitz Abetted Mortgage Mess," *Wall Street Journal*, December 31, 2007. According to campaign finance records, the Mortgage Bankers Association contributed nearly $43,000 in the two years following the introduction of Fort's bill; the Money Tree gave $24,250. Contributions from Wells Fargo, the Georgia Bankers Association, Bank of America, Wachovia, Washington Mutual, and Southstar Funding helped Republican Sonny Perdue boot Roy Barnes from office.

153 *would no longer rate pools of mortgages*: Diana Henriques with Jonathan Fuerbringer, "Bankers Opposing New State Curbs on Unfair Loans," *New York Times*, February 14, 2003.

Chapter 7: Huffing the Fumes

156 *"What is the best way to make money in real estate?"*: Frank D'Alessandro, "Market Watch: Investment More than Just Money," *Fort Myers News-Press*, September 15, 2002, p. 1G.

158 *private circles of investors*: Dick Hogan, "99 claims filed against D'Alessandro estate," *Fort Myers News-Press*, January 24, 2008.

163   *Frank D'Alessandro's body*: Ed Johnson, "D'Alessandro's Death Accidental Drowning," *Fort Myers News-Press*, September 17, 2007.

163   *"just a matter of education"*: Katie S. Betz, "First Place," *Gulfshore Business*, February 2004.

167   *Lisa went on Marketwatch.com*: http://www.marketwatch.com/news/story/sunshine-state-has-best-us/story.asp.

167   *expansion of the airport and Florida Gulf Coast University*: Frank D'Alessandro, "FGCU Big Growth Generator," *Fort Myers News-Press*, December 5, 2004.

168   *GM's mortgage operations*: "Record Earnings for GM's Mortgage Operations," *National Mortgage News*, February 6, 2006.

169   *indicted for fraud*: USA v. Cabrera, U.S. District Court, Middle District of Florida, 2:08-CR-94-FM-34DNF, Indictment.

169   *Hovnanian proceeded to claim*: Sewell v. D'Alessandro & Woodyard et al., U.S. District Court, Middle District of Florida, 2:07-cv-343-JES-SPC, Defendant K. Hovnanian First Homes, LLC's Motion to Dismiss Class Action Complaint. Hovnanian's attorneys asserted that the company had merely bought the assets of First Home, but public statements by CEO Ara Hovnanian referred to the Fort Myers company as an acquisition (see Bob Ivry, "Hovnanian Posts Loss on Canceled Home Deals," Bloomberg News, March 9, 2007).

169   *"worst housing market in the country"*: Q4 Hovnanian Enterprises, Inc. Earnings Conference Call, FD Wire, December 19, 2007.

170   *young adman named Gerald Gould*: Gerald Gould interview.

171   *Cape Coral was the creation of Leonard and Jack Rosen*: David E. Dodrill, *Selling the Dream: The Gulf American Loan Corporation and the Building of Cape Coral, Florida* (Tuscaloosa: University of Alabama Press, 1993).

172   *selling Florida swampland*: Leslie Allan, *Promised Lands: Subdivision Development in Florida* (New York: Inform, 1976), p. 3.

172   *grand sales banquets*: Dodrill, *Selling the Dream*, p. 43.

172   *separated husbands from wives*: Gerald Gould interview.

172   *made his customers swear on the Bible*: Eileen Bernard, *Lies That Came True: The Amazing Creation of Cape Coral, Florida* (Ocoee, Fla.: Anna Publishing, 1983), p. 93.

173   *"about as salable as a half-finished nuclear power plant"*: John Craddock, "Uncle Sam Tries Hustling Property at Lehigh Acres," *St. Petersburg Times*, July 9, 1990.

173   *high school buddies from Anaheim*: Matthew Padilla, "Partners Pitch Land for Homes—Via Infomericals," *Orange County Business Journal*, November 15, 2004. Jeff Frieden and Robert Friedman went on to found the Real Estate Disposition Corporation auctioneers (see chapter 6).

173   *free junkets to Florida*: Brian Melley, "Land Sales in Left-for-Dead Subdivisions: 'Worst Deal I Ever Made,'" Associated Press, December 28, 2004.

173 *number one buyer of tax liens*: Carie L. Call, "Tax Liens Put Lots up for Grabs," *Fort Myers News-Press*, February 20, 2004.

174 *$40,000 for the full "platinum" package*: johntreed.com.

174 *dialed their credit card companies*: Randall Patterson, "Russ Whitney Wants You to Be Rich," *New York Times*, March 18, 2007.

174 *grossing upward of $100 million*: Whitney Information Network, Inc., Form 10-K filing with Securities and Exchange Commission, 2006. By the end of 2006, the company was grossing $225 million and for the first time paid a dividend to shareholders.

174 *informed them that if they acted now*: *Acciard v. Whitney*, Circuit Court of the Fifth Judicial Circuit, Lee County, Florida, 07-CA-002190.

175 *$210 million in defaulted loans*: Ed Roberts, "NCUA Holding the Bag for Failed Real Estate Deals," *Credit Union Journal*, March 31, 2008.

177 *aquifer is drying up*: Minutes of the Lehigh Acres Community Planning Corporation, July 12, 2006.

181 *$1.5 million (plus expenses) a speech*: Dan Fost, "Trump on the Stump: World-Famous Billionaire Turns Speechmaker," *San Francisco Chronicle*, March 7, 2006.

183 *he guesses twenty-seven million*: Chris Palmieri, "Rich Dad's Advice," Hot Property blog, *BusinessWeek*, August 28, 2007.

CHAPTER 8: TENANTS NO MORE

186 *roughly 173,000 apartments in New York City*: New York City Rent Guidelines Board, "Changes to the Regulated Housing Stock in New York City, 2007."

189 *covered by some kind of rent control*: Peter Dreier, "Rent Deregulation in California and Massachusetts: Politics, Policy, and Impacts," 1997, p. 9. This section is indebted to Dreier and, for the New York account, human rights attorney Craig Gurian and his *Fordham Urban Law Journal* article "Let Them Eat Rent Cake: George Pataki, Market Ideology, and the Attempt to Dismantle Rent Regulation in New York" (2004).

189 *middle-class renters started feeling the heat*: "Rental Housing: A National Problem That Needs Immediate Attention," Comptroller General of the General Accounting Office, November 8, 1979, reprinted in *Rent Control: A Source Book* (Santa Barbara, Calif.: Foundation for National Progress, 1981).

190 *Los Angeles asked the RAND Corporation*: C. Peter Rydell, C. Lance Barnett, Carole E. Hillestad, Michael P. Murray, Kevin Neels, and Robert H. Sims, *The Impact of Rent Control on the Los Angeles Housing Market*, RAND Corporation, prepared for the City of Los Angeles, August 1981.

190 *banned rent controls outright*: Dreier, "Rent Deregulation," p. 14.

190   *Reagan administration's own housing commission*: U.S. President's Commission on Housing, Interim Report, October 30, 1981.

190   *"discourages affluent tenants"*: Peter Salins, "Rent Control's Last Gasp," *City Journal* 7, no. 1 (1997). To the limited extent that this question has ever been examined in the real world, there's no evidence that this is true. One report, prepared for the City of Santa Monica, noted that it actually saw *more* housing construction than neighboring communities after rent controls went into effect (cited in Ned Levine et al., "Who Benefits from Rent Control? Effects on Tenants in Santa Monica, California," *Journal of the American Planning Association* 56, iss. 2 [1990]: 140–152).

190   *rent hikes consistently rose higher*: "Rent Destabilization Study II: An Analysis of the Fairness to Landlords of Rent Increases Granted by the Rent Guidelines Board for Stabilized Apartments," Office of Public Advocate Mark Green, 1997.

191   *"rent regulations were necessary"*: David Firestone, "Rent Regulations Firmly Supported in New York City," *New York Times*, June 11, 1997.

191   *no dispossessed in the streets*: As mass homelessness became a national phenomenon in the 1980s, several scholars attempted to assess—inconclusively, in the end—whether rent regulations contributed to the growth of homelessness. But as rent regulations deteriorate, homelessness has persisted and, by some accounts, is growing. In 1989, one study estimated the number of Americans living in shelters or on the streets at 500,000 to 600,000. Martha Burt and Barbara E. Cohen, *America's Homeless: Numbers, Characteristics, and Programs That Serve Them* (Washington, D.C.: Urban Institute Press, 1989). The U.S. Department of Housing and Urban Development now estimates the national homeless population at nearly 700,000.

191   *major landlord lobbying group*: Richard Perez-Peña, "Landlords Quietly Increased Donations to Fight Rent Law," *New York Times*, May 5, 1997.

191   *New York City Democrats in Harlem*: Glenn Thrush, "Wedge City," *City Limits*, January 1997.

191   *"An atom bomb"*: Kimberly Schaye, "Pol Eases Bid to End Rent Rules," *New York Daily News*, December 31, 1996.

191   *"disease of the mind"*: William Tucker, "How Rent Control Drives Out Affordable Housing," Cato Institute, Cato Policy Analysis No. 274, May 1997.

191   *"mutated into an entitlement"*: "A Generational Rent Gap," *New York Times*, June 13, 1997.

192   *spent more than $1 million*: Dreier, "Rent Deregulation," p. 11.

192   *California's landlords heaped*: Ibid., p. 21.

193   *"enhance the profile of such units and raising rents"*: GE Commercial Mortgage Corporation, Series 2007-C1 Trust, Prospectus Supplement, filed May 4, 2007.

193   *sent eviction papers*: Timothy Williams, "As Landlord Grows, So Does Criticism," *New York Times*, September 3, 2006.

194   *sold to foreign investors*: Paul Harris, "Britons Buy Slice of the Big Apple," *Observer*, November 18, 2007.

194   *more than sixty thousand new condos*: *The Real Deal New York Real Estate Data Book 2007*.

195   *cost of buying property in New York*: In the second quarter of 2008, the price per square foot of Manhattan real estate was $1,263, up from less than $900 in 2003. Miller Samuel Real Estate Appraisers, July 2008.

195   *average salary of nearly $340,000*: "The Securities Industry in New York City," Office of the State Comptroller, October 2007.

195   *fixed-income compensation tripled*: Compensation at Merrill Lynch, Goldman Sachs, Bear Stearns, Lehman Brothers, and Morgan Stanley, calculated based on SEC filings, in Kevin Connor, "Wall Street and the Making of the Subprime Disaster," National Training and Information Center et al., 2007.

195   *repackaged apartment buildings, shopping malls, and mobile home parks*: Fitch Ratings, 2008 Global Structured Finance Outlook; US CMBS 2007 Outlook.

198   *significantly more likely to fall behind*: The MarketPulse, LoanPerformance, June 2007 data, p. 14.

198   *issued a special advisory*: Interagency Guidance on Nontraditional Mortgage Product Risks, U.S. Department of the Treasury et al., October 2006.

198   *total amount of home mortgage debt*: Federal Reserve, Flow of Funds Report, 1Q2007.

198   *took out a much bigger loan*: Survey of Consumer Finances, Federal Reserve, 2004.

199   *taking out $1.2 trillion*: Alan Greenspan and James Kennedy, "Estimates of Mortgage Originations, Repayments and Debts on One-to-Four-Family Residences," Federal Reserve Board 2005 (paper 2005-41), pp. 20–21.

199   *home equity borrowing and refinancing*: Joint Center for Housing Studies, "State of the Nation's Housing 2008."

199   *about one quarter of all new home loans were "jumbo"*: Thomas Zimmerman, UBS, to the American Enterprise Institute, "Why Such a Large Market Size for Subprime and Alt-A?," in "The Deflating Mortgage and Housing Bubble, part II," October 11, 2007, slide 2.

199   *typical Manhattan apartment sold for $800,000*: Miller Samuel, reported in the *Real Deal New York Real Estate Data Book 2007*, p. 20 (median sales price).

203   *London property prices multiplied*: Nationwide Building Society Web site, http://www.nationwide.co.uk, "House Price Index: How Much Is Your Property Worth?"

206   *on West 126th Street in Harlem*: For much more on the rampant abuse of the HUD 203(k) program in New York City, see Kemba Johnson, "The Harlem Shuffle," and her subsequent series, for *City Limits* magazine, http://www.citylimits.org.

207 *collusion of sellers, financers, and appraisers*: The People of the State of New York v. First American Corporation, U.S. District Court for the Southern District of New York, 2007-CV-10397.

207 *"the system is a joke"*: Max Abelson, "New York's Longest-Running Real Estate 'Joke,'" *New York Observer*, June 11, 2007.

Epilogue: Returning Home

213 *securitizing mortgages does not lower their interest rates*: Steven Todd, "The Effects of Securitization on Consumer Mortgage Costs," *Real Estate Economics* 29, no. 1 (2001): 29–54; Andrea Heuson, Wayne Passmore, and Roger Sparks, "Credit Scoring and Mortgage Securitization: Implications for Mortgage Rates and Credit Availability," *Journal of Real Estate Finance and Economics* 23, no. 3 (2001): 337–363.

214 *study coauthored by a Federal Reserve economist*: Heuson et al., "Credit Scoring and Mortgage Securitization."

214 *top fifth has had its wealth jump sharply*: Lawrence R. Mishel, Jared Bernstein, and Sylvia A. Alegretto, *State of Working America 2006/2007* (Washington, D.C.: Economic Policy Institute, 2006).

214 *average securities industry* bonus *in 2006*: "New York City Securities Industry Bonuses," January 2008, and "The Securities Industry in New York City," October 2007, New York Office of the State Comptroller.

215 *nine out of ten could not identify the total charges*: James M. Lacko and Janis K. Pappalardo, "Improving Consumer Mortgage Disclosures: An Empirical Assessment of Current and Prototype Disclosure Forms," Federal Trade Commission, Bureau of Economics, June 2007.

215 *home equity loans alone pumped up the gross domestic product*: Estimate by Calculated Risk, calculatedrisk.blogspot.com.

216 *nation's homes were collectively worth $19 trillion*: Robert Denk, "Homeownership, Financial Flexibility, and Wealth," National Association of Home Builders, Washington, D.C., July 2006.

216 *another $1 trillion in home equity loans*: Alan Greenspan and James Kennedy, "Estimates of Home Mortgage Originations, Repayments, and Debt On One-to-Four-Family Residences," Federal Reserve Board of Washington, 2005; see also Greenspan and Kennedy, "Sources and Uses of Equity Extracted from Homes," Federal Reserve Board of Washington, 2007.

217 *More than half of the $400 billion goes to the small minority*: President's Advisory Panel on Tax Reform, Final Report, November 2005.

217 *average deduction of nearly $35,000*: Robert D. Dietz, "Local Use of the Mortgage Interest and Real Estate Tax Deductions," National Association of Home Builders, June 2006.

217 *allowed the owners of more than three hundred thousand apartments*: Calculation by National Housing Trust, Washington, D.C.

218 *nearly seven hundred thousand Americans*: U.S. Department of Housing and Urban Development, "The 2007 Annual Homelessness Assessment Report," July 2008.

218 *spending more than half its income*: Center for Housing Policy, "The Housing Landscape for America's Working Families," 2007.

218 *Americans are devoting more of their income to housing*: Joint Center for Housing Studies, Harvard University, "State of the Nation's Housing 2008."

219 *In L.A., following a nearly one-third drop*: California Association of Realtors, August 2008 Median Home Prices, from DataQuick Information Systems data.

219 *city that lives by the old limits of sane borrowing*: Joint Center for Housing Studies, "State of the Nation's Housing 2008," Median House Price/Median Household Income Ratio, 1980–2006.

220 *an astonishing eight million foreclosures*: Crédit Suisse Fixed Income Research, "Foreclosure Update: Over 8 Million Foreclosures Expected," December 4, 2008.

221 *In 1950, all the home mortgages in the nation*: Richard K. Green and Susan M. Wachter, "The American Mortgage in Historical and International Context," *Journal of Economic Perspectives* 19, no. 4 (2005): 93–114.

222 *head of the FHA's team of land planners*: Seward H. Mott, "Land Use Requirements and Subdivision Planning Under Section 203," *Proceedings of the Realtors' Housing Conference Discussing the National Housing Act,* March 17–19, 1938.

223 *"one detached single family dwelling and a one- or two-car garage"*: Federal Housing Administration, "Planning Neighborhoods for Small Houses," July 1936.

224 *"strewn with printouts of spreadsheets"*: David Wessel, "Greenspan Sees Bottom in Housing, Criticizes Bailout," *Washington Post,* August 14, 2008.

224 *Greenspan frequently pored over such documents in his bathtub*: Michael Hirsh, "Greenspan's Folly: The Former Fed Chief's Culpability in Wall Street's Woes," *Newsweek,* September 17, 2008.

225 *study sponsored by the Federal Transit Administration*: "Costs of Sprawl 2000," Transit Cooperative Research Program (with data from Center for Urban Policy Research, Rutgers University), sponsored by the Federal Transit Administration.

225 *finance and real estate industries together spent nearly $2 billion*: Center for Responsive Politics, www.opensecrets.org: Figures for contributions and lobbying from finance, insurance, and real estate, with insurance figures deducted.

226 *much of that money would have gone into other parts of the economy*: In his 1984 testimony supporting the Secondary Mortgage Market Enhancement Act, Federal

Reserve Board governor Preston Martin acknowledged that steering more capital to mortgages through securities would likely drain resources from other areas of the economy: The law "should encourage more capital to flow to the private sector and less to flow to other private sectors. If this process altered capital allocation away from plant and equipment, there could be some impact on business productivity growth over time."

227   *one in every ten working Americans*: Daniel Gross, "Economic View: As the McMansions Go, So Does Job Growth," *New York Times*, November 20, 2005.

INDEX

A

ACC Capital Holdings, 93–94. *See also*
     Ameriquest Mortgage; Argent Mortgage
ACORN (Association of Communities for
     Reform Now), 22–23
Adelman, Fred, 125–26
adjustable-rate mortgages (ARMs)
     option ARMs, 218, 240, 241
     overview, 233
     resetting interest rates, 241
     subprime mortgages as, 57, 66
     teaser rate, 88, 242
advertising campaigns, 44–46, 125–26,
     172–74, 191–92
Alt-A mortgage loans (NINJAs), 67, 233, 239
American Banker, 43
American Dream, 6, 33, 48, 66, 216
American Greetings, 82
American Institute of Real Estate Appraisers
     (AIREA), 7
Ameriquest Mortgage
     and Argent, 91, 92
     and Arnall, 93–94
     account executives' illegal practices, 92–93,
          94–95
     flipping in Cleveland, 83
     and Freddie Mac, 71
     lobbying in Washington, 153
     mortgage pools of, 94
     refinancing for more and more, 122
     as reincarnation of Long Beach Mortgage, 63
     states' lawsuit against, 93–94
     See also Argent Mortgage
Ameristar mortgage company, 136
amortization, 53, 127, 168, 233, 239
Anderson, Lance, 56, 57

appraisals, 47, 92, 110, 234. *See also* appraisers
appraisal fraud
     from $32,000 to $250,000 for same house,
          151–52
     appraisers complaining about, 207
     Atlanta mortgage scam, 139, 142–43
     FBI investigation of, 141
     for flippers, 2, 97, 99, 152
     HUD's too little, too late approach to,
          206–7
     kickbacks to, 10
     and mortgage brokers, 89
     in Ohio, 90–91
     overvaluing property, 84, 90–93, 95–96,
          97, 118, 135, 144
     refinancing boon, 83
appraisers
     FHA's original monitoring of, 222, 223–24
     income from fees, 83
     liability for lying on paperwork, 145
     overview, 234
     Realtors' power over, 140, 142, 158
     state licensing, 90, 142–43
Argent Mortgage, 84, 91–97, 99–100
ARMs. *See* adjustable-rate mortgages
Arnall, Roland, 59–61, 62–64, 93–94
Asian investors, 48
Associates First Capital, 68–69, 70
Association of Communities for Reform Now
     (ACORN), 22–23
Atlanta Journal-Constitution, 25, 43
Atlanta, suburbs and exurbs
     appraisal fraud, 135, 139, 142–44, 151–52
     flipping homes, 135–39, 152
     foreclosures in, 69, 139, 143, 148–52
     home construction in, 146, 147–48

Atlanta, suburbs and exurbs (*continued*)
    inadequate resources for pursuing fraud,
        145
    mortgage fraud schemes, 132–40, 142–43,
        148–49
    real estate market, 140–41, 145–46,
        147–48
    St. Ives, 129–31
    St. Marlo, 131–33
    Wolf Creek, 145–47
auctions in Atlanta area, 150–52
Austin neighborhood, Chicago, Illinois, 1
automated underwriting, 47–48

B
Bank of America, 16–17, 70
banks. *See* commercial banks; investment
        banks; savings and loans
Bardis, Christo and Rachel, 113–14
Barnes, Roy, 152–53, 154–55
Bass, Adam, 153
B&C lending, 234
Bear Stearns, 87–89, 94, 119, 149–53,
        225
Berresford, Susan, 46
Black Entertainment Television, 45
black homeownership rates, 40, 44
blockbusting (panic peddling), 9–10, 13, 83,
        96–97, 208
blogs, 208–12
Bocchicchio, Mike, Jr., 123–24, 126, 127
Boiler Room (movie), 93
bond investors, 18, 50–51. *See also* mortgage-
        backed securities
bond-rating agencies, 19
bond-sales business, 2
Boortz, Neal, 154
Bring Back the 70s Street Club, 79–80
Brooklyn, New York, 41, 185–86, 188, 208,
        209–10
Broward County Convention Center, 177
Brownstoner real estate blog, 209–12
Bruno, Joe, 191
Bucha, Stephen, 82
Buckhead area of Atlanta, 137
Buckley, John, 44–45
Buckley, William F., Jr., 8
Burnham, Don, 179
Bush, George H. W., 30, 42
Bush, George W.
    Arnall's contributions to, 93
    and GSEs, 72–73
    increase in mortgage debt, 198–99
    meeting with new homeowners, 75–76

prohibiting states from regulating financial
        institutions, 154
public housing cutbacks, 217–18
Butler, Jonathan, 209–10

C
Cabbage Patch Kids, 18
Cabrera, Samir, 164, 165, 169
California, 127, 187, 192, 218–19. *See also*
        Sacramento suburbs and exurbs
California state pension fund, 105–6
Cape Coral, Fort Myers, Florida, 160–62,
        166–69, 170, 171–75
Carl, Bernard, 19
Carrington Park condominium, Atlanta,
        137–39
Case-Shiller Index, 219
cash-flow as a verb, 174–75
cash out refinancing, 241
CDOs (collateralized debt obligations), 76,
        220, 234, 239. *See also* mortgage-backed
        securities; tranches
Centex, 111, 126, 127
Central Park West, New York City, 186–87
charities providing down payments, 99
Chertoff, Michael, 112
Chicago, Illinois, 7–9, 13, 69, 81, 140
Chicago Freedom Movement, 7
Chicago's West Side, 1–2, 7, 10–11. *See also*
        Cincotta, Gale
Cincotta, Gale
    belief in regulations, 15–16
    biographical information, 12
    on Clinton's National Homeownership
        Strategy, 37
    and doughnut effect due to Fannie Mae
        policies, 21–22
    and National People's Action on Housing,
        13–14
    objective of making communities, 226–27
    organizing urban activists, 1, 10–11, 13,
        22–23
    at U.S. Congressional hearings, 12–13, 25,
        226–27
Cirinelli, Pam, 58
Cisneros, Henry, 30–31
Citigroup, 70, 87–89, 94
Cleveland, Ohio
    Cleveland Heights, 90
    foreclosure rate in, 83, 90
    National City Mortgage, 136
    Shaker Heights, 90–91
    sheriff's foreclosure sales, 80, 82, 84–86,
        95, 98–100

Slavic Village, 78–86, 90, 95–97, 149
South Euclid, 90
Cleveland Housing Network, 96, 98, 101
Cleveland Plain Dealer, 65
Clinton, Bill, and Clinton administration
    addressing Realtors' conventions, 36
    and FTC's Operation Home Inequity, 68–69
    and GSEs low-income buyers requirement,
        72
    naïveté of, 213
    reelection campaign, 28–29
    reminiscing about his first house, 37
    on society, 213
    welfare system overhaul, 33
    See also National Homeownership Strategy
Clinton Economic Plan, 29, 31–32, 33–37
Clinton Hill, Brooklyn, 209–10
collateral, 67, 133, 149–50, 220, 234
collateralized debt obligations (CDOs), 76,
        220, 234, 239. *See also* mortgage-backed
        securities; tranches
"Color of Money, The" *(Atlanta Journal-
        Constitution)*, 25, 43
Commerce Department, 3
commercial banks, 13, 22–23, 70, 72–73
community development corporation, 46
Community Empowerment Agenda, 33
Community Home Buyers (Fannie Mae
        program), 24–25
Community Reinvestment Act of 1977
        (CRA), 13, 14–15, 22–23, 234
commuting and greenhouse gases, 110
Conaway, Patty, 138, 139–40
condominium conversions in New York,
        185–88, 192, 194–95, 200–202
conforming loans, 235
consumer debt, 4–5, 51, 216
conventional loans, 235
co-op boards in New York City, 196
Corbett, Michael, 178
Corcoran real estate agency, 196, 201
Corinthian Homes, 113–14
corporate socialism, 225–26
Countrywide Home Loans, 35–36, 43, 56, 70
Countrywide Mortgage, Full Spectrum division,
        64
Court Street Lofts, Brooklyn, 185–86, 188
CRA (Community Reinvestment Act of
        1977), 13, 14–15, 22–23, 234
credit card debt, 51
credit default swaps, 220
credit scores, 88, 233, 235
Crédit Suisse, 220
Cuomo, Andrew, 72, 206–7

Curbed real estate blog, 210–11
Cuyahoga County, Ohio, sheriff's foreclosure
        sales, 80, 82, 84–86, 95, 98–100

D
D'Alessandro, Frank, 156–58, 163
Davis, Terry, 112–13
Dayton, Ohio, 140
Deane, Albert L., 6
debt surge pumping up GDP, 215
deed, 235
default, 235
delinquency, 235
Delta Funding, 68–69
deregulation, 16, 19–21, 25, 33, 192–95
derivatives of mortgage-backed securities, 83
discrimination, 25, 36, 43, 62, 79
Disney, Walt, 107
Donewar, Renee, 130
down payments
    applying rent toward, 96–97, 101
    Fannie Mae lowering to 3 percent, 44
    for FHA-insured loans to minorities, 10, 36
    flipper's loan for, 99
    for homebuyers in 1920s, 5
    and inner city doughnut hole, 22–25
    overview, 235
    homebuilder lingo for, 105
    second mortgages as, 5, 53, 82, 126–27, 240
    using rent vouchers for, 41, 80
Dragmen, Steve, 99
Dr. Seuss, 107

E
East Garfield Park, Chicago, Illinois, 2
East Side Organizing Project, 80–81
Eccles, Marriner, 3–4
Edgewater (Marysville, Ca.), 113–14, 121
Eisner, Adele, 91, 94
Elk Grove, Ca., 109, 121–26
Equifirst, 76
equity. *See* home equity
Estrada, Erik, 173
Express Funding, 135

F
Fairbanks, Shannon, 18
Fannie Mae (Federal National Mortgage
        Association)
    advertising campaign, 44–46
    and doughnut effect, 21–22
    Ford Foundation insurance fund for, 46
    history and role of, 14–15
    instructions to lenders, 47

Fannie Mae (*continued*)
  on minority and new homebuyers, 69
  misrepresentations on loan applications,
    141
  opposition to bill attributing responsibility,
    153
  overview, 6, 236
  profits from loans to low-income people,
    49
  Showing America a New Way Home
    program, 43–46
  technology investment, 47
  and urban activists, 21–26
  See also government-sponsored enterprises
Fast Funding, 152
FBI (Federal Bureau of Investigation), 141
Federal Bureau of Investigation (FBI), 141
federal deposit insurance, 60–61
Federal Housing Administration (FHA)
  and Clinton Economic Plan, 41–42
  discrimination against poor neighborhoods,
    6–7
  down payments as low as 3 percent, 235
  first twenty years, 6
  as front in the War on Poverty, 9
  Home Owners' Loan Corp. as antecedent,
    5–6
  insuring more than double previous
    amounts, 221
  overview, 236
  in Roosevelt's time, 222–23
  speculators benefiting from, 10
  accounting for only 1 dollar in every 50 in
    mortgages, 95
Federal Housing Finance Agency, 237
Federal Reserve, 13, 17, 67–69, 214, 237
Federal Trade Commission (FTC), 68–69,
    215
Federal Transit Administration, 225
Feeling Called Home, A (video), 35
FHA. *See* Federal Housing Administration
FICO credit score, 235
Financial Edge seminar series, 183–84
Find It, Fix It, Flip It (Corbett), 178
First Alliance Mortgage, 68–69
First American Corporation, 206–7
First Fidelity Bank, 22–23
First Home Builders, 163–69, 173
flipping homes
  areas affected by, 219
  in Atlanta, 135–39, 152
  in Chicago, 81, 83, 140
  co-op boards' prevention of, 196
  homes won't sell, 161–63

in New York City, 208
  overview, 135, 236
  shows on TV about, 158–59
flipping loans, 94
Flip This House (TV program), 180
Florida. *See* Fort Myers, Florida
Ford, Henry, 4
Ford Foundation, 46
foreclosure mills, 148–49, 151–52
foreclosure rescue specialists, 155
foreclosures
  in 1930s, 4–6
  in Atlanta, 139, 143, 148–52
  in Cleveland, 83
  Fed/Greenspan's failure to prevent, 67–68
  from inability to pay tax bills, 149
  as incidental threat to the lenders' boon, 76
  and job loss, 218
  as lenders' opportunity to make money,
    51–53, 63, 82–83
  overview, 236
  parts stripped from homes, 79
  predictions, 220
  procedure, 98, 100
  resulting in legal limbo for homes, 96
  seminars on how to benefit from buying,
    178–81
  sheriff's sales in Ohio, 80, 82, 84–86, 95,
    98–100
  in Slavic Village, Cleveland, 79–82, 84–86
  in Wolf Creek, Ga., 147
foreign investments in New York City real
    estate, 194
Fort, Vincent, 153
Fort Myers, Florida
  Cape Coral, 160–62, 166–69, 170,
    171–75
  home construction in, 158–61, 175–77
  Lehigh Acres, 159–60, 163–66, 170, 173,
    176–77
  real estate market, 156–59, 163–69
Freddie Mac (Federal Home Loan Mortgage
    Corporation), 71, 236–37. *See also*
    government-sponsored enterprises
Frieden, Jeff, 150
FTC (Federal Trade Commission), 68–69, 215
Fulmer, Ann, 145

G
GDP (gross domestic product), 215, 221
GE Capital, 193
General Motors Acceptance Corporation, 4
Georgia, 142, 145, 151, 153–54. *See also*
    Atlanta suburbs and exurbs

Georgia Real Estate Fraud Prevention and
    Awareness Coalition (GREFPAC), 145
Georgia Residential Mortgage Fraud Act
    (2005), 145, 153–54
Gingrich, Newt, 32, 42
Ginnie Mae (Government National Mortgage
    Association), 10, 17, 237
Glass-Steagall Act, 70
Gonzalez, Henry, 25
Gould, Gerald, 170–71
Gould, Julie, 23–24
government
    bailout for investment banks, 225–26
    and nation's debt addiction, 221
    New Deal era, 222–23
    preventing foreclosures in 1930s, 5–6
    propping up real estate prices, 220–21,
        227–28
    See also regulations; entries beginning with
        "federal"
government-sponsored enterprises (GSEs)
    and Bush, G. W., 72–73
    domination of safe mortgages, 58
    federal government takeover, 223–24
    Ginnie Mae, 10, 17, 237
    mixed mortgage pool investments, 71–73
    and mortgage-backed securities, 17
    overview, 237
    participation in creating tranches, 21
    on prime borrowers with subprime loans,
        68
    purchasing larger and larger mortgages, 221
    racial quota, 72
    Reagan's attempt to undermine, 18
    See also Fannie Mae
grading system for subprime loans, 50, 234,
    242
Gramlich, Ned, 68
Gramm-Leach-Billey Act (1999), 70
Great Depression, 3–4, 5
Greenspan, Alan, 32, 67–68, 69, 181, 224
Greenwich Capital, 55–56, 61
gross domestic product (GDP), 215, 221
GSEs. See government-sponsored enterprises
Gulf American Corporation, 172

H
Habitat for Humanity, 41
Hall, Bill, 136
Harlem, New York, 193
Herrholz, Eric, 157–58
Hill, Phillip, 133–40, 143
Hills, Carla, 13
Holland, Michigan, 27–29, 38

homebuilders
    IRS credit for, 115
    low interest rates as gift to, 48–49, 110
    National Association of Home Builders, 30
    propping up real estate market, 220–21
    publicly traded, 105–6, 111, 115, 169–70
    survival of mega builders, 115–16
    See also home construction; Lennar Corpo-
        ration; real estate market
"Home Buying for Hipsters" seminar, 196
Homecomings Mortgage, a GM company, 168
home construction
    in Arizona, 74
    in Atlanta, 146, 147–48
    Clinton's push for, 30–37
    cutting corners, 113–14, 122–25, 127–28
    failure of private market, 221, 224–25
    Fannie Mae financing of, 23–25
    FDR's push for, 3–4
    in Fort Myers, Fla., 158–61, 175–77
    in Sacramento area, 102–7, 108–10,
        111–14, 123–26
    subcontractors blamed for substandard
        quality, 125–26
home equity
    Home Owners Equity Protection Act, 64,
        67, 237
    negative equity, 5, 219–20, 239
    overview, 86–87, 235, 237
home equity loans, 51, 56–57, 65–66, 215–16,
    235, 237
homelessness in U.S., 218
Home Mortgage Disclosure Act of 1975
    (HMDA), 13, 237
home mortgage interest income tax deduction,
    216–17
Homeowners Equity Protection Act of 1994
    (HOEPA), 64, 67, 237
homeownership
    affordable housing vs. affordable home-
        ownership, 32
    as behavior modification technique, 8–9,
        32–35
    boom of late 1990s to mid-2000s, 48–49
    feasibility for renters, 39–40, 44
    naïveté of new owners and minorities, 69
    predictions about homeowners' responsibility,
        8–9, 32–35, 38–40
    rate of, 46, 48
    riots in Chicago lead to plan for the poor,
        7–9
    size and distance from work, 110
    social conditioning for, 6, 33, 48, 66, 216
Homeownership for Women (HOW), 41

Home Owners' Loan Corporation (HOLC),
    5–6, 222, 238
home price declines, 40, 140, 219–20
home price increases
    defying logic, 116
    in Fort Myers, Fla., 158
    in Harlem, 206
    housing boom in 1920s, 4
    from increasing customer pool, 73–74
    from interest-only mortgages, 218–19
    lenders and investors' reliance on, 82–83,
        141
    in New York City area, 186–87
    overview, 219
    in Sacramento suburban areas, 109, 113, 114
    trading up, 76
Hoover, Herbert, 3, 216
Household Finance, 54, 80
Housing Choice Vouchers from HUD, 41, 80,
    97, 242
housing development
    in Great Depression, 3–4
Hovnanian, K., 169
How to Own Your Home (Commerce
    Department), 3
HSBC
    acquisition of Household Finance, 70
HUD. See U.S. Department of Housing and
    Urban Development
Hudson, Mike, 52
Humboldt Park, Illinois, 2
Hyland, John, 184

I
IndyMac Federal Bank, 114
infomercials, 172, 173–74
installment plans, 4–5
interest-only mortgages
    for building customer base, 116
    dependence on rising prices, 127
    finite length of interest-only aspect, 204
    as mortgage brokers' recommendation, 197
    overview, 197–98, 238
    recasting, 241
    resulting price increase, 218–19
    tax code support for, 216–17
Interest Only PLUS program (California), 127
interest rates
    and Clintonian economics, 29
    effect of SMMEA, 19, 20
    Federal Reserve pledge for lowering, 13
    opportunistic use of, 48–49, 51–53, 110
    post-September 11, 2001, terrorist attacks,
        73

rising in mid 1990s, 50
    and savings and loan crisis, 51
    as unfulfilled promise, 213–14
    and war on inflation, 17
Internal Revenue Service (IRS), 51, 115, 149,
    170, 216–17
International Association of Investors, 179
International Capital Group, 175
investment banks
    attempt to hold responsible, 152–53
    culpability of, 141, 155
    government bailout, 225–26
    as home owners, 149–52
    and lawsuit against Ameriquest, 94
    overexposure in MBS market, 119
    paying penalties instead of upkeep,
        130–31
    process for purchasing MBSs, 152
    profits from fees and minimal risks, 88–89
    propping up real estate market, 220–21
    retail banking operations vs., 70
    salaries and bonuses for workforce, 195,
        214
    shortage of raw material, 214
    and wealth gap, 214
investors
    California state pension fund, 105–6
    in Hill's Atlanta real estate scam, 135, 136
    of pension funds, 16, 20, 50, 105–6, 141
    pump-up seminars for, 174–75, 178–81,
        184
    renting out overvalued houses, 118–19
    in Sacramento housing boom, 116–17
    See also mortgage-backed securities
IRS. See Internal Revenue Service
issuers, 238. See also mortgage-backed
    securities

J
Johnson, James A. "Jim," 42–50
Johnson administration, 9
Joint Center for Housing Studies (Harvard),
    38–39
JTS Communities, 118–19, 120
judicial vs. nonjudicial foreclosures, 151, 236
jumbo mortgages, 238

K
Kensington, Brooklyn, 208
Kerner Commission, 7
Kerry, John, 53
Kiyosaki, Robert, 183
Kruger, John, 135
Kucinich, Dennis, 79

L

Larios, Kim, 114
Laudermill, Christine, 135–36
laundering money with real estate scams, 139,
    140
Learning Annex Real Estate and Wealth Expo,
    178–82
Lee County, Florida. *See* Fort Myers, Florida
Lehigh Acres, Fort Myers, Florida, 159–60,
    163–66, 170, 173, 176–77
Lehigh Acres Corporation, 170–71
Lehman Brothers, 43, 87–88, 119, 149
lending guidelines, 20, 55–59, 67, 141,
    222–23
Lennar Corporation
    buying up California, 106–7, 111–13
    charging losses against previous earnings, 115
    home construction, 102–5, 122–25, 127–28
    management style, 107–8
    model homes, 109–10
    overview, 115–17
    as publicly traded mega builder, 106, 107
    suing subcontractors, 125–26
    and Universal American Mortgage, 116,
        126–27
Lennar Renaissance, 108–10, 114–15, 124–25
leveraging, 74–77, 86
Levittown, New York, 109–10
Liar's Poker (Lewis), 16
liens, 173, 238
Lincoln, California, 102–5, 117–21, 120–21
lincrusta, 210
Livnat, Eyal, 152
loan guidelines, 20, 55–59, 67, 141, 222–23
"loan shark," 13
lobbies in Washington, 153, 225–26
Logue, Pat, 163–64
Long Beach Mortgage
    acquisition by WaMu, 70
    development from S&L to mortgage
        company, 59–62
    fees on subprime loans, 63
    founder of, 59–61, 62–64
    lawsuit against Palazzo, 59, 63
    mortgage fraud in Atlanta area, 132–39
    staff members move to other companies,
        58–59
    subprime mortgages of, 54–56, 57, 63–64,
        65
    See also Ameriquest
Long Beach Savings & Loan, 60–62
low-doc loans, 238, 242
low-down-payment mortgages, 24–25, 36, 44,
    49–50, 88, 99

low-income homeowners, 39–40, 43–45, 48, 91
Lucky Lee Ranch, Fort Myers, Florida, 170

M

"Make a Fortune Rehabbing Fixer-Uppers"
    seminar, 179
Manhattan, New York, 194, 208–11
market research, 38–40
Marketwatch.com, 167
Marshall Reddick Real Estate Network, 175
Martin, Gerald, 179
Marysville, California, 113–14, 121
Massachusetts, 187, 192
Maxwell, David O., 21–22
MBSs. *See* mortgage-backed securities
McCord, Ron, 65–66
McDonald, Stewart, 6
McGill, William "Bill," 129–30, 131, 133–37,
    139
Merrill Lynch, 94
Miller, Stuart, 106–8
Millionaire University, 174–75
minorities
    and Bush, G. W., 72, 75–76
    discrimination against, 25, 36, 43, 62, 79
    as subprime customers, 55, 68
Money Dance, 177–78
Monteleongo, Armando, 180–81
Moody's ratings agency, 19, 63
mortgage-backed securities (MBSs)
    and Ameriquest's illegal practices, 94
    appraisals, appraisers, and value of, 234
    and Chicago of 1970s foreclosure crisis, 2
    commercial pools, 193, 195
    derivatives of, 83
    Fannie Mae packaging of, 236
    financing construction in Florida, 175–76
    fine print protection, 141
    investment bank profits from, 87–88
    laws on, 241–42
    lenders' benefit from, 82–83
    making investment banks responsible, 152
    origin of, 17–18
    overview, 239
    and post-9/11 low interest rates, 73–74
    profitability leading to overexposure of
        investment banks, 119
    and real estate boom of 1920s, 4
    reliance on rising value of real estate, 82–83,
        86–87
    securitization, 16–17, 88, 213–14
    as sink hole for nation's dollars, 226, 227–28
    and S&L crisis, 60–61
    studies of results, 213

mortgage-backed securities (*continued*)
    Wall Street-generated, 51, 71–73, 82, 83,
        87–90
    warnings to buyers, 89
    See also tranches
Mortgage Bankers Association, 30, 31–32,
        35–36, 39–40, 50–51, 65
Mortgage Bankers Association of Georgia, 153
mortgage brokers
    Argent's "account executives," 92
    culpability of, 141, 155
    customer pool, 50, 55, 58–59, 88–89
    exceptions to lending guidelines, 55–56,
        57, 141
    fabrications on paperwork, 2, 84, 89, 92,
        166
    fees paid to, 57, 62, 89, 136–37, 155
    foreclosure mills, 148–49
    increase in firms from 1987–2004, 89
    in New York City, 196–99
    overview, 239
    yield spread premiums, 57, 239, 243
mortgage debt, 43–46, 48, 86–87, 198–99,
        214–16
mortgage disaster of early 1970s, 1–2, 3
mortgage fraud
    and appraisers, 89, 142
    in Atlanta area, 132–40, 142–44, 148–49
    business environment conducive to, 226
    falsifying paperwork, 92–93, 94–95,
        99–100
    FBI focus on, 141
    FBI investigation of, 141
    foreclosure rescue specialists, 155
    inflating borrower's income, 92–93, 99–100
    investor and fund managers' shield from
        responsibility, 154
    overpricing loans, 62, 68
    overview, 140–41, 144–45
    statistics on, 142
    See also appraisal fraud; flipping homes
mortgage lenders
    attempt to hold responsible, 152–53
    credit and administration vice president's
        concerns, 54–56
    culpability of, 141
    discrimination against minorities, 25, 43
    effect of SMMEA, 20
    Fannie Mae's instructions to, 47
    overview, 239
    and payment-option mortgages, 218–19
    profit from fees, 50–52, 63, 67, 83, 136–37
    providing down payments, 99
    See also Long Beach Mortgage

mortgages
    in 1920s, 5
    funding with investors' dollars, 17
    interest income tax deduction, 216–17
    jumbo mortgages, 238
    lending guidelines, 20, 55–59, 67, 141,
        222–23
    low-doc loans, 238
    low down payment, 24–25, 36, 44, 49–50,
        88, 99
    overview, 238
    and price of homes, 86
    refinancing, 64, 82–83, 122, 241
    removing taint of shame from, 4–5
    stated-income, 242
    See also mortgage fraud; *specific types of
        mortgages*
Mozilo, Angelo, 35, 71
municipal bonds, 118, 119–20
My Community Mortgage program
        (Fannie Mae), 43–46

N
naïveté, 213
National Advisory Commission on Civil
        Disorders, 7
National Association of Home Builders, 30
National Association of Realtors, 30, 217, 219
National City Mortgage (Cleveland, Ohio),
        136
National Homeownership Day, 29, 35
National Homeownership Strategy
    lenders signing up for, 35–36
    mass behavior modification goal, 32–35
    mixed results, 38–42
    in New York City, 206–7
    origin of, 29–32
National Mortgage News, 49
National People's Action on Housing, 13–14
National Recreational Properties, 173
Natomas basin, Sacramento, 112
NBA teams and Fannie Mae, 44–45
negative amortization, 53, 127, 168, 239
negative equity (underwater), 5, 219–20, 239
Nehemiah Program (Bronx and Brooklyn), 41
neighborhood evaluations
    by S&Ls and AIREA, 7
New America Financial, 135
New Century Mortgage, 64, 109
New Deal response to mortgage crisis, 222–23
New York City, New York
    apartment to condo conversions, 185–88,
        192, 194–95, 200–202
    appraisal fraud in, 206–7

blogs, 208–12
buying a home, 202–6
Central Park West, 186–87
and Clinton's revitalization program, 205–7
co-op boards, 196
foreign investments in real estate, 194
homeowning as reasonable choice, 194–95
home restoration, 209, 210
mansion tax, 203
mortgage brokers in, 196–99
overview, 207–8
real estate blogs, 208–12
rent decontrol, 192–95
rent regulations, 186–87, 189–92,
    199–202
See also Brooklyn, New York; Wall Street
New York Times, 191–92
NINJA loans (no income, no job, [no] assets),
    67, 233, 239
no-doc mortgages, 135, 140–41, 215,
    240, 242
no-money-down mortgages, 10, 50, 116
nonjudicial foreclosures, 151, 236
North Carolina, 70–71
notice of default, 235
NovaStar Mortgage, 57

O
Obama administration, 115, 217
Office of Low- and Moderate-Income Housing
    (Fannie Mae), 23–25
Ohio
    appraisal fraud, 90–91
    Dayton, 140
    sheriff's foreclosure sales, 80, 82, 84–86,
        95, 98–100
    See also Cleveland, Ohio
Operation Home Inequity (FTC), 68–69
option ARMs, 218, 240, 241
Option One Mortgage, 64
Otte, Bryce, 134, 136, 137
Outlaw, Dennis, 143–44
Ownership Society of G. W. Bush, 75–77

P
Palazzo, Manny, 54–59, 63
panic peddling (blockbusting), 9–11, 13, 83,
    96–97, 208
Park Slope, New York City, 202
Parra, Leah, 58
Patel, Steve, 151
payment-option mortgages, 218–19
Peaks Mason Mints factory, New York City,
    193–94

pension fund investors, 16, 20, 50, 105–6,
    141
Percy, Charles, 7–9
Perdue, Sonny, 154
Perry Ranch (Elk Grove, Ca.), 123
Phoenix, Arizona, 76
piggyback loans, 5, 53, 82, 126–27, 240
Pittman, Jan, 130–31
Placer County. *See* Sacramento suburbs and
    exurbs
PMI (private mortgage insurance), 235, 240
Poetsch, Robert, 120–21
Polite, Michelle and Joe, 151
political action committees, landlords', 191
Praedium Group, 193–94
predatory lending practices
    Georgia attempts to assign responsibility
        for, 145, 153–54
    Greenspan on, 69, 181, 224
    industry's intent to police offenders,
        70–71
    of United Companies Financial, 66, 67
    See also appraisal fraud; mortgage fraud;
        subprime mortgages
prepayment penalties, 65, 240
prepayment risk, 18–19
President's Commission on Housing, 17–18
private mortgage insurance (PMI), 235, 240
Proxmire, William, 13
public housing, 187, 217–18
publicly traded homebuilders, 105–6, 111, 115,
    169–70. *See also* Lennar Corporation

Q
QuickCredit mortgages, 59

R
Raines, Franklin, 68, 72–73
RAND Corporation, 190
Ranieri, Lewis
    on abuse by mortgage securities brokers,
        20
    belief in deregulation, 16, 20–21
    biographical information, 15–16
    and home mortgage debt, 86–87
    profits for Salomon Brothers, 19–20
    and Reagan administration, 17–19
    and tranched MBSs, 51
ratings agencies, 19, 66, 153, 240–41, 243
Ratner, Lee, 170–71
Reagan administration, 15, 17–21, 30, 190
real estate blogs in New York City, 208–12
real estate lobbies in Washington, 153,
    225–26

real estate market
    in Atlanta, 140–41, 145–46, 147–48
    bankers' and builders' attempts to prop up,
        220–21
    failure of private market, 221
    foreign investments in New York City,
        194
    in Fort Myers, Fla., 156–59, 163–69
    Greenspan on, 181, 224
    home price declines, 40, 140, 219–20
    increasing value supports lenders, 82–83,
        86–87, 220–21
    and rent regulation, 190
    rising prices drying up customer pool,
        88–89
    See also home construction; home price
        increases
real estate speculators
    and appraisers, 2, 90–91
    blockbusting/panic tactics, 9–11, 13, 83,
        96–97, 208
    co-op boards' prevention of, 196
    foreclosures as opportunity for, 51–53, 63
    and Fort Myers, Fla., 163–69
    profits from SMMEA, 20–21
    See also flipping homes; mortgage fraud
Realtists, 35
Reasor, Lawrence, 97
recasting mortgages, 241
Rector, Les, 140
redlining, 11. See also blockbusting
refinancing, 64, 82–83, 122, 241
regulations
    on banks and S&Ls, 60–61
    federal banking agencies in 2001,
        too late, 70
    Georgia Residential Mortgage Fraud Act,
        145, 153–54
    on loan charge information, 215
    prohibition on state consumer protection
        laws, 154
    rent regulations, 186–87, 189–92
    skewering S&Ls, 60–61
    on subprime mortgages, 64, 67
Renaissance Homes, 105
Reno, Nevada, 114–15
rent decontrol, 192–95
renters
    apartment to condo conversions, 185–88,
        192, 194–95, 200–202
    as second-class citizens, 187–89, 191–92
rent regulations, 186–87, 189–92, 199–202
Rent Stabilization Association, 191
Resendez, Ed, 56

resetting interest rates, 241
Retsinas, Nicolas, 36–37, 42, 227
reverse redlining, 52
Reynen, John, 113, 114
Reynen & Bardis, 113–14
Rich Dad/Poor Dad books and products, 183
Robbins, Tony, 178–79, 181–82, 182–83
Rocklin, California, 118
Roosevelt, Franklin Delano, 3–4, 222–23
Rosen, Jack, 171–72
Rosen, Leonard, 171–72
Roseville, California, 118
Rubin, Robert E., 31

S
S&Ls. See savings and loans
Sacramento River, 112
Sacramento suburbs and exurbs
    building in flood plain, 112
    Elk Grove, 109, 121–26
    homebuilders cutting corners, 113–14,
        122–25, 127–28
    home construction in, 102–7, 108–10,
        111–14, 123–26
    home price increases, 109, 113, 114, 116
    housing boom in, 102–5, 108, 109–10
    land grabs, 106–7, 111–13
    Lincoln, 102–5, 117–21
    Marysville, 113–14, 121
    and subprime mortgage crisis, 115
Salins, Peter, 190
Salomon Brothers, 15–18, 20–21, 51, 213.
        See also Ranieri, Lewis
San Francisco, California, 109
savings and loans (S&Ls)
    crisis of 1980s and 1990s, 24–25, 60–61
    and high interest rates in late-1970s, 17–18,
        51
    and Home Mortgage Disclosure Act, 13
    map of acceptable vs. redlined areas, 11
    overview, 12, 241
    subprime loans from, 65
Saxon Mortgage, 56–57
Schraw, Tom, 23–24
Schwartz, Faith, 71
Schwarzenegger, Arnold, 127
"Scratchings from the Little Red Hen"
        (anon.), 107–8
Secondary Mortgage Market Enhancement
        Act of 1984 (SMMEA), 19–20, 241–42
second mortgages
    for buying a home in the 1920s, 5
    as down payment, 5, 53, 82, 126–27, 240
    overview, 241

silent seconds, 126, 242
See also home equity loans
Section 8 tenants, 80, 242
Securities and Exchange Commission (SEC),
16–17, 19, 72–73
securities laws. *See* regulations
securitization, 16–17, 88, 213–14. *See also*
mortgage-backed securities
September 11, 2001, terrorist attacks, 73
Shaker Heights suburb of Cleveland, 90–91
Sheerar, Geoff, 195–99
Sheets, Carleton, 174, 182
Sherraden, Michael, 34
short sales, 119, 242
Showing America a New Way Home, 44
Showing America a New Way Home program,
43–46
Siedlecki, Christopher, 97
Sierra Club, 112–13
silent seconds (piggyback loans), 126, 242
$imply $olved, 183–84
Slavic Village (Cleveland, Ohio), 78–86, 90,
95–97, 149
S&Ls. *See* savings and loans
SMMEA (Secondary Mortgage Market
Enhancement Act of 1984), 19–20,
241–42
Smoot, Courtney, 182–84
social conditioning
homeownership as "American Dream," 6,
33, 48, 66, 216
homeownership as behavior modification
technique, 8–9, 32–35
home prices go up, 82–83, 104, 141
South Euclid, Ohio, 90
Southstar Funding, 143–44
Spence, Roy, 44
Spitzer, Guy, 105–9, 115–17
Spitzer, Jeff, 105–8, 111, 127–28
Spitzer, Joni, 104–5
Standard & Poor's ratings agency, 19,
63, 153
stated-income mortgages, 140–41, 242
state laws
on appraiser licensing, 90, 142–43
federal prohibition on consumer protection
laws, 154
and judicial vs. nonjudicial foreclosures,
151, 236
on subprime mortgages, 70–71
Stegman, Michael, 34, 40
Stephanopoulos, George, 30
St. Ives area of Greater Atlanta, 129–31
St. Marlo area of Greater Atlanta, 131–33

subcontractors blamed for substandard quality,
125–26
subprime consumer loans, 51
subprime home equity loans, 51, 56–57,
65–66
subprime mortgage crisis, 69–70, 143–44.
See also appraisal fraud; mortgage fraud
subprime mortgages
with adjustable rates, 57, 66
Citigroup's share of, 87–88
foreclosure rates, 66, 69, 89
and Freddie Mac, 71, 237
grading systems, 50, 234, 242
of Long Beach Mortgage, 54–56, 57, 63–64
multiple mortgage lenders for, 64
origin of, 50–51
overview, 54–56, 242
predatory lending practices, 56, 64–65, 240
for prime borrowers, 62, 68
pushing up price of homes, 88–89
seconds as, 127
suburban areas, 110–11. *See also* Atlanta
suburbs and exurbs; Fort Myers, Florida;
Sacramento suburbs and exurbs
Summers, Larry, 227

T
Tagalakis, Ted, 136–37, 139
teaser rate, 88, 242
terrorist attacks (9/11), 73
thrift institutions. *See* savings and loans
tranches
commercial pools, 193, 195
Fannie and Freddie allowed to participate,
21
marketing of, 20
origin and growth of, 18–19, 65–66
overview, 239, 243
tax-exempt trading, 51
See also mortgage-backed securities
Trump, Donald, 181, 183
Tsakopoulos, Angelo, 111–13
turf wars in New York City, 208–9, 211–12
Tyson, Laura, 37

U
underwater (negative equity), 5, 219–20, 239
underwriting system, automated, 47–48
United Companies Financial, 66, 67
Universal American Mortgage, 116, 126–27
urban activists
Bring Back the 70s Street Club, 79–80
in Chicago, 1, 10–11, 13, 22–23
East Side Organizing Project, 80–81

urban activists (*continued*)
    GSEs forced to purchase low-income
        homeowners' loans, 25–26
    See also Cincotta, Gale
urban areas
    benefits and risks of homeownership in,
        39–40
    Chicago, Illinois, 7–9, 13, 69, 81, 140
    Chicago's West Side, 1–2, 7, 10–11
    as consumer base of last resort, 31
    doughnut hole effect of GSE practices,
        21–22
    as Fannie Mae's focus on, 43–48
    homeowners prefer suburbs to, 110
    as unsuitable for home loans, 7, 12
    See also Cleveland, Ohio; New York City
U.S. Commerce Department, 3
U.S. Congress
    repairing damage from deregulation, 25
    responsibility for subprime mortgage crisis,
        154, 226–27
    and subprime mortgages, 64, 67
    support for securities deregulation, 19
    vote to make GSEs purchase low-income
        homeowners' loans, 25–26
U.S. Department of Housing and Urban
        Development (HUD)
    activists takeover briefing at Chicago office,
        13
    and Clinton Economic Plan, 31–32,
        35, 41
    creation of, 8–9
    and foreclosures in Chicago, 1–2
    and GSEs, 72, 73
    Housing Choice Vouchers, 41, 80, 97, 242
    mortgage interest deduction as higher
        priority, 217
    overview, 243
    Republicans' attempt to eliminate, 32, 42
    See also Federal Housing Administration
U.S. Senate. *See* U.S. Congress

V
value engineering, 114, 126
Vestri, Ermete, 59, 64
Veterans Administration (VA), 6, 236
vouchers from HUD, 41, 80, 97, 242

W
Wall Street
    awareness of mortgage fraud, 207
    MBS generated by, 51, 71–73, 82, 83,
        87–90
    salaries and bonuses affecting New York,
        195, 214
    See also investment banks
War on Poverty, 9
Warrington, Pennsylvania, 164, 165
Washington Monthly, 52
Washington Mutual, 64, 94, 206–7
Washington Post, 224
wealth gap in the U.S., 214–15
Wealth Intelligence Academy International
        Hall of Fame, 174
Weiss, Marc, 29–32
welfare system overhaul, 33
West Side Coalition, 10–11, 13
Whitney, Russ, 173
Whitney Information Network, 173–75
Whitney's Wealth Intelligence Academy,
        174–75
Wirth, Tim, 19
Wiseman, Mark, 84–86, 90
Wolf Creek exurb of Atlanta, 145–47
Works Progress Administration, 4

Y
yield spread premiums, 57, 239, 243

Z
Zigas, Barry, 42–43, 45, 72
Zion Investments, 151
Zogby poll, 218

ABOUT THE AUTHOR

Alyssa Katz teaches journalism at New York University and works with the Pratt Center for Community Development. Formerly the editor of *City Limits*, a magazine about New York and its neighborhoods, she currently writes for *Mother Jones*, *New York*, the *Nation*, and other publications. Alyssa lives with her family in Brooklyn, in a co-op apartment they own.